# "Charity Signs for Herself"
*Gender and the Withdrawal of Black Women from Field Labor, Alabama 1865-1876*

Carol Lemley Montgomery Ph.D.

1991

Copyright © 1991 by Carol Lemley Montgomery Ph.D.

Published by CaryPress International Books

All rights reserved. This book or any portion thereof may not be reproduced or used in any manner whatsoever without the express written permission of the publisher except for the use of brief quotations in a book review

# Table of Contents

*Curriculum Vitae* ............................................................................................................. v

*Introduction* .................................................................................................................. ix

Chapter 1 – Prologue ................................................................................................ 13

Chapter 2 – "I know you will play your part bravely" ............................................. 21

Chapter 3 – "Able Men to be Rulers or Thousands, & Rulers of Hundreds, & Rulers of Fifties, & Rulers of Tens." ..................................................... 59

Chapter 4 – "Remember me to Adeline and tell her I saw her mother..." ................ 99

Chapter 5 – "A Contract-for Carrying on the Faunsdale Plantation" ....................... 149

Chapter 6 – "12 March, 1867...The 3 squads parted, & began planting…" ............. 179

Chapter 7 – "Jan. 6 Charity began work for 1/2 the crops, on self-maintenance, 1/2 the mules, & 1/2 their risk" ........................................................... 221

Epilogue ..................................................................................................................... 253

Bibliography .............................................................................................................. 255

Carol Lemley Montgomery .......................................................................................... 269

# Curriculum Vitae

I. **Home Address:**
Carol Lemley Montgomery
642 S. 4th Avenue
Kure Beach, NC 28449

II. **Education:**
   A. **Ph.D.** - University of California, Irvine, (UCI), 1991
        **Primary Field:** United States History, with a special focus on Southern and Women's' History
        **Secondary Field:** England from the Industrial Revolution to World War I
        **Methodological Field:** Social History
   B. **M.A.** - University of California, Irvine, 1983
   C. **B.A.** - Armstrong State College, 1981 (Summa cum Laude)
        **Major:** United State History
        **Minor:** Historical Archaeology, Preservation and Museum Studies (Material Culture)

III. **Ph.D. Dissertation:**
   A. **Title** - "Charity Signs for Herself: Gender and the Withdrawal of Black Women from Field Labor in Alabama, 1865 - 1877"
   B. **Committee** - Michael P. Johnson (director), Mary P. Ryan and Jonathan Wiener

IV. **Fellowships and Honors:**
\* American Association University Women Fellow, 1985 \* Dissertation Fellowship, UCI, 1984
\* Regent Fellowship, UCI, 1981-82

V. **Professional Experience:**

January - May 1999
Instructor for University of North Carolina, Pembroke at Richmond Community College, US History

Summer 1998
Instructor for University of North Carolina, Pembroke (Pilot Site) at Sandhills Community College, Us History

January - May 1998
Professor of History Methodist College in Fayetteville, North Carolina; Western Civilization, US History,

January - May 1997
Instructor Richmond Community College, Hamlet, North Carolina; US History

January - May 1996
Professor of History full-time temporary replacement Peter Murray, Ph.D. (head of History Dept.) while on sabbatical;

March - May 1995
Instructor, Richmond Community College, Hamlet, North Carolina, "Ethics and the Criminal Justice System"

February - August 1994
Assistant Editor, Jane Addams Papers Project; acted as Researcher and writer to prepare the papers and letters of Jane Addams and other relevant persons for publication

August 1992 - February 1994
Instructor Richmond Community College, Hamlet, North Carolina; taught United States History, African-American History and Western Civilization

August 1991 - June 1992
Instructor Campbell University; Western Civilization
Instructor Methodist College; American History

August 1990 - December 1990/ January 1992 - June 1992
Fayetteville State University; "Critical Thinking"

1983 - 1985
Teaching Assistant, University of California

**VI. Volunteer/Community Involvement**

US Department of Interior - Volunteer
National Park Service, 2014

- Aztec Ruins National Monument, NM, Visitor services

US Department of Interior - Volunteer
US Fish and Wildlife Service, 2012

- Sevilletta National Wildlife Refuge, Visitor services, Education, Biological assistance and Maintenance assistant

US Department of Interior - Volunteer
Bureau of Land Management, 2010 & 2015

- Dripping Springs Natural Area, Resident Host of Recreation Site, Las Cruces, NM District

NC State Parks – Sea Turtle Volunteer

- Ft Fisher State Recreation Area

Cape Fear Community College –

- Foundation Board of Directors

# Introduction

The withdrawal of black women from field labor in the postwar South is the historical question being addressed with a gender analysis as the theoretical framework. Primary sources used have been drawn from Somerset plantation, North Carolina and Faunsdale plantation, Alabama. This research adds to the literature of women's history, gender studies, black history, and the Reconstruction era of Alabama. It adds to the growing body of knowledge of the way gender relations interact with class and race to influence variations of gender roles for both women and men within different social classes and races. The development of the squad system as an integral phase in the general movement toward single-family-based sharecropping is also explored.

By the 1880s, family-based sharecropping was the dominate organization of agricultural labor in the cotton South. Informed by a gender analysis, this research focuses on the immediate postwar decade, 1865 to 1877, on one plantation-based community in Marengo County, Alabama. Faunsdale plantation, the white household and black freedwomen and men, form the community under study. The research reveals the persistence of male dominance among black freedmen as evidenced in their gender relations and ranking of squad members.

## PHOTOS

*Somerset House*

*Somerset Slave*

*Faunsdale House*

*Faunsdale Slave*

# Prologue

On the 24th of April, 1872 the Rev. William Stickney of Faunsdale Plantation in Marengo County, Alabama, made this entry in his plantation day book, "Wed. Afternoon discharged Josiah and Boston, Lavinia's boys, mainly to get rid of her."[1] Stickney's note provides a convenient point from which to view the historical problem of the withdrawal of black women from field labor after emancipation. The confrontation between Lavinia, the black female field worker, and Stickney, the white male ex-master, had been a long time in the making. She had been a productive, defiant, disobedient, troublesome field hand who was not easily managed by Stickney. And he had been a master accustomed to obedience and compliant responses from his dependents. Lavinia was an unmarried mother of two sons with no man through whom Stickney could expect to help him in keeping her under control. She was a strong and consistently good cotton picker who could also command the labor of her sons. Although she was a valuable worker, Stickney fired her because he had too little control over her.

To get Lavinia off the plantation, Stickney had to fire her sons. He had not hired her for 1872, and yet she remained on his place with her two sons. Since Josiah and Boston, Lavinia's boys, were still under contract with the old master in 1872, Stickney had to fire them to assure ridding himself of their mother. This kind of loss of black female field workers was not taken into consideration by Roger L. Ransom and Richard Sutch when they assumed in <u>One Kind of Freedom</u> that black women who worked in cotton fields left field labor because they wanted to carry out domestic labor for their families.

In analyzing how sharecropping came to dominate the postwar southern agricultural economy and why the cotton South remained so poor, Ransom and Sutch assumed that the causes of discontent and deprivation for freed black men were mutually applicable to freed black women. They subsumed all freedpeople under the male experience when they stated that "[h]e had gained his social freedom . . . yet the black man was the poorest of farmers."² Black women had gained no political or economic freedom, nor were they released from the constraints of gender as <u>women</u> as soon as they were freed. And despite the various charts Ransom and Sutch included in their book that clearly showed that the withdrawal of field labor was a gendered problem, they offered no gender analysis.

Emancipation brought freedom from racial slavery for the freedpeople, but it also carried new restraints for freedwomen. They were free to marry, to become part of the patriarchal institution that recognized a woman and her children as existing under the control and direction of the male head of household, the ruler of his own little commonwealth. In his comparative study of slavery, <u>Slavery and Social Death</u> Orlando Patterson characterized slavery as being an institution having three distinctive attributes for the slaves; powerlessness, natal alienation, and an absence of honor. These characteristics were not limited to the nineteenth-century institution of racial slavery, but were also found, to a lesser degree, in the condition of all free women in the antebellum South. Once freed from the restraints of slavery, black women still had to deal with the well-entrenched patriarchy of the elite white planter class and the developing male dominance among black men. If freed black women were to assume the same gender role as white women, then black women would also suffer the same type of natal alienation that legal marriage caused white women; black women would continue to assume the political non-existence experienced by all white women; and black women would have to accept that their social position, their status, would be determined by either that of their father or husband. If freed black women assumed the same gender role as free white women, they still would not be free.

In his argument against locating the current condition of black families in the historical roots of slavery, Herbert Gutman's <u>The Black Family in Slavery and Freedom 1750 - 1925</u> relied in part on slave records from populations of plantations that had remained stable over several generations. His study revealed much about the central importance of kinship for slaves and the persistence of family structure during slavery and in freedom. What he overlooked, however, was the possibility that the standard by which he measured a "normal" black family either in slavery or freedom was heavily influenced by a white model that failed to consider the strength of African cultural survivals.

Slavery distorted the social relations and gender roles that had existed between African men and women in their societies before they were enslaved. The cultures which nurtured and supported them could not be replicated once they reached North America. And after slavery ended and the interference and control of masters was reduced, freed African-Americans were left to sort out for themselves much of what had been forced on them. It is my argument that while the gender system which developed between freed African-Americans in the postwar South differed in some ways from the one in place within the dominant white culture, the subordination of black women by black men remained a prime feature.

An asymmetrical gender system which allows for subordination of women by men cannot claim the specialization of labor along gender lines as the root of its inequality when both sexes are performing the same jobs, as slave women and men did. The proven ability of slave women to perform the same quantity and quality of work as slave men and to produce even more wealth than did the men should destroy the assumption that labor and specialization of work <u>alone</u> provide an adequate explanation for the persistence of asymmetrical gender systems. I have used the transition from slavery to freedom as a testing ground for a monocausal explanation for an unbalanced gender system. I have not found the single cause for the reshaping of the gender system between freed black women and men, but I am convinced that performing the same amount of labor did not create equality in social, economic, or political rewards for women and men.

Karl Marx provided a theoretical framework by which the struggle between economic and social classes can be analyzed, but that theoretical model lacks adequate explanatory power for the struggle between the sexes. Gender-blind theories of history are as inadequate in their explanatory power as are those which ignore the role of human agency. Neither provides a comprehensive critical analysis of the dialectical process in society which goes on between the men and women who <u>are</u> society and between human beings and the material conditions into which they were born.

While Marx stated the dialectical nature of the relationship between the material world and humans as agents of change, he explicitly spoke in the voice of a man of his own time, subsuming the reality of the lives of women under the "generic term" of men. Marxist theory did not take gender into consideration. Neither his work nor those who have applied it exclusively in class terms have successfully explained why men hold dominant positions in society and women do not. It has long been apparent, at least to feminist scholars of many disciplines, that a marxian critique of society cannot successfully explain female subordination in monocausal terms. Although industrial capitalism is shored up by the lingering remnants of patriarchal values, male dominance is not a by-product of that mode of production.

In <u>The Creation of Patriarchy</u>, Gerda Lerner addresses the unsuitability of a single-cause explanation for the historical subordination of women by men. Lerner encourages historians to use gender as an analytical tool, but cautions that

> {w)e must think about gender historically and specifically as it occurs in varied and changeable societies... Approaching the quest as historians, we must abandon single-factor explanations.[3]

Lerner charges historians to recognize the primacy and centrality of gender in the formahons of society. She also reminds her audience that good history is built upon solid evidence as well as strong theory. I have taken that charge seriously and examined a specific time and place in postwar Alabama.

In seeking to gain deeper knowledge of the lives of women by examining gender "historically and specifically as it occurs," I studied Faunsdale plantation and its community of people during a critical time period. The central focus of the study were historical sources elated to the slave and freed population of Faunsdale, Marengo County, Alabama, from 1843 to 1875, with emphasis on the immediate postwar decade from 1865 to **1875**. The Collins Papers in the State Archives in Raleigh, North Carolina also held valuable material for this dissertation.

I argue that while black women did <u>choose</u> to leave field work upon emancipation, many were <u>forced</u> out. I also argue that the freed women of Faunsdale Plantation had several reasons for not signing labor contracts with Stickney and not continuing to perform field labor. Stickney's obdurate refusal to accept such women as Lavinia and his encouragement of domestic male dominance among the black families who worked on the plantation formed a strong barrier for freed women to overcome. Stickney helped force many black women out of wage-earning field work. As black men shook off the bonds of slavery, they took up dominance within their own families.

I have organized this work in an unconventional structure that permits development of topical themes within each chapter rather than following a strictly chronological one. I deliberately chose this organization because of the disparate nature of the data that are scattered throughout a massive collection of plantation documents. It has also been a deliberate choice because I had to weave together the stories of the black and white families who constituted the Faunsdale household and plantation. In doing so, I have often moved forward and backward in time within one chapter, knitting together the various strands of my multi-causal argument.

Chapter one introduces the research thesis that while the asymmetrical gentler system in operation between women and men of the dominant culture of the 19th-century South was adopted in part by freed black women and men, race had already affected gender roles during slavery. It focuses on legal marriage as the "glue" for society as well as the later means by which black men assumed and exercised domestic male dominance.

The second chapter traces the establishment of Josiah Collins' wealth and family in colonial North Carolina and their development in the nineteenth-century. The chapter thesis is that precapitalistic mercantile ventures, reliance on slave labor, and accumulation of property through marriage was the basis for the Collins family's wealth. This chapter brings together the dominant social and economic forces that supported the prevailing patriarchal slave system in the nineteenth-century South.

Chapter three focuses on the network of kinship ties that existed among the Faunsdale slaves. Most of these families persisted long after their departure from Somerset, North Carolina, for Faunsdale, Alabama in 1843. Some had been coherent family groups since the late eighteenth-century. The chapter thesis is that kinship ties that probably existed between white and black members of the household could not have been recognized by white family members because of the barrier of race. Familial and kinship relations could not overcome race for white members of the family, but black women accepted the primacy of the bond between a mother and her child regardless of the race of the father. Race took the primary position within the white family while kinship prevailed for black women. Within this chapter the strength of African cultural survivals is also highlighted.

With the fourth chapter, I focused more on the postwar era. The chapter deals with the limited success of the application of a standard device of market relations, labor contracts, by the Episcopal priest and planter William Stickney. It reveals how Stickney, the manager of his wife's plantation, began what would be a successful forty-year role as the plantation manager and labor lord. The thesis is that his religion-soaked ideology supported his authority and that he used labor contracts to maintain social control over the free labor force in the first postwar decade after emancipation.

In chapter five, I have continued to narrow the focus to the reorganization of labor on the plantation that began in 1867. This chapter addresses the significance and probable provenance of the squad system that led to sharecropping at Faunsdale. It also shows that Stickney actively encouraged black male dominance as a means of exerting social control and that opportunities were withheld from black women.

Finally, the last chapter focuses on one woman who "signed for herself," the freedwoman Charity Paine. In emphasizing the term "signs for herself," found in the labor contracts signed by Faunsdale field hands, I mean to point out that Charity acted for herself without husband or father to represent her with the old master. The chapter includes material on other female field hands who signed for themselves and some who had a man sign for them. The thesis is that only single women were allowed to act independently.

# END NOTES

1. Plantation Day Book 18Z2, April 24, Stickney box VII, folder 10, Faunsdale Plantation Papers, Linn-Henley Research Library Archives, Birmingham Public Library, Birmingham, Alabama

2. Roger L. Ransom and Richard Sutch, <u>One Kind of Freedom: The Economic Consequences of Emancipation</u>, (Cambridge University Press, 1977), pp.1-2.

3. Gerda Lerner, <u>The Creation of Patriarchy</u>, (Oxford University Press, 1986), p. 37.

# CHAPTER ONE

# "I know you will play your part bravely"[1]

Thomas A. Harrison, lately of Virginia, passed the second night of what would be a fifty-day journey in October, 1843 camped within a mile of the Chowan River near Winton, North Carolina. Having eaten a supper of "soaked crackers ham & coffee," he made a temporary writing desk of an over-turned water trough and wrote a letter to his bride who had remained in the North Carolina town of Edenton.[2] Louisa Mckinlay Collins, daughter of the late Josiah Collins II and Ann Daves Collins, had married Harrison ten months earlier in December, 1842. This trip marked the second long separation for the couple in less than one year after their marriage. The first had been to find suitable land to buy and this second one was to transport goods and slaves from North Carolina to the newly-purchased plantation in Alabama. The establishment of a home at Faunsdale plantation in Marengo County, Alabama, would begin Louisa and Tom's life together as an independent married couple and separate household.[3]

Properly exercising his patriarchal prerogative, Louisa's brother Josiah Collins III had objected to her choice of Harrison as a suitable marriage partner, but Tom and Louisa overcame his objections and those of her two other brothers and married. However, need to prove himself capable of replicating the kind of life expected for a daughter of the wealthy Collins family weighed on him. The Collins were part of a tidewater community of elite families that included Pettigrews, Iredells, and Camerons. Harrison was aware that his wife's male kin had disapproved of the match and he must have felt concern about his relationship with the eldest brother and head of the family, Josiah Collins, since Harrison knew that he needed the good will of Collins and his friends.[4]

Putting his concerns aside, Harrison left his bride in her brother's care and the company of Josiah's family and headed toward what was still a wild frontier of the United States. In his first letter written to Louisa enroute, Thomas cautioned her to remember her role during their separation:

> If I could only see my dear Lou one hour each day (if no more) & kiss her & comfort her I should be happy. And now how fares it with you dear Wife? I know you will play your part bravely, & bear up under our separation, hoping and believing we shall never be separated so long again.[5]

As members of the landed elite, Louisa and Thomas both knew their places and each had been trained to fulfill their roles. For the elites of this hierarchical society, places and roles were very clearly defined, unambiguous, and gender- and race-specific.

Thomas Harrison's role was the young patriarch - husband to a woman of his own class, father of children to carry on his estate, master of slaves, political representative for his class and race interests, and lord of his landed domain. Harrison was suited for the life of southern patriarch and gentleman, according to the oral family history known among descendents of the Collins-Harrison marriage. They locate Berkeley, the Virginia estate of Benjamin Harrison, as the place where Thomas Alexander Harrison was born.[6] Harrison attended William and Mary College under the sponsorship of a man who had married one of the Harrison daughters, George Minge, and kept a close association with Minge's family during the doctor's lifetime. Harrison's own expectations were those of a gentleman even if he lacked the material means to live as one. A letter written by Harrison to Louisa during their engagement in 1842 reveals just how much he was relying upon marriage to provide a material base necessary to become a member of the planter elite and live as the gentleman he aspired to be. The letter was a response to Louisa's proposal that they delay their marriage for a year.

Harrison thought that suggestion came from those members of her family who objected to the match and reminded her that he was in the midst of searching out land to buy in preparation for their life together:

> I must settle a farm before you can marry me. Now I am in search of a farm to be settled by servants belonging to you - how therefore... can I <u>settle a farm,</u> till by our <u>marriage</u> I acquire the <u>control</u> of those servants. ...The fact is, that in consequence of so large a portion of your fortune consisting of slaves, I am almost <u>forced</u> by every consideration of providence, to devote my attention to agriculture.[7]

Serious and prolonged opposition to their marriage had colored Louisa's letters to her kinswoman and confidant, Martha Pride, in which she made veiled references to exactly who opposed the marriage. Even during the period of their engagement, Louisa knew that her decision was not one that her brothers accepted readily and their opposition strained her relationship with Tom Harrison.[8] It is also possible that what she expressed to Martha Pride may have been her own doubts that she could not openly admit to having. Even if Dr. Thomas A. Harrison was a legitimate member of the highly respected Harrison family of Berkeley, he needed more than good breeding to win approval from Louisa's brothers. To the Collins men, good blood lines must not have been sufficient if the one possessing them appeared to be a fortune hunter or simply lacking in a good business sense. Being of the family which had produced one of colonial Virginia's signers of the Declaration of Independence and a president of the United States would not make him a good manager or pay the bills.

Harrison's desire and determination to become part of the elite class and live as a gentleman were great enough that he acquired the means and he probably also had the training. Louisa Collins was a woman of high standards and would not have settled for a man who lacked the social graces of her own class. He knew what was expected of an elite white landowner. In this class, owning land, slaves, and marrying well were the avenues to wealth and political advantage. Although he had been educated to be a medical doctor at the College of William and Mary, Harrison took up the role of a planter whose marriage gave him a work force of slaves. His letter to Louisa (where he objected to her proposal to delay their marriage) pointed out the only reason he might choose to practice medicine:

> Take for example the reason why you propose to defer our marriage. "That it will take me one year to establish myself as a physician, & that I ought not to marry till the expiration of that time." Now you know my dear Lou, that I did not come to St. Louis for the purpose of practicing medicine but for the purpose of establishing a farm & that if I did practice at all, it would only be whilst I was engaged in locating a farm.[9]

For men of his class, marriage might possibly include the expectation of affectionate compatibility, but it would certainly include the expectation of financial addition and family support. Harrison necessarily expected his wife's family to provide him with financial backing and connections when he needed credit. A good name and ties to a financially healthy family meant as much as cash in an age where loans were based on connections. A dashing and handsome young swain's courtly manners might impress the lady of his choice, but her father or guardian would want strong evidence of more concrete talents. If a beau won the affections of the girl and failed to impress her male guardian, the courtship usually ended. In spite of her maturity (she was in her mid-twenties) at the time of marriage, Louisa was aware of the importance of her brother Josiah's approval of her "Tom."[10]

Louisa's indecision toward Harrison troubled Martha Pride who thought it reflected a side of Louisa's personality that she had never seen. Pride chided Louisa more than once about her failure to make a commitment to Harrison after revealing her deep feelings for him. From a letter to Louisa in March, 1842, Martha tried to console her "dear cousin," all the while chastising:

> I am truly grived to hear of your troubles and at the same time mightily inclined to scold you for your want of what Danton called "l'audace"! My dear, I could not have believed you were deficient in either will or decision. And I cannot comprehend how a woman of sense and spirit—as I believe I told you in my last—could at the very first show

of opposition in her friend—give up tamely a man she loves and <u>believes worthy of her</u>![11]

Martha and Louisa had developed a deep, emotionally intimate relationship built on long visits and letters. When Louisa wrote of her intention to wed, Martha was frank in her jealousy of the man whom she had not even met, and she did not wish to see her beloved Louisa taken away from her. Martha expressed disdain for marriage and often told Louisa that she would not give up her freedom for marriage. Once her dear friend made it plain that she loved enough to wed, Martha again expressed her sympathy with Louisa for what her brothers had put her through and questioned why she cared so for Josiah's opinion:

> But who on earth could have imagined—could have conjectured such a state of affairs as you tell of—My cousin I am so astounded, so overwhelmed by your communication that I hardly know what to say or do... this much I can say, however, that it was natural & proper in your brother Josiah to desire that your property be settled on you.... There are two things...that I must say are incomprehensible to me. The first is your fear & dread for your Brother's opinion. ...Now the second thing is this...I am alarmed at the vacillation of your feelings...one moment ready to accept & the next to renounce.[12]

While mentioning several men's names to Louisa as possible suitors, Martha seems to have rejected them all. Perhaps she had a keener awareness for what they had their eyes on than did Louisa and remained an unmarried daughter in her father's company and household.[13]

As an aspiring southern patriarch, Harrison had to do more than just marry well. He had to own land, slaves, and a large enough residence to house his dependents. The larger the number of dependents, black and white, the greater was his authority and status. Growing wealthy and powerful in antebellum Alabama meant more than just growing cotton for English mills. members of the elite class secured their superior social position informally by increasing their personal power and formally by electing peers to the state legislature. One of the main strengths of Harrison's role in upholding patriarchal institutions was in controlling his dependents. He would take part in public activities that served to maintain the class and community consensus necessary to keep a small minority in control of a vast majority of people. In short, all elements for the role of patriarch were taken up by Thomas A. Harrison.[14]

Louisa's role was as gender-bound as her husband's. A lady of the South shared many of the characteristics as those defining the northern ideal of true womanhood.[15] Like her northern sister, a southern lady was the emotional center of her family, religious instructor to the children of the household, whether her own, slave, or servant, and a "helpmeet" to her husband, the lord and master of her life.[16] Louisa Collins Harrison would certainly have been expected to live up to the ideal for southern ladies that required they be "sexually pure, pious, deferent to external authority, and content with their place in the home."[17]

Race influenced the role of the southern lady in ways that differed from that of the northern "true woman". Race made role expectations in nineteenth-century slave states take a different track, so southern women were bound by racial constraints as well as by class and gender rules. These restraints worked toward holding apart black and white women as well as white women *of* different economic classes. Louisa had been born into a family of great wealth, high social status, and political influence. As devout and active members of the Episcopal (Anglican) Church, they often housed and entertained the bishop when he visited Edenton.[18] Her paternal grandfather, Josiah Collins I, emigrated from Somerset, England and carried a deep sense of the weight of English history with him to North Carolina.[19] Louisa was able to live richly and comfortably as an intelligent woman who was very well educated and musically trained. While many planters' wives had a life of demanding tasks and childbearing, she had one child and turned over the housekeeping to a slave woman named Adeline. She lived a life of sheltered ease through the efforts of the labor of others.

As a southern lady, Louisa was hardly expected to do physical labor. Depending on her own talents and domestic training, a southern lady would oversee the domestic labor of her "servants." But to perform household tasks was considered to be demeaning of her position.[20] Parents of young brides often "gave" their daughters a housekeeper to alleviate some of the burdens of creating and managing a new household. Although both of Louisa's parents had died by the time of her marriage, she had the benefit of owning several mature black women such as Hannah, Adeline, and Margaret, as part of her inheritance. With the help of a trained staff of black women to carry out the domestic labor, Louisa was free to practice achievement of the feminine ideal for her class and race. She could play the piano and guitar, write letters, and visit relatives. With necessary work being done by slaves, Louisa could focus on those gentler arts of being a lady who inspired gentlemen.[21]

There was one responsibility that even the often praised slave Adeline could not take for Mistress Louisa. While any of the female slaves could produce more laborers for the master's fields, only his wife could bear a legitimate heir for his wealth and property. Only Louisa could have children who would assume all the prerogatives of family membership. For a woman to be in the kind of 17 situation that Louisa occupied as her time to deliver the baby drew nearer, bereft of her intimate circle of supporting female kin to get her through the fear of childbirth before and to educate her to motherhood afterwards, it would be a lonely and frightening event.[22] Shortly before the birth of her first and only child Louise, Louisa's sister Henrie Collins wrote a letter of satisfaction and approval of the arrangements made by Louisa in anticipation of the birth. Louisa had hired a nurse to help with the baby in place of her women relatives who would have been her support system had they been close enough:

> ...one thing however gave me more comfort than almost anything else was that you had procured a Nurse - one that you seemed pleased with & one with whom there was some association with this section of the U.S.A. - I sincerely hope she will prove herself competent to the task - & a comfort to you in the absence of all female friends.[23]

If the nurse hired by Louisa to take the place of her absent female relatives and friends was black, it was just one more way in which an elite woman such as Louisa Harrison relied upon the labor of black women. One of those absent female relatives was Louisa's eldest sister Nancy Collins Shepard who had married a year before in May, 1843 and was also pregnant with her first child. Forty years old and pregnant for the first time, Nancy's own fear of childbirth shows through in her letter of congratulations to Louisa as she sought reassurance from the younger but tried veteran of a woman's ordeal:

...as soon as you are able, you must write me how you bore the crisis so trying to most women, & if your fortitude & resolution forsook you. I have been very anxious to hear from you...[24]

Nancy successfully gave birth to a boy, Willie, who married his cousin Louise Harrison in 1866. However, Nancy did not survive to see the event because she died following the birth of her second child in June, 1848.[25]

Just as the members of the ruling class had ideals and roles to fulfill, so had they expectations for their slaves who worked for them. Crafting the role for enslaved <u>black</u> men gave free <u>white</u> men some uneasy moments, especially when such slavery ideologues as George Fitzhugh recommended enslavement along class lines as well as racial ones. In spite of the supposed inferiority of the entire race, the generally accepted tenet of belief in male superiority created an ideological conflict for white patriarchs who took male dominance as a natural and God-directed phenomenon. Racial difference between master and slave eased the transgression against male solidarity. The deepest function that physiological difference serves may be the consolidation and reinforcement of class dominance. What men in ancient societies discovered about slavery by enslaving a sex, men of modern times perfected by the enslavement of a race. White slave-owning patriarchs had to create ideological justifications for degrading other males. Black men, as enslaved laborers in southern states, were seen by their masters as less than human, yet possessing a peculiar set of contradictory human personality traits. They were considered to be both guileless, simple children and sly, savage, dangerous brutes.[26]

The role which masters expected black men to play was straightforward enough: they were to work, obey orders, and render perfect loyalty to their masters. Black men were to labor and create wealth for white men and provide them with a class of dependents whose very existence proclaimed the power of the masters. Most carpentry, smithing, masonry and other such craftwork was done by slave men while others performed the various jobs involved in producing a crop. Artisans were frequently hired out to neighboring plantations or even sent into nearby towns so that their skills could provide additional profit to the master. Thus by 1843, the role that black men were to play was well in place. If white males did feel occasional concern cover the subordination of other men, they were still clear about what was demanded of their male slaves: labor, obedience, and loyalty.[27]

There was an area in which some planters expressed ambivalence regarding the nature of slaves. Some masters questioned whether or not slaves possessed souls and if those souls would benefit from religious instruction. Possession of a soul was not considered to be a gender-related characteristic, but who might influence and instruct souls was. If slaves were allowed to meet for worship, they would need preachers and that was a gendered role. It was one by which much prestige and respect were obtained in any community and, naturally, masters did not wish to see any of their male slaves grow in authority. If a master believed that his slaves needed religious instruction and worship, then he had to provide and oversee such activities or run the risk of a competing authority figure within the slave community. And white slave-owning men had no reason to encourage autonomy among their male slaves. Undiluted social power based on the assumption of racial superiority with supporting institutions and personal authority derived from male dominance held in place through marriage gave the white master absolute authority. He dared not weaken it by recognizing his male slaves as fully men.[28]

If indeed the systemic enslavement and domination of other men gave white males uneasy moments of doubt, no such conflict was likely to have troubled the masters regarding enslavement of black women. White males were accustomed to occupying a position of dominance and control over the women of their own class and race: the extension of that power over racially subordinated women was automatic. Had white women resisted the ideal of true womanhood and denounced the confining role of ladyhood, the extension of power over black women may have been problematic for white men. The inherent contradictions within planter-class ideology that dealt with gender roles according to race seems to have been too patent for anyone to miss. However, since white women shared the class rewards gained by their men, they could overlook the similarities between their true position and that of their black "sisters."[29]

Sisterhood was denied and black women gained no support from white women. If black women were not expected to live up to the female ideal and be "the angel in the house" or "true women," what was the role of the black women in slavery? She, just as a male slave, was a producer of wealth by means of her own labor. She also possessed skills which added to the master's wealth by weaving, spining, dying, sewing, cooking, midwifery, doctoring, nursing, cleaning, and producing cash crops. Unlike her white lady mistress for whom work was degrading, the black slave woman was defined by labor. Because of her race, gender expectations differed for her in spite of her sex. Because she was perceived to be less than. a true (white) woman and much less than a lady (elite white) she performed roles that were otherwise though to be unfit for women and would "unsex" them.[30]

One of those roles unfit for ladies was foisted onto slave women. If ladies were too pure to enjoy sexual acts, then black women must revel in them. It was easier for the masters to use their female slaves as sexual partners, albeit unwilling ones, if they saw black women as the obverse of their own white wives. Many white masters bestowed the very characteristics upon black slave women which their class ideology denied ladies. Black women were portrayed as shameless and highly sensual beings who lacked the restraint of libido that was part of the lady's role to play. More than one writer of fiction has implied that black and white women of the big house were jealous of one another's particular freedom. This truncated version of the basic female nature, that each woman was either a "good" woman who was pure and uninterested in basic human desires or a "bad" woman who was sexually available and enjoyed such acts is at least as old as Judeo-Christian doctrine. This set of beliefs saw the ouster from Eden, humanity's perfect relationship with God, as the result of Eve's behavior and one that recognized the female nature as dichotomous. According to this ideology, a women was either a voluptuous, disobedient, and bad Eve or a pure, deferential, and good Mary. The casting of antebellum Southern women into two distinct roles of good and bad with each role determined by skin color was less a result of slavery than the patriarchal way of defining the nature of all women. The obvious difference of skin color between white women and black simplified the process. Finally, black women were the reproducers of the labor force. By means of their reproductive ability they could continue to provide wealth in the form of new workers for the masters. As a slave, what she produced and reproduced was claimed by the white males who dominated southern plantations, northern towns, and English mills.[31]

By laborious rhetorical contortions, the elite class fashioned a gender ideology which was filled with contradiction. They managed to overlook these contradictions and allowed for all of the human personality demonstrating purity, passivity, fragility, sensitivity, meekness, and dependence to accrue to those who were female - unless they were black. Through their need to maintain power and authority, white patriarchs remained blind to the contradictions embedded in their gender system. They idealized specific characteristics as inherently female, yet denied those same characteristics to certain women. They effectively bifurcated the nature of females into two separate roles: one to be played by their female slaves and the other by their own wives.

Despite Harrison's desire to be with his wife and his unhappiness at their separation, he was not alone on his long trek. With him were approximately fifty adult slaves who made up part of Louisa's inheritance from her grandfather's estate.[32] These adults, some with very young children, were making the move with Harrison to Alabama on a trip, probably on foot, that lasted for fifty days.[33] What each one of them felt about the move is not a matter of record. No letters are extant to reveal either the joy or pain with which they made the move. Somerset, the Collins plantation, had been their home for several generations and long-time friends and relatives would be left behind. Possibly some anticipated escaping such a proud and autocratic master as Josiah Collins III and hoped for a lighter hand under the new owner. But the hopes or fears of the slaves cannot be read, only imagined.[34]

Harrison did mention some individual slaves by name and did make general comments on their welfare as they traveled—as he did about the welfare of another valuable asset:

> We have an old house in which they will sleep (last night I pitched a tent for them under which they passed the night very comfortably—Negroes I think never sleep). They are all in very fine spirits & travel well. My horses also behave well.[35]

He also remarked on the condition and behavior of two or three of the slaves who had been domestic workers for the Collins. One of his comments inadvertently serves as a grim reminder that insanity among slaves was not uncommon:

> The servants who had chills when I left Edenton have missed them today under the use of Quinine & Hannah sends word to Adeline that she feels better of her pains than she has in some time. Margaret is entirely sane, & attends me in a very satisfactory manner.[36]

Since no letter from one of the slaves can tell her impressions of how well she regarded the move or indicate what her real "spirits" were, Harrison's description must suffice. His ideas of how they felt about it all fail to tell us if his charges were chained together in the odious coffle or not. Nor do his letters indicate how heavily laden they were as they traveled. It is not even clear how they traveled.[37]

Hannah, fifty-four at the time the letter was written, was sending a message back to her daughter Adeline. Perhaps Adeline, twenty-five, had remained in Edenton only as long as her mistress Louisa did, in order to wait on her. Adeline's name does show up on the first list of slaves working on the Faunsdale plantation in Alabama in 1844 and her name continued to be carried on several Faunsdale slave lists until emancipation.[38] The message sent from Hannah to Adeline simply acknowledges their existence for us: it does not convey the texture of their relationship nor does it express their feelings about leaving their home for a new and unknown place.[39] And Harrison probably misidentified the slave suffering from insanity since Margaret and Nancy were twin sisters. Later documents show that it was Nancy and not Margaret who suffered from frequent bouts of insanity.[40]

The Alabama plantation to which Harrison and his caravan traveled was located in Marengo County in the rich cotton-growing district that stretched across the southwestern portion of the state. Prior to Harrison's purchase, Faunsdale was owned by a man named in one of Harrison's letters to Louisa simply as "Colonel Pearson". He left a small but substantial house for the new owner as well as cabins for slaves, living quarters that were available on the plantation as soon as all arrived. When they did arrive by boat in December, the new household goods could not be moved from the riverside dock to the plantation because the roads were impassable from the rain.⁴¹ Harrison was unable to leave Faunsdale for Somerset until the weather lifted and the roads dried. The tone of his letters to Louisa during the winter days of waiting was that of a man under pressure. Perhaps Louisa grew impatient with the long delay and let him know it.

Apparently the man to whom she referred to as "the Major" had influenced Harrison to seek land in the Southwest, yet he had not so impressed Louisa. In a letter to Harrison her doubts about the wisdom of his choice are obvious:

> I have already changed the current of my thoughts, & informed bright anticipation of my future home which I am glad now you have started in search of. I hope you will not curtail your investigations, for as yours is to be a selection for life & you have now the whole country presented to you, I would see it all, it seems to me before I decided.⁴²

In a subsequent letter she remonstrated that he should act with caution before buying land in Alabama. The remark that his selection was one for a lifetime was a reflection of her own selection of a lifetime. A poor choice of land by a man could more easily be remedied than a poor choice of a man by a woman. Tom Harrison was Louisa's economic and social base for existence just as the plantation was his. She pointedly reminded him of her own sacrifice for him:

> …yet by going to Louisiana & Mississippi you may find some place in those parts preferable, …and as I have given up my native land, I care not a rush where I sojourn, so long as you are with me.⁴³

In spite of her brave-wife words, Louisa continued to express concern over what her husband was doing. She clearly thought that he might be acting too hastily and without giving the matter ample thought. Again she urged careful consideration of his choice of land in a letter of April 6, 1843 when she wrote advice to him, wondering had not "the Major" exerted too much influence and prejudiced the selection of land. Harrison stayed with his plan to buy and settle in Alabama, but must have later regretted it. In the early 1850s he bought another established plantation, but his accidental death ended those plans.

Somewhat ironically, the new plantation which proved to be such a burden to Louisa later was in one of the states that she had once urged her husband to investigate years earlier:

> You know best I am sure, but yet I felt desirous you should have visited the other states before you decided & I have heard the merits of Louisiana & Mississippi so much cried up since you have been gone that my anxiety about your decision made me perhaps fear you might overlook advantages elsewhere, by contenting yourself with Alabama. You will doubtless think now that you are the best person to judge the propriety of your own course in the matter & I assuredly agree with you, my love, & am more over happy to abide by any decision you shall see fit to make. [44]

Louisa's cautionary advice was always tempered by conciliatory words to assure her husband that she had not overstepped her place and was not attempting to tell him what to do. It was not even a matter of her being too timid to speak her own desires, but a case of his seeming to ignore what she did say. Her desire that her husband at least visit the other states is easily discerned. In light of the fact that her property was to provide part of their joint economic base, she assumed that she might have a say in the decision of where they settled. Almost every slave used to work the Alabama plantation came to Harrison through Louisa, yet her considerable economic contribution to their venture granted her very restricted authority to say where that contribution would be applied. That was not unusual: Harrison acting under his wife's direction would have been more unusual since the legal system and custom both supported his actions. Married women could not own property in North Carolina or Alabama in 1843. Harrison acted as the men of his class did and utilized the assets marriage had given him. Marriage was a serious business.[45]

Depending upon the class and race of those involved, marriage served various functions for men. One function marriage served for all men, free or not, was the creation of kinship ties between male members of the uniting families; only free men could take advantage of the important family connections that marriage with the daughter or sister of another man of wealth would bring. The financial bonding between men through marriage created a web of absolutely essential ties that could be achieved in no other fashion.[46] Enslaved men could not act in a true patriarchal capacity because they were not free to exert one of its essential prerogatives.[47] The economic, social, cultural, and juridical systems which constituted patriarchy required that the fathers have the power and authority to marry into the families of their own social class, with their own kinswomen marrying out to other families within that class. Unfree men could establish emotional bonds and a sense of familial duty toward their wives' families, but they could not execute that specific male prerogative of free exchange of women. The white masters had pre-erupted it. The white assumption of racial superiority and subsequent usurpation of all male authority denied black males a share of the public role of that authority. This usurpation caused an ideological and physical separation between the men of both races. Enslaved black men were witnesses to, yet barred from, the public authority derived from systemic female subordination. For black men to exercise the general male prerogative of subordination of females, they would either have to do so in privacy or wait until their access to public authority altered.[48]

In the nineteenth century, marriage bound free white elite males together in alliances that allowed for financial backing and the credit essential to their individual economic ventures. For working-class men who required less in terms of future investments than present needs, marriage provided them women and children who performed domestic labor without wages. If the women or children of a working-class man or yeoman farmer earned wages outside the family, he rightfully expected dependent family members to hand over their earnings.[49] Again, depending on the class and race of men involved, marriage provided various benefits: it could provide the locus for the transformation of raw materials into consumable or salable goods through domestic skills of wives; marriage sanctioned sexual activity and allowed for the legitimate reproduction of members of a class and the replication of its ideology; marriage provided a structured and orderly method for distribution of property from one generation to the next; and marriage gave men the right to control women and womens' sexual activities. As Gerda Lerner has written, marriage helped sustain male dominance since "male power is as contingent upon the availability of sexual and economic services of women in the domestic realm as it is upon the availability and smooth performance of military manpower."[50] Men relied on marriage, but in a different capacity than did women. It was not the material base for their existence nor was it the primary determinant of their social class as it was for women.

Marriage was the single institution which formed the matrix for all the diverse elements which constituted the material conditions and psychology for nineteenth-century white women of all classes. An unmarried woman belonged to the social class of her father while a married one depended on her husband's. Men gained their class position based on their relationship to the means of production, while women gained theirs based on their sexual ties to a man.[51] While marriage served different functions for women than for men, it served the same functions of enforcing social order and the protection of private property in society. For all of the reasons that marriage was central to the creation and continuation of a patriarchal society in the nineteenth-century South, slaves were not permitted to marry.[52]

Harrison had no racial barriers to his marriage to Louisa but he did have to please the male who acted as guardian of her wealth. For Harrison marriage meant selecting a woman who not only had an inheritance of her own, but making the all-important connections with the men of her family. Rich and well-connected male in-laws were needed to help provide financial backing and political standing for men who were starting up new plantations and in need of capital. Since there were few credit institutions for individuals and securing large loans from banks required the equivalent of a co-signer to vouch for the borrower's reputation and reliability, turning to a male relative was critical. Those same relatives would naturally want to assure the success of the husband of a kinswoman if only for her sake.

For the white elite class, marriage also provided socially sanctioned creation and socialization of the next generation. It provided the necessary services for the legal off-spring of that union. Marriage was the "glue" of society that held together the little commonwealth that each family was thought to be. The basic unit of society upon which all other institutions rested and depended was not the individual, but the family. Into a family created by marriage children were born, socialized, and fully incorporated into society, each child ideally replicating the gendered role of the parent of the same sex. Each generation was to inculcate its own belief system within the rising one and rise above or at least maintain their crass standing. In the dominant white culture children belonged to their fathers and looked to their mothers for the emotional and religious training coincident with their class. It was from within the family that a free child was prepared to become an economically self-sufficient and productive person.

Depending upon their class and gender expectations, children were either apprenticed, educated, or trained at home by their parents to assume a future place in society. Only as the product of a legal union could a child be assured of inheriting his or her financial support and social status. Children born outside of marriage were not entitled to the same benefits as those born within it. Marriage provided a family which in turn gave the opportunity for a young boy to learn a trade, buy land, or attain a profession. It also trained young women to take care in their selection of a man to marry. Legally sanctioned marriage and the ownership of children by their parents did not apply to the condition of slaves.[53]

For white elite women like Louisa Collins Harrison, marriage was also the primary economic base from which they gained support. Few alternatives presented themselves to white women in mid-nineteenth century America, and most especially those living in the overwhelmingly rural southern states. Those financially able could create a separate estate or trust fund for single women of the family to insure their economic independence and protect them against a husband's possible profligacy, but such options were not available to most families.[54] The majority of white women in the early nineteenth-century United States did marry and were trained to the domestic skills which made their unpaid labor so valuable.[55] Few women had the skills to earn wages and those who did left their wage-paying work once married.[56] And according to Alabama common law of the 1840's, had a married woman such as Louisa earned wages, they would have belonged to her husband. But no woman of her class expected to support herself through her own labor. She had abundant black slaves for that.[57]

Even those methods available to women of garnering a living by means other than the economic dependency of marriage existed as an extension into the public sphere of the private domestic services which women provided within a marriage and family. Women who kept boarding houses did so for those who lacked the material means to establish homes of their own.[58] Even prostitutes offered a service that was expected within marriage. Had sexual activity not been restricted to the confines of marriage, prostitution would not have offered an alternative. Prostitution certainly existed well before the fourth decade of the nineteenth century and functioned in other capacities than just as a sexual alternative to marriage. But by the time and in the place of antebellum North America, it lost any symbolic religious meaning and had no place in communal value systems as a power to invoke fertility or appease gods. By the time of Thomas and Louisa Harrison, prostitution served men as an alternative to marriage for their sexual needs and a way of making money for women. It was one in which women were paid direct wages instead of entering the barter arrangement of marriage where patriarchal values dominated. In patriarchal marriage, a woman's sexual services were the exclusive right of her husband. He provided her material support and in return had exclusive access to her sexually. That white masters could assume the same sexual use of enslaved black women might not have been openly acknowledge but was known among white women of the South. White men owned their black slaves directly as chattel property, but women of their own race and class were owned in a less direct, less brutal, yet more complex manner.[59]

 Women, married or single, had no formal political existence. Thus marriage did not directly affect their access to formal political power. Neither class nor race barred them from exercising the franchise or holding public office. Restrictions against them were as a sex. There were forms of informal, personal influence which women exerted in the male-dominated society and in their own "separate spheres" women wielded increasingly larger degrees of control. But the private sphere of women's culture did not permit them access to public arenas of market, pulpit, academy, or legislature.[60]

 Finally, since marriage was a legal contract, the state had a vested interest in recognizing and upholding its sanctity. By considering marriage to be a contract, the state could exert its public authority deeply into the private lives of individual members of the society. Parties entering the contract had to be of age to act on their own, or with consent of those legally responsible for them.

 Immediately upon entering the contract of marriage, the state rendered one of the contracting partners legally dead. Common law of antebellum Alabama regarded a married woman to have lost her legal and civil existence. She could "...not enter a contract, her lack of capacity of being akin to infants and persons of unsound mind."[61] Or, as in English common law from whence the Alabama concept derived, she experienced civil death.[62] Once a woman married, all of her property passed from her ownership to that of her husband and she could not act to buy or sell what was no longer hers. She could not represent herself in court nor enter into a contract once married. The children of a marriage were regarded as the property of their father: even in such a clear case of disregard for marriage as Pierce Butler exhibited toward Fanny Kemble Butler, he still won custody of their two daughters.

In 1832 Frances Anne Kemble, an English actress and member of the renoun Kemble family so well known to English theatre audiences, first met Pierce Butler. She was beautiful, talented, and deeply opposed to slavery, yet she married a man whose chief source of income was derived from the slave labor of his southern plantation. They met while she and several members of her family toured the United States, performing plays in Philadelphia, New York, Baltimore, Washington, and Boston, and married in 1834. In 1837 she accompanied her husband to his rice plantation on the sea islands of Georgia for the winter months. There she came face to face with the reality of slavery and it profoundly affected their marriage. As deeply as her abolitionist convictions cut into their marriage, so did his egregious marital infidelity also damage it. Although Fanny was well aware of his adultery, she would not use it against him in hopes of protecting herself and two daughters from further public embarrassment. Because he was their father and had the power of custom behind him, Butler gained custody of their children.[63]

Marriage did not cost enslaved black women the same degree of autonomy as white women because, as slaves, they had none. Nor did marriage provide them with the economic support, childrearing possibilities, or social respect which it usually gave to white women of any class. As long as black women were enslaved, marriage did not mean the same for them in material terms as it did their white sisters. Masters had an absolute authority to interfere in the most intimate decisions of a slave's life. A master could dictate the choice of a marriage partner for one of his slaves, or forbid their association. He could separate a man and woman from each other or from their children or parents. As long as masters had so much control over the personal lives of the enslaved workers, interference or even the threat of it hung over any familial relationship.

Depending upon his interest in slaves' lives or his economic need to produce more workers, the actions of a master regarding the personal lives of slaves could cover a wide range. He could go so far as matching likely-looking men and women in a sort of crude eugenics or be so lenient as to allow slaves to select their own mates and remain together at will as long as no problems arose.[64] The master could also remain as such a remove from the lives of his own slaves that he had no involvement in their marital arrangements. Enslaved men and women could and did take control over their own intimate decisions such as choosing a marriage partner without regard for the master—but the point must be reiterated that it lay within the authority of a master to keep families together or force them apart just as he could do with a married couple.[65]

In spite of the overwhelming potential power of the masters to command and their possible intent to obviate their slaves' own cultures, elements of African material culture survived. The artifacts made by human hands may be seen and recognized; the mental set of instructions for the personal and social ties that are also part of any culture are fleeting and their traces very difficult to locate.

However, because the material culture did survive, one may assume that much of the abstract did also and survived especially well in such remote and culturally isolated areas as the sea islands of Georgia and the coastal plantations of the Carolinas. The evidence that much of African culture did remain with slaves is irrefutable, but that is not the critical question. To what extent those cultural elements were applied by slaves to their own personal relationships and family structure is. If what had been a prevailing way of organizing most African societies, corporate families and polygamous marriage, continued to be the ideal for the Africans who became slaves at Somerset and then Faunsdale, then mothers and fathers living with their own children who were produced only after marriage was not what they would have remembered. Aunts, uncles, and grandparents would have been more important as family than just the marital pair of parents and their offspring. However, the coercion of slavery rendered such decisions impossible for the slaves to make until they were free of a master's control.[66]

Whether recalling older patterns of behavior or adapting to the new environment, slave men and women continued to live as satisfying a life as possible for them under the oppressive conditions of slavery. Some masters were lenient in their control and gave their slaves some degree of choice in making personal decisions. One example of how slaves used this relative freedom in selecting a marriage partner was captured in the memories of some of the elderly ex-slaves interviewed in the mid-1930's. Exercising one of their few options, young men went courting. According to these accounts, courting had rules and a certain protocol to be observed which required that the male make the first move and call on the girl or woman. Gaining the master's permission to leave his own plantation and visit her if she lived on another one was just the first step. Gaining her favor and her family's approval were all hurdles that had to be overcome by observing the proper cultural restrictions. Perhaps some of the older African mores that required respect of the older generation from the younger still prevailed:

> "Dem's moral times," said Amos Lincoln, and others confirmed that courting was as much a matter of gaining the parents' approval as of winning the girl's heart. While Peter Clifton was keeping the Ashford road hot, he was also practicing the arts of diplomacy on his sweetheart's mother and father. "I had to ask her old folks for her before' she consent,..."[67]

In spite of the patriarchal overtones of this method of establishing a marital partnership, one may still conclude that most of the forces which compelled white elites to marry had no function in the lives of black slaves. Since the slaves could expect no financial improvement in their lives from marriage, no greater access to public and political power via a well-planned alliance, no improvement in social status, no parental authority to direct the lives of their own children, no greater freedom or opportunity for women, and no relief from hard work or poverty by marrying a man of high status, marriage must have had a different dynamic and meaning for slaves:

> When folkese got married den dey was a-thinkin' bout makin' sho' 'nough homes for deyselfs and gittin' married meant sompin sort of holy.

Marriage in those days was looked upon as something very solemn, and it was mighty seldom that anybody ever heard of a married couple trying to get separated.

When I was young...young folks took their time and went together a long time and (when] they married they stayed married.[68]

The psychological and sexual reasons for seeking a long or even permanent relationship with another person were probably present for slaves in spite of the oppressive nature of slavery. Slaves may have regarded their marital and familial ties more highly <u>because</u> slavery took so much away from them.

Because slavery had robbed black men and women of so much of their personal freedom and supporting social institutions, the intimate and familial aspects of their lives probably took on greater importance.

For slave women, marriage may not have been the most significant emotional bond in their lives, as one historian has posited:

"...motherhood was still the black girl's most important rite of passage, and mothers were still the most central figures in the black family.[69]

The mother-child relationship was most likely to be, as among their African grandmothers, the real emotional center of an African-American slave woman's life.[70]

This does not necessarily mean that marriage was not an integral element of the African-American woman's life, but it does cast a different light on what would constitute a "normal" marriage among slaves and among freedwomen and men. What they had experienced as slaves was not necessarily that would persist once they were freed. African-American history has often been studied and discussed from a cultural bias of what constituted a family or a marriage. Frequently the criteria used to evaluate these institutions reflected the historian's own culture. He applied the criteria he found most familiar without taking into consideration possibilities like surviving African cultural elements. These surviving African cultural elements may have formed a tenuous link between Africans and enslaved black women and men in North America, but freedom brought about opportunity to cast off what had been lived as a slave and take up what was desired as a free person. Depending upon the gender of the freed slave, what was desirable could vary widely.[71]

African-American women were not held in the same regard in terms of their gender role as were white farm wives or plantation mistress or urban women., For their masters and mistresses, a slave woman giving birth to children did not carry the same meaning as it did for married white women. Slave women were workers first who could also reproduce the work force as well as produce the crop, so the concept of female frailty or the distinct separation of male and female spheres into the private and public realms that helped keep white women economically dependent on men did not apply to black female slaves. It remained to be decided by the freedwomen whether or not they saw hard work for themselves as freedom.

Not only were black women not allowed to occupy the same gender role as white women, the much-touted familial ties did not extend from the white household to black relatives. Mary Chestnut pointed out how sharp was the eyesight of many white mistresses who saw the kinship between some mulatto children and other white masters while obviously suffering from myopia when it came to their own lords and masters. While kinship ties were the most pervasive organizing structures in antebellum southern culture, those ties could not reach across the racial barrier and bridge the chasms that separated white and black children of the same father. Within the Faunsdale household was a black domestic slave who might easily have been a kinswoman of the white mistress, but family ties could not be stretched that far. The primacy of family to which slave-owners clung had been carefully crafted to circumscribe a color line over which no sister, brother, or cousin could step unless they were legitimate members of the white family. Only the maintenance of slavery kept many slave women outside one half of their family.

What African-American women experienced in slavery is not the focus of this study, but rather a limited set of experiences possible for freedwomen during the Reconstruction decade on one plantation in Alabama. The main focal point is the direction in which their developing gender system was headed after ten years of the restricted freedom that followed emancipation. For the freedwomen of Faunsdale, the changing economy of which they had been a part while slaves could have opened new opportunities for them since they had not been bound while slaves by the same gender restraints as their white mistresses. Competing ideologies were also opening up new paths to them to consider during that decade. Many of their actions were based on repeating what was known and familiar, but even more must have been carried out as a result of what they witnessed going on about them and their deep desires to own themselves and their children. "Freedom" is a relative term and condition. Theirs was restricted in two distinct ways: one was a conscious and deliberate creation by the members, especially the men, of the ruling class who had recently been their owners; the other set of restrictions acting on the now "free" black women were of the same nature which acts on all human beings who are all subjected to those "definite, necessary relations which are independent of their will," but with one refinement; black women were further restricted as the dominant patriarchal family model which was being transformed into a type of black male dominance intruded more and more into their lives.[72] Elements of African culture that may have survived in the isolation of such great tracts of land as Somerset and Faunsdale under slavery were unlikely to survive the onslaught of market capitalism. When this ineluctable force combined with the steady pressure from the dominant culture's ideology, Africanisms were unlikely to prevail. The combined ideologies of the Protestant work ethic, male dominance, and egregious racism fused together into a formidable barrier for the freed women of Faunsdale.

# END NOTES

1. Thomas A. Harrison to Louisa Collins Harrison, Oct. 25, 1843; Correspondence of Louisa Collins Harrison, Harrison box 1, folder H 1; Faunsdale Plantation Papers (FPP), Linn-Henley Research Library, Archives, Birmingham Public Library (BPL), Birmingham, Alabama. The Collins owned a home in the town of Edenton, North Carolina as well as their plantations. Somerset Plantation, home to Louisa's brother Josiah Collins, is still located at Lake Phelps, near Pettigrew State Park, and open to the public is a historic site.

2. Ibid.

3. Passim, Correspondence between Louisa Collins Harrison and Thomas A. Harrison, March 7, 1843 through January 5, 1844.

4. Josiah Collins, HI to Louisa Collins Harrison, July 8, 1844; Correspondence of Louisa Collins Harrison, Harrison box 1, folder H 1; FPP, BPL, Birmingham, Alabama; Collins opposed the matched before they married. This letter, written after they married and moved to Alabama, does not refer directly to his objection, but advised her to be certain to protect her interests and those of any children she might have in the future. He also reminded her of the slaves which were part of her "maiden inheritance."

5. Op. cit., T.A. Harrison to L.C. Harrison, Oct. 25, 1843.

6. The records are not clear on the relationship between Thomas Alexander Harrison, born May 1, 1814 and the Benjamin Harrisons of Berkeley. A search of land tax lists for Charles City County, Virginia from 1782 to 1840 was made in effort to establish Harrison's place in the Benjamin Harrison family, but to no clear conclusion. A copy of the report may be found in the inventory box, FPP, BPL.

7. "My dear Lou," from Th. A. Harrison, St. Louis, Sept. 13, 1842, Harrison Box 1, folder H 1, FPP, BPL

8. Numerous references to the problems encountered by Louisa and Thomas during their courtship and engagement may be found in the correspondence between Louisa Collins and Martha Pride during 1842 as well the letters between Louisa and Harrison in the same year.

9. Op. cit., "My dear Lou," Sept. 13, 1842

10. For an example of the problems of southern planters, state banks, and credit, see William A. Blair and W. A. Clark, <u>A Historical Sketch of Banking in North Carolina and the History of thBankingin Institutions Organized in South Carolina Prior to 1860</u> (rep. Arno Press, New York, 1980), pp. 15-16 on the by-laws of the proposed Bank of North Carolina. "Each note must have, except in special cases, two good sureties, residents of North Carolina, or stock collateral. ...If paper was not paid nor renewed no name on it could be accepted for another loan."

11. "My Sweet Pigeon," Martha Pride to Louisa Collins, Wyoming [Martha's family plantation in South Carolina], March 8th, 1842, Harrison Box I, folder 1, Louisa M. C. Harrison "Correspondence," FPP, BPL

12. Op. cit., "My dearest, My most beloved Cousin," Martha Pride to Lousia Collins, Wyoming, May 16, 1842

13. Ibid.

14. Harrison was trained as a medical doctor, but the Southern road to wealth and social prominence was the one taken by planters rather than physicians. Bertram Wyatt-Brown, <u>Southern Honor: Ethics & Behavior in the Old South</u> (Oxford University Press, 1982), recognized community consensus as a necessity for white planters, the minority, to maintain control over slaves who were the majority on large plantations.

15. Works analyzing the gender role of nineteenth-century white northern women may be found as well as an overly-abundant amount of contemporary descriptive and proscriptive literature for white women of the South. For more on the image as well as reality of life for the Southern lady, see Anne Firor Scott, <u>The Southern Lady: From Pedestal to Politics</u> 1830-1930 (University of Chicago Press, 1970), pp. 4-21; Catherine Clinton <u>The Plantation Mistress: Woman's World in the Old South</u> (New York, 1982); Elizabeth Fox-Genovese <u>Within the Plantation Household: Black and White Women of the Old South</u> (University of North Carolina Press, 1988). For a comparison and analysis of possible origins for the two <u>different</u> regional concepts, see Anne Goodwin Jones, <u>Tomorrow Is Another Day</u> (Baton Rouge, 1981), pp. 3-13.

16. The term "helpmeet" occurs too often in nineteenth-century letters, books, and diaries in reference to a woman's correct attitude toward her husband to try and cite the usage. The origins of the concept (and possibly the exact term) probably lies in the King James version of the Protestant Bible, Gensis 2:18.

17. Jones, <u>Tomorrow is Another Day</u>, p. 14

18. Passim, Correspondence Louisa Collins Harrison

19. For an account of an event in the life of the elder Josiah Collins, see the typewritten copy of "The Story of Washington County," John Darden, v.2, pp.2 - 6, Somerset Plantation, Creswell, North Carolina. Included in the MS is a copy of a letter dated July 6, 1790 from Dick Thorne to his father, Abraham Thorne, in which he described Collins' celebration of 4 July, 1790.

20. Seldom is the term "slaves" ever used in the letters or contemporary written materials of the white planters or their family members. The euphemistic "servant" was used instead.

21. Louisa's guitar is now in the possession of her great, great, great granddaughter who lives in the same house as did Louisa at Faunsdale. In a

conversation with her, she repeated information from family tradition that Louisa Collins Harrison was an unusually intelligent woman with fine musical talents. Her interest in music is evident in many of her letters.

22. For more on the history of social support and development of medical practices surrounding childbirth in the United States, see Dorothy C. and Richard W. Wertz, Lying-In: A History of Childbirth in America. (New York, 1979). For more on the specifics of nineteenth-century women and their attitudes of the dangers of childbirth, see Judith Walzer Leavitt, "Under the Shadow of Maternity: American Women's Responses to Death and Debility Fears in Nineteenth-Century Childbirth," Feminist Studies. 12, n. 1, (Spring, 1986) pp. 129- 154.

23. "My dearest Lou," H.E.C. (Henrietta Elizabeth Collins) to Louisa Collins Harrison, Edenton, June 12, 1844, Harrison Box 1, folder 2, FPP, BPL

24. "My beloved Lou," A.D.P. [Ann Daves "Nancy" Collins Page) to Louisa Collins Harrison, Elizabeth City, June 21 [18)/44, Harrison Box 1, folder 2, FPP, BPL

25. "My own precious Sister," E. Alethia Collins to Louisa Collins Harrison, Edenton, June 22, 1848, Harrison Box 1, folder 6, FPP, BPL

26. On the origins of slavery, see Gerda Lerner, The Creation of Patriacrhy (New York, 1986) and Orlando Patterson, Slavery and Social Death: A Comparative Study (Cambridge, 1982).

27. Many of the histories which purport to analyze the institution of slavery and the nature of slave-master relations actually focus on the relationships between men. Even the important and path-breaking work done by Eugene Genovese's Roll, Jordan, Roll: The World the Slaves Made (New York, 1976), does exactly that. While Genovese makes it clear that masters needed much more from their slashes than just their labor, he analyzes the relations along class lines, paternalism, rather than the gender lines which underlay the patriarchal structure of slave society.

28. In one of the first contracts between the old master of Faunsdale and the laborers who had been his slaves, a two page list of fines was included. The offense which carried the greatest fine was for preaching or conjuring. And as valuable as cotton was in 1867, the fine for breaking a cotton stalk was .10 while the fine for preaching was $20.00. See Labor Contracts, Stickney box VII, folder 15 for Faunsdale contracts for 1865, 1866, 1867, 1872, and 1874. See Genovese, esp. pp. 255-270 on the role of black preachers during slavery.

29. On the subordination by white southern women of gender interests for class position, see LeeAnn Whites, "Women, War, and Southern Culture," War and Southern Society, (University of Mississippi Press, forthcoming). For a contemporary view of slave women from the perspective of an elite slave owner's wife, see C. Vann Woodward, Mary Chesnut's Civil War (ed., New Haven, 1981), p. 243. Chesnut wrote, "There will never be an interesting book with a negro heroine down here. We know them too well. In fact they are not picturesque- only in fiction do they shine. Those beastly negros beauties. Animals..." However, according to The Private Mary Chesnut: The Unpublished Civil War Diaries (ed. C. Vann Woodward and Elisabeth Muhlenfeld, New York, 1984), p. xv, she wrote in March, 1861 of slavery as "a curse to any land. Summer said not one word which is not true." Also see Minrose Gwin, Black and White Women of the Old South: The Peculiar Sisterhood in American Literature (University of Tennessee Press, 1984) esp. pp. 3-5, 111-115, and 171-174; Joan Kelly, Women, History, and Theory (University of Chicago, 1984), esp. p. 61.

30. For the particular skills of the black women of Faunsdale, see Register of St. Winifred's Family and Day School, Stickney box v, folder 55, pp. 21-23 for a list of taxable slaves drawn up in 1864 for the Confederate Government, FPP, BPL.

31. Minrose Gwin, op. cit., writes eloquently on p. 45 that "the nineteenth-century southern mythos demanded moral superiority from white women and sexual availability from black,..." She devotes an entire chapter, pp. 45-

109, to obverse images of mistress and slave. For more on the nineteenth-century sexual ideology as applied specifically to white women, see Nancy F. Cot, "Passionless: An Interpretation of Victorian Sexual Ideology, 1790 - 1850," <u>A Heritage of Her</u> <u>Own</u> (ed. Nancy F. Cott and Elizabeth H. Pleck, New York, 1979) pp. 162-181.

32. Heirs of Josiah Collins, Senior, Harrison, Louisa (Mrs. Thomas), Private Collections, Raleigh provides a list of all of those slaves belonging to Louisa Collins Harrison as of October, 1843 just before Harrison's departure for Alabama. There are fifty-nine names on the list with each family grouped as a unit.

33. There were eleven groups of names, ten of which I have identified as husband and wife or parent(s) and child(ren). Of the enare group that traveled to Alabama, at least 12 were under six years of age, and several women gave birth within the year after reaching Alabama.

34. Although one letter from a family member to Louisa Collins Harrison stated that another letter was enclosed from one slave to another, it is not in the family papers. Most letters between the white female members of the Collins family included messages to special slaves.

35. Thomas A. Harrison to Louisa C. Harrison, Oct. 25, 1843, FPP

36. Ibid.

37. Herbert Aptheker, <u>American Negro Slave Revolts</u> (New York 1964) pp. 287-288, wrote of an incident in which a slave woman helped to free two male slaves who were part of a coffle of ninety (a coffle was a group of enslaved persons chained together to prevent their escape as they walked to their destination). That particular coffle was on its way from Maryland to the South for sale. Sherley Anne Williams used it, plus another historical event in which a free white woman in the South hid runaways, for the basis of her novel <u>Dessa</u> <u>Rose</u>.

38. List of Negroes 1848, List of Negroes 1857, Faunsdale box 1, folder 4, FPP, BPL

39. Hannah, b. circa 1788, did not live at the Somerset Plantation, but at "the Homestead" in Edenton. Her daughter, Adeline, b. 1819, was probably a domestic "servant" as well. For their status in 1864 at Faunsdale, see St. Winifred's register, p. 21 which lists Adeline as a "House servant" and Hannah Paine as "too old for work." Hannah must have been a house slave earlier since her name is not on any of the lists for field workers, yet she was definitely taken to Alabama.

40. No evidence suggests that Margaret was ever insane, while Nancy was still being noted as having periods of insanity as late as 1883. The information that Nancy and Margaret were twins comes from the "List of Negroes belonging to Josiah Collins in the town of Edenton and County of Chowan, April 1838," Slave Papers, Josiah Collins' Papers, Private Collections, Department of Archives and History, Raleigh, North Carolina. The information about Nancy's condition is scattered throughout various documents in the Faunsdale Papers, but especially in the diaries of William Stickney.

41. Thomas A. Harrison to Louisa C. Harrison, January 5, 1844

42. Louisa C. Harrison to Thomas A. Harrison, March 7, 1843

43. Ibid.

44. Louisa C. Harrison to Thomas A. Harrison, April 6, 1843

45. For more information on the importance of marriage as a means of securing financial connections between elite southern males, see Bertram Wyatt-Brown, Southern Honor: Ethics and Behavior in the Old South (Oxford, 1982), esp. pp. 199 - 217. May Ryan also includes some remarks on the same relationship, but for northern men of the developing middle class in Cradle of the Middle Class (Cambridge, 1981), pp. 137, 138.

46. For more on the exchange of women and the patriarchal family, see Gayle Ruben, 'The Traffic in Women: Notes on the 'Political Economy' of Sex," Toward an Anthropology of Women (ed. Rayna R. Rapp, New York, 1975) pp. 157-210; Joan Kelly, Women History and Theory (The University of Chicago Press, 1984), esp. "The Social Relations of the Sexes," pp. 1-18; Gerda Lerner, The Creation of Patriarchy (New York, 1986).

47. I am indebted to Elizabeth Fox-Genovese for pointing out this critical difference in the use of the term "patriarchy" and its inappropriate application to black men while they lacked public authority. For want of a better term to express the sanctioned subordination of women by men, I have taken her suggestion and used "male dominance" when referring to the black male's role and position in the family after emancipation.

48. As yet, no one has, to my satisfaction, determined how pervasive were such attitudes among black freed men as reported by Laura M. Towne, Letters and Diary of Laura M. Towne (ed., Rupert Sargent Holland, rep., Negro University press, 1969), pp. 183-184 when she wrote in June, 1867. She repeated a black man who told her that "...the womens will stay at home and cut grass [while the men took part in a political meeting]," Town then editorialized: "It is too funny to see how much more jealous the men are of one kind of liberty they have achieved than of the other! Political freedom they are rather shy of, and ignorant of; but domestic freedom - the right, just found, to have their own way in their families and rule their wives - that is an inestimable privilege!"

49. For the postwar challenge to that right of working class women to "own themselves" and thus retain their wages, see Amy Dru Stanley, "Conjugal Bonds and Wage Labor: Rights of Contract in the Age of Emancipation," The Journal of American History (vol. 75 no. 2, Sept. 1988), pp. 471-500.

50. Lerner, op. cit., p. 100

51. Ibid., esp. pp. 215 - 219

52. For more on the nature of slavery and its intrinsic requirement to break kinship ties, see Orlando Patterson, Slaved and Social Death (Cambridge, 1982).

53. Authority over their children did not necessarily accrue to the freed women and men in the first years after emancipation. For several years following emancipation a battle was waged between black adults and white ex-masters over "orphan" black children. These children, many of whom actually had at least one parent, became another method by which whites attempted to hold onto their waning control over black women and men.

54. Brother Josiah seems to have harbored some suspicion regarding his brother-in-law Harrison. According to a document in the Collins Papers, Archives, Raleigh, Harrison granted a power of attorney to Josiah for the express purpose of having all property surveyed which had belonged to Louisa before marriage. It reads in part: "...all other lands owned by, or being in the possession of my wife at the time of her marriage & to have such line or lines run around said lands, as he [Collins] may think necessary & proper, more clearly to define the boundaries between them..." Susan Lebsocks's The Free Women of Petersburg: Status and Culture in a Southern Town, 1784-1860 (New York, 1984), provides an authoritative source for more on women'

55. For more on womens' domestic labor in rural or agricultural areas, see John Mack Faragher, "The Midwestern Farming Family, 1860," Women's America (ed. Kerber and Mathers, New York, 1982), pp. 114 - 129; Julia Cherry Spruill, Womens' Life & Work in the Southern Colonies (New York, 1972); Catherine Clinton, The Plantation Mistress: Woman's World in the Old South (New York, 1982).

56. Wage work was scarce for women of the antebellum South. The economy was primarily agricultural - which was carried out either by slaves or yeoman farm families—and towns small. No industrial work of any significance offered women opportunities for wages either. Most scholarly attention focused on this topic has been turned in the northern direction to mill workers as seen in Thomas Dublin, Women At Work (Columbia University

Press, 1979). For a very small bit on southern wage-earning women, see Anne Firor Scott, <u>The Southern Lady: From Pedestal to Politics 1830 to 1930</u> (University of Chicago Press, 1970), pp. 35- 36.

57. As Amy Dru Stanley observes, the social context which could permit recognition and clarification of the relationship between a woman's right to own her wages and her right to own herself had not developed by the mid-nineteenth century.

58. Running a boarding house was one of the "hidden" ways in which women, esp. in towns and cities, worked. I refer to it as hidden because its true economic nature seems to have been hidden for so long from those who sought to evaluate work done by women to earn money or to survive. Alice Kessler-Harris, "Where Are The Organized Women Workers?" (Woman's America, op. cit.), p. 238, n. 3, writes "Such occupations as taking in boarders, homework, and working on husbands' farms or in family business are not counted by census takers.

59. Lerner, op. cit., with a nod in the direction of Engels, recognizes the significant relationship between sexual control and social control. "...the sexual control of women has been an essential feature of patriarchal power. The sexual regulation of women underlies the formation of classes and is one of the foundations upon which the state rests." (Lerner, p. 140)

60. The body of literature on the analytical concept of separate spheres is far too great to list here. Some historians who have successfully applied it, as well as pointed out its drawbacks, are the following: Nancy F. Cott, <u>The Bonds of Womanhood: "Woman's Sphere" in New England, 1780 – 1835</u> (New Haven, 1977); Carroll Smith-Rosenberg, "The Female World of Love and Ritual: Relations Between Women in Nineteenth-Century America," <u>A Heritage of Her Own</u> (New York, 1979) pp. 311-342; Mary Beth Norton, "The Paradox of 'Women's Sphere'" <u>Women of America: A History</u> (ed. Carol Ruth Berkin and Mary Beth Norton, New York, 1979) pp. 139-149; Mary P. Ryan, <u>Womanhood in America: From Colonial Times to the Presents</u> (New York, 1983) pp. 113-165; Ellen DuBois, Mari Jo Buhle,

Temma Kaplan, Gerda Lerner, and Carroll Smith-Rosenberg, "Politics and Culture in Women's History: A Symposium," Feminist Studies (v. 6, n. 1, Spring 1980) pp. 26-64; and Linda Kerber, "Separate Spheres, Female Works, Woman's Place: The Rhetoric of Women's History," The Journal of American History (v. 75, n. 1. June 1988) pp. 9-39.

61. "Legal Status of Women in Alabama," p. 2 (published by Ida D. Rosenthal, 1940, Birmingham, Alabama. The pamphlet is part of the archival holdings (which are relevant to the history of women in the South) in the Linn-Henley Research Library, Birmingham Public Library, Birmingham, Alabama. I am much indebted to Jane Keeton for pointing it out to me.

62. Since property ownership comes under state jurisdiction, to accurately trace changes in married women's property rights in the United States would require a state-by-state assessment. For a general view of changes in married women's property rights in the post-war South, see Suzanne D. Lebsock, "Radical Reconstruction and the Property Rights of Southern Women," Journal of Southern History XLIII (May 1977) pp. 195-216. For a general overview of married women's property rights outside the South in the nineteenth-century, see Norma Basch, In the Eyes of the Law: Women, Marriage, and Property in Nineteenth-Century New York (Cornell University Press, 1982). Suzanne Lebsock, Free Women of Petersburg (New York, 1984), includes such information and many secondary sources related to women owning property specifically in antebellum Virginia.

63. Fanny kemble's own account of her stay in Georgia, Journal of a Residence on a Georgia Plantation in 1838-1839a (Reprint, Athens, 1984), while married to Pierce Butler makes no reference to her marital difficulties. For more on her personal life, see Margaret Armstrong, Fanny Kemble: A Passionate Victorian (New York, 1938) and Malcolm Bell, Jr.'s Major Butler's Legacy: Five Generations of a Slaveholding Family (University of Georgia Press, 1987). Bell unequivocally states "The underlying cause of their troubles was the ownership and treatment of the Butler slaves at Hampton and Butler's Island Plantations. The second basic cause for the

breakup of their marriage was Pierce Butler's infidelity" (p. 307), which was apparently well-known.

64. For primary sources, see <u>We are Your Sisters: Black Women in the Nineteenth Century</u> (ed. Dorothy Sterling, New York, 1984), pp. 31-36.

65. The debate over the nature of North American slavery, or in the words of Ann J. Lane, "what did slavery do to the slave?" opened with publication of Stanley M. Elkins' <u>Slavery : A Problem in American Institutional and Intellectual Life</u> (Chicago, 1959). Since then, a great deal of heat and some light has been generated over this quintessentially American problem. For a single work which lays out the bare tenets of Elkins argument and how various historians have responded to it, see Ann J. Lane, ed. <u>The Debate Over Slavery: Stanley Elkins and His Critics</u> (University of Illinois Press, 1971). Somes of the essays are precis for the authors' later monographs on slavery.

66. I am indebted to Dr. Theresa Singleton of the Smithsonian for aid she has generally given on this issue. Writing about possible African survivals in African-American slave cultures and societies is treading, metaphorically, a minefield of intellectual and political dangers. It is not my argument that seventeenth- or eighteenth-century African cultural institutions survived intact within African-American societies, nor that their persistence shaped American black family structures in the middle of the twentieth century. I am arguing that some significant African cultural elements did survive and were manifested among the slaves of coastal North Carolina, South Carolina, and the sea islands of Georgia. For more on African survivals, both material and ideological culture, see Dr. Edward Warren, <u>A Doctor's Experiences on Three Continents</u> (Baltimore: Cushings and Bailey, 1885) passim; Melvin Herskovits, <u>The Myth of the Negro Past</u> (Boston, 1958); John M. Vlach, <u>The Afro-American Tradition In Decorative Arts</u> (Cleveland Museum of Art, 1978), whose text and photographs of the artifacts, made it a very valuable document; Albert J. Raboteau, <u>Slave Religion: The 'Invisible Institution' in the Antebellum South</u> (Oxford University Press, 1978) esp.

pp. 3-92; Lawrence W. Levine, Black Culture and Black Consciousness: Afro-American Folk Though from Slavery to Freedom (Oxford University Press, 1978) esp. chapters 1, 2, and 3; John Blassingame The Slave Community: Plantation Life in the Antebellum South (Oxford University Press, 1979), esp. pp. 5-48, 71-75, 98-100, 177-183; Paul D. Escott Slavery Remembered: A Record of Twentieth-Century Slave Narratives (University of North Carolina Press, 1979) pp. 95, 100-110; Charles Joyner, Down by the Riverside: A South Carolina Slave Community (University of Illinois Press, 1984); Deborah Gray White, Aren't I a Woman?: Female Slaves in the Plantation South (New York, 1985) esp. chapters 3 and 5; Sterling Stuckey Slave Culture: Nationalist Theory & The Foundations of Black America (Oxford University Press, 1987) chapter 1.

67. Escott, Slavery Remembered, p. 53.

68. Ibid, p. 49.

69. White, Aren't I a Woman?, p. 108.

70. Ibid., p. 107.

71. In 1786 eighty "new Africans" were transported directly from Africa to Josiah Collins' Lake Company plantation of Somerset. By looking at a current map of North Carolina, one may see the isolation of the site. The Lake Phelps area was once part of the Great Dismal Swamp, a name which aptly describes the environment. Until the canals were completed, access to the area and transportation of produce out of it were very difficult. Since it was his policy to keep slave families intact, the eighty who came directly to Somerset from Africa in 1786 probably infused the slave community there with strong reminders of Africa. It was from that same community of enslaved people, that Louisa Collins Harrison and husband took about sixty slaves to Faunsdale Plantation, Marengo County, Alabama. Some of their descendants live in Marengo County today.

72. Karl Marx, the preface to <u>A Contribution to the Critique of Political Economy</u> as quoted by Thomas Dublin in <u>Women at Work,</u> (Columbia University Press, 1979), p. 2.

CHAPTER TWO

# "Able Men to be Rulers or Thousands, & Rulers of Hundreds, & Rulers of Fifties, & Rulers of Tens."[1]

The sternly disciplined Protestant clergymen of the northern communities of colonial and eighteenth-century North America who so personified the Protestant work ethic and patriarchal ideology would have recognized William Augustus Stickney as one of their ideological descendants. If any nineteenth-century southern clergyman of the Episcopal Church could have felt part of their community, it would have been the Rev. Stickney. Although he had been an Episcopal priest since 1847, Stickney seemed closer to the Mathers than the Beechers in his theology and rigid adherence to an earlier ideal that every family was "little commonwealth" over which the husband and father ruled as benign despot. William Stickney managed to hew to both a form of Calvinistic self-discipline and patriarchal authority over dependents that would have marked him as one of their own with the stern old men of eighteenth-century New England.[2]

His father, Joseph Blodgett Stickney, had moved to Alabama in 1820, just one year after its creation from the remains of the once far-reaching Creek Indian nation that had covered Alabama, Mississippi, Tennessee, part of Georgia, and the Carolinas and brought his New England ideology with him. Getting in his bid on 840 acres of land from General Count Charles Lefevre Desnouettes between the exodus of the defeated Creeks and disheartened French, the elder Stickney, also a priest of the Episcopal Church, settled in Greensboro, Alabama and was a founding member of St. Paul's Episcopal Church. Thus the younger Stickney was exposed from his childhood to the ideology of his father's own training.[3]

Born in 1824 in Alabama when it was still the frontier for the rest of the white nation, Stickney graduated from the state university in 1844, then attended General Theological Seminary in New York until he was ordained as an Episcopal priest in 1847. He spent the rest of his life in Alabama, dedicated to what he considered missionary service to slaves and then freedpeople. What brought him into the sphere of the Canebrake planter elite that was developing in the southwestern section of Alabama was a decision to conduct a parochial school for boys in Marion, a town in Perry County. His school was successful enough that it stayed at capacity and kept a standing list of those who wished to enter when a vacancy opened until he gave it up in 1863. Since that was the time of his marriage to Louisa Collins Harrison, his new responsibilities as manager of her plantation added to his duties as a priest were probably the reason he left the school. After his acquisition of a wife and plantation with two hundred slaves, he refocused his priestly concerns toward the slaves of the area for whom he had ministered as a missionary since 1858. Into his new calling he carried what was locally known as a strict regard on matters of sexual morality. It was said of him that when a single man himself, he advocated that all clergymen should remain celibate.[4]

With his marriage to Louisa Collins Harrison, Stickney became the manager, but not the owner of Faunsdale. He had known her for some time before they wed since she had been an active member of the church for many years before her husband's death in 1858. Harrison's death left her the sole executor of his estate and legal guardian of their child, Louise. Louisa had no child in her marriage to Stickney and after Louise died in 1872 at age twenty-eight, ownership of the plantation eventually passed to her daughter (Louisa's granddaughter), Lou Harrison Shepard. It is likely that a separate estate to protect the interests of Harrison's child had been devised through a pre-naptual agreement which settled the property on his daughter, by-passing Stickney. Since the death of Dr. Harrison in 1858, the plantation has not been owned by a man.[5]

It was not Stickney's marrying a land- and labor-rich widow that merits attention since rich widows were a common path for men of ambition wanting to raise their station in life; it was his successful postwar management of her plantation and its labor force along the lines of a biblically informed patriarchal model that imbues him with significance. Once it was clear to him that to control the new social class of free labor he had to devise methods that differed from the threat and punishment of slavery, he resorted to what he knew from theological training. William Stickney's combined roles of priest and labor master cohered and meshed without missing a beat as he delivered a sermon in 1866 based on the following verse from Exodus; 8, 21, with the title "How to rule the masses and hold the negro to us":

> Moreover, Thou shalt provide out of all the people able men, such as fear God, men of truth, hating covetousness & place such over them to be rulers of thousands, rulers of hundreds, rulers of fifties, & rulers of tens.[6]

Stickney's specious interpretation of the biblical patriarch's admonition and how it must be taken up and adapted to the use of those nineteenth-century men who continued to regard themselves in the same light formed the body of his sermon.

Calling up his pedagogical experience, Stickney proposed to his congregation that they, the best, the kind of "able" men of whom the heathen priest spoke, act on their gender responsibility and "act like men," to force the issue, seize the initiative, and use their dependents. Only in backing down, being 5t weak, failing to achieve their own will would the white patriarchs who listened to his sermon suffer the great weakness of being unmanly:

> There's always a way, if we only act like men to find it out, as has been said. And if we are but half true to ourselves, we can hold this people to us for all our uses until their extermination. It is backing down from exertion, & thereby providing unworthy of a man's position or a man's reward, to give up & cry out "we can do nothing with them now they are free,..."[7]

He acknowledged how difficult a position they, the "able men" to whom he was preaching, were in because in the few months' time that had elapsed since the war ended, they were still in a state of shock, still stunned over their loss, yet were expected to direct and manage their own masses. He continued on in the text of the sermon to remind the congregation of the old set of relations that had existed, that if left alone, they could solve any problems "between Master and Servant" because only they could understand that relationship:

> Were we let alone, with the dissolution of sacred authority time honored in its inheritance & transmission, there were time allowed for calm second thought to assist us. But insane fanaticism is sending its emissaries among us to eradicate all ties of the old relationships existing between Masters & Servant.[8]

The defunct class of masters were to reassert control over free workers through education - for their own uses - that would re-establish "able men" as the masters of their minds if not their bodies until the black race destroyed itself:

> Whether they can be educated or not is not the question for us at this stage...of their importance to our own deepest interests. We do know they can be educated in the vast department of usefulness to us, our families, our children. And we ought to be selfish enough to say no more, to be moving rapidly enough in the direction of contravening the efforts of the radical fanatic by receiving them within schools under the control of our own best people. Where they may be taught all their capacities can receive, & especially their place as Servants. Equality is the first idea the New England radical would inculcate. Then all our past pains are lost. We no longer have <u>Servants</u> but <u>equals</u> to wait on & serve us. Avert this. For we may & can, not by talking but acting.[9]

The rest of the sermon was directed toward his instructions on how to "hold the negro to us" by means of education and class responsibility. He charged the "best people" to take up the work of educating free black workers. As Stickney described the work, it was still the role of the white elites to take charge for the good of their society, especially to protect themselves against incursions from northern radicals. Stickney correctly identified the threat they presented to his class's need to control laborers and what would happen if freed black workers realized their leverage and bargained for what they wanted.

> [A]ble men must be picked, men of truth &: excellence, to be put over the masses. Teachers of such order may get the reins in hand or command not this respect of our better people. Will they foster respect in these servants toward our higher, better people? Will they not rather draw them away & alienate them so entirely from us that in the scarcity of labor, they will rule by various vile artifices & monopolize all? ...Keep things as you would have them while you can. A very little time & you may not have the matter within your hands.[10]

Stickney was expressing concerns for what he had lost and knew that he still could lose. His sense of importance and authority which had flowed unimpeded from his position as the head of the household of Faunsdale and manager of the plantation and its work force of two hundred slaves was bad enough; the grim prospect of also losing economic power was too dose to be denied.

As the nominal master of the plantation and actual head of the household, Stickney had only two years to practice being the master of the large enslaved labor force before he would have to deal with the workers as free laborers. Stickney's sermon, his own words preached to his congregation, stated his ideological guidelines for the kind of relationship he would have with freed women and men, if he could. He envisioned himself as a patriarch much as his canon invested him with all of the authority in his society based upon his race, class, and sex. As his dealings with freed workers expanded over the years, he never relinquished his hold on his authority as a male, as master of a household, as a white man, and as a priest in his dealing with his workers. All that informed his sermon in 1866 continued to fuel his actions with his "servants."

William Stickney had also meant to keep his "servants" in the fold and under his hand in the early spring months of 1865 as news of approaching Union armies had spread through southwestern Alabama. Intending to protect his authority while trying to hold onto the plantation labor force, Stickney sent the slaves into hiding before the dreaded Yankees arrived. His efforts were both unnecessary and futile. Although the Canebrake had no actual combat before that spring, Federal armies were moving inexorably into those counties. Once they arrived, anxious slave-owners could not preserve slavery simply by hiding their slaves. Selma, which was thirty-three miles from Faunsdale Plantation, fell on 2 April when its three thousand defenders could not hold back the superior force of nine thousand commanded by Gen. J. H. Wilson. Driving various locally mustered militia and Confederate regulars before them, Wilson's raidiers left their Tennessee Valley stronghold in northern Alabama on 22 March, 1865 and secured their primary goal of Selma ten days later.[11]

As Wilson's raid from northern Alabama brought war into the heart of the state, other federal forces closed in from the southwestern front of Louisiana and Mississippi. On 4 May Confederate forces east of the Mississippi River under command of General Richard Taylor officially surrendered to Union armies commanded by General Edward R. S. Canby in Citronelle in Mobile County.[12] The combined Confederate defeats of that spring in Alabama roughly coincided with Lee's surrender of his army at Appomattox County Courthouse in Virginia, effectively ending the war, slavery, and the Confederacy. As the moribund Confederacy passed, William Stickney struggled to maintain mastery of slaves as well as his own threatened authority. Four days before Lee's surrender on 9 April, Stickney made this entry in his diary:

> All the land upset...Very busy weighing all the meat to negroes. Dispatched all the men and certain women with four wagons, all mules, some cows, for the hill county below. Oliver in charge...[I spent) till 11 o'clock digging & securing valuables & no house servants retained.[13]

Stickney's diary entry reveals both his fear of loss as the federal troops drew closer to the plantation and his inability to grasp the profound changes that were taking place between masters and slaves.[14] When he hid the valuables without the aid of even the most trusted of all slaves, the "house servants," his decision showed his distrust of them. Yet at a time when escape must have been on the mind of every slave, Stickney sent them into hiding under the supervision of slave Oliver. Stickney's slaveholder's ideology could admit, even expect, that slaves may steal from a master, but it also necessitated belief in his own authority over them. His authority derived in part from a deeply held faith that as long as he remained master, slaves would be either too dependent or too frightened to run away. Ideology alone could not hold a majority in thrall; it must be constantly reinforced with raw force and violence. Threats of invasion and subsequent loss of authority and power to federal agents pushed Stickney and other men of his class to permit slaves unaccustomed freedom of movement that would not have happened in normal times.[15]

By the 6th of April, two days later, Stickney had regained confidence in his own mastery of the situation to the point that "all slaves returned from the woods" and guns were given to four slaves who were set out as guards for the night. And those mules were indeed safe from the Yankee soldiers because they were taken by Confederates instead. On 15 April Stickney noted the return of slaves who had been impressed to work in Confederate salt mines. A tersely expressed diary entry for 23 April, 1865 leaves much unsaid, noting only that he had a long talk with S'vts (men) about going to army." He must have referred to the United States Army whose continued presence a long day's walk away remained a great threat to Stickney's mastery of his "S'vts." and his society.[16]

In spite of the maelstrom of change eddying about them, members of the Faunsdale community continued tending to ordinary and mundane events of life. Stickney did not turn to his diary as a way of relieving his worries resulting from the larger political and military events taking place in the state. It reveals instead immediate and intimate indigenous events of his household such as his performing the marriage ceremony of "s'vts William and Jane," on the evening of 29 April. The material concerns of his family and household took precedence in William Stickney's mind over larger but distant concerns of war. His diary for 1865 reflects almost no concerns beyond the boundaries of the plantation. And while such personal decisions were being made by so many other Williams and Janes to trust in their own future, military and political decisions were being made by men who were surrendering their past. No longer would the old patriarchal relations of master and slave serve to mediate between white masters and black workers; relations between the new social classes remained to be established. Nor would the race-specific gender systems remain unaltered. The social fabric of the South was rent and required much alteration and repair.

The diary entries written by William Stickney in the spring months of 1865 reflect neither the larger events that were bringing an end to his familiar world nor the persistent urge of his servants to begin shaping a new world for themselves. One can easily detect Stickney's determination to maintain old social relations between himself and the servants, but their resistance to his effort are more subtly, even inadvertently, included in his private writings. Reading his diary entries for May, one easily discerns that he was not ready to relinquish the authority which he had known as master. He still used force to maintain control over his "servants."

> May 12 [H]earing from negroes running to Selma to the Yankees. Mine all silent yet.
>
> 16 At noon had s'vt Albert punished. Negroes leaving for Yankees all round. Not yet mine.
>
> 19 Yankees in Uniontown [five miles away).
>
> 24 Had Austin Sex-slave) punished for going off. Three soldiers at night took horses.
>
> 27 S'vt George (house) gone. S'vts Mark & Fanny still about the roads.
>
> 29 ...Rode to U'town to see Yankee Col. (Brittain) about getting back Geo. to jail. Succeeded.
>
> 30 ...Got the S'vt George duly delivered & tied. Sent him to jail... Put out s'vt guards for night with guns, Henry, Hiram, & Oliver.[17]

Soon the presence of soldiers of the Army of the United States, particularly that of Lieutenant Colonel W. B. Brittain, was felt by white landowners in Marengo County. The newly created federal agency, the Bureau of Refugees,

Freemen and Abandoned Lands would soon intervene in the working out of social relations between free black labor and white ex-masters, but that relationship was most immediately influenced by federal soldiers. Although the Freedmen's Bureau was not fully operational in Alabama until late in the summer of 1865, some of the policies and practices used by certain general officers who had commanded Union armies in the southwestern theatre of war were adapted to fit immediate needs of the incipient Bureau.

When faced with the exigencies of occupation of Louisiana early in the war, General Benjamin F. Butler and his successor General Nathaniel P. Banks had reacted to immediate problems by cobbling together some practical solutions into a cohesive policy. Labor contracts were one of the devices employed by Generals Butler and Banks to ease the social tensions resulting from the ruptured relations between quasi-free black workers and masters while Louisiana was under federal military occupation. Conflicts flared repeatedly between various social groups when northern armies were garrisoned in the midst of southern slavery, giving rise to many of the expeditious practices which remained in place. By the time Lt. Col. Brittain and his forces reached Marengo County, Alabama, labor contracts between ex-master and ex-slaves were not a new practice - at least among Yankee officers.[18]

Across the state Union officers such as Brittain had assumed powers that usually accrued only to elected officials of a state government. However, since Alabama's war government had been imprisoned and "union" and "secession" men were jockeying for the right to rule, President Johnson appointed Lewis E. Parsons Provisional Governor on 21 June, 1865. For the next three years Alabama's state government rose and fell in response to Presidential and Congressional Reconstruction plans. For several months following the war's end, inhabitants of Alabama lived in a rather confused, even desperate state of affairs while three overlapping political and military entities vied for authority in a state where personal authority of planters had been the rule. Union armies, the federal agency of the Freedmens' Bureau, and a provisional state government all wrestled to solve the most immediate and pressing problems created by a war whose damage was too great for all of them to ameliorate. Exactly how much authority officers and Freedmens Bureau agents in Alabama were to have was yet to be defined in the summer of 1865, but males of the planter class such as William

Stickney did not relinquish their accustomed authority over their society and "servants" readily, not even to the most obvious dispensers of authority and order in sight.[19]

Freedwomen and men were quick to turn to Union soldiers only to learn that federal officers were not <u>automatically</u> their champions. Turning to the federal men was a gamble. Sometimes it paid off for the ex-slave, but more often Union officers were trying to keep the worker out of the towns and on the plantation and remind the over-proud planters who was currently in command. Protection of the safety and rights of black men and women by Union officers was too idiosyncratic and dependent upon personal beliefs to be reliable for the freed women and men. When some of Faunsdale's ex-slaves took their complaints of William Stickney's wrongdoing to the garrison at Uniontown, Lt. Col. Brittain was quick to threaten Stickney with punishment if he continued to abuse his hands. However, they were returned to the plantation by Brittain's soldiers with little protection from departing soldiers against Stickney's wrath.

Although his diary was private, Stickney's efforts to reassert his authority over his "servants" were of public significance and represented a primary concern of the elite men of the planter class:

June 2 Called on by Yankee guard…about S'vt Geo.

9 First sign of Yankee poison among the negroes - 4 ran off to U'town & returned by noon. A Yankee Capt. out to investigate, "No complaint to make" (quoting his frightened workers].

10 2nd fuss with the negroes at noon hour & further at night. Whipped 3 & tied 2.

12 5 negroes there (Uniontown) - nothing to them.

13 Those 5 negroes all back. Took their rations away.

15 Had all negroes up at night for making contract. Left 5 out.[20]

Lieutenant Colonel Brittain's rather different view of the same events was revealed in his letter of June 15, 1865. He wrote to Stickney that he was aware of what had happened at Faunsdale and warned that it lay within Brittain's jurisdiction to render decisions when conflicts arose between land owners and free labor. Brittain cautioned that such draconian measures as had been taken by Stickney were not going to be tolerated:

> Should I have another complaint from your plantation I will send an officer to investigate the whole affair. And if you are found to be at fault you will be ameaditely [sic] arrested and punished. You will be required to keep the Negroes until the crops are gathered.[21]

In the case of this particular complaint and the officer to whom it was made, the freed men and women who wished to live and work at Faunsdale had an ally. However, real sympathy with and support for the problems faced by ex-slaves was sacrificed in Alabama under General Wager Swayne's command. Brittain's letter to Stickney could scarcely be interpreted as a reflection of the "cordial terms" with which Elizabeth Bethel characterized social relations between General Swayne and the planters who made up the constitutional convention of September, 1865. But one harsh letter does not deny the cooperation which Swayne gave to the planter class of Alabama. General O.O. Howard's organization was not the effective tool of the most radical element of the United States Congress which advocated redistribution of plantations. Free labor may have been the concept envisioned by federal policy makers, but the Union officers and Bureau agents who carried out the policies more often served the interests of planters concerned about keeping black laborers anything but free. And when officers whose personal beliefs compelled individual support for the rights of freed black men and women left their assignment, that support vanished.[22]

Stickney's diary shows that Union soldiers occasionally helped him retrieve workers who had left Faunsdale "without permission." Compelling the old master to keep them on his land for six more months may not have been the result desired by Sal, Cassius, Edward, Tom, Anderson, London, Peter, Howitt, Wilson, Austin, Christopher, and Barney when they went to the soldiers in

Selma and complained.[23] Perhaps they had expected the victors to aid them in gaining ownership of land rather than a new form of bondage. In time hired black agricultural workers in the South would gain some concessions from the old masters, but real freedom for black men would be hard to win in the postwar South; harder yet for black women.[24]

The end of racial slavery in the southern states did not set black women free of restraints embedded within an asymmetrical gender system any more than being white satellite women free of theirs. Nineteenth-century southern society was gendered, i.e., separated into distinctly male, or masculine roles, and female, or feminine ones. Factors of race and class created separations within each gender so that there was no single monolithic concept which addressed the universal feminine or masculine gender role. This mutability of perceived roles for males and females according to their race and class presents prima facie evidence that this process did not arise of its own accord from unalterable biological differences. Malleable gender roles, with race and class refinements, eased the process of ordering and maintaining such a hierarchical society as existed in the nineteenth-century antebellum South. Maintaining social control over such dependents as wife, children, family members, slaves, or lesser white men, was a responsibility of a class of men whose vision of themselves and their society was drawn from the biblical Patriarchs. These nineteenth-century versions of patriarchy held the power necessary to control their society and acted accordingly to consolidate their authority by protecting their own gender and class interests. Keeping women, black and white, as well as all lesser men, in economic, social, and political subordination formed the basis of their superiority and maintained a necessary imbalance of power.[25]

Mid-nineteenth century gender roles had not followed the mythological example of Pallas Athene and sprung full-grown into existence from the mind of a creator, but had grown and adapted as necessary. Whatever other needs gender roles may have filled, their primary function served to impose and perpetuate an imbalance of economic, social, and political power which succeeded in splitting society along several fracture lines. The antebellum South's lines of fracture were of gender, race, and class with every woman and man who were society materially located within their own space. Louisa McKinlay Collins was caught as firmly in the requirements for women of her class and race as was her slave Charity Paine and all the black women owned by Louisa. Although Louisa and Charity lived during the same time and on the same plantations in North Carolina and Alabama, material conditions of their lives differed markedly. As long as slavery combined with patriarchy to provide the economic and social base of Southern society, women such as Louisa and her slave Charity Paine had few options other than those allowed by gender as it was mediated by class and race. For either woman to escape the confines of her social place and alter her life, systemic changes would have had to occur in the social institutions which shaped each life. Individual women could act against prevailing social constraints, seeking their own solution, but those few could not alter society by escaping it.[26]

Louisa Collins left no evidence of dissatisfaction with her position. Born to Josiah Collins II and Rebecca Ann Daves Collins in 1817, she was, respectively, granddaughter, daughter, and sister of three wealthy and prominent men of Edenton, North Carolina. Her paternal grandfather, Josiah Collins, was born in the Somerset county town of Taunton, England, to Joan and David Collins in 1735. Collins' marriage to Ann Lewis of Staffordshire in 1761 produced three children, Josiah in 1763, Ann in 1764, and Elizabeth in 1769 before Ann's death in 1770. Her death may have been the catalyst which spurred Collins to leave England for the colonies because he soon left infant Elizabeth in England and sailed with the two older children for Boston.[27]

Collins did not settle immediately in Edenton, North Carolina upon his arrival in America. He lived briefly in Rhode Island and then moved to the North Carolina town of Halifax. His name appears with those of seven other men, who were swearing their allegiance to North Carolina on 17 June, 1777. Two of those men had previously held crown offices, so possibly Collins had also occupied an office of the crown during the time he lived in Halifax. In any case, Collins publicly swore in June, 1777 that his loyalties now lay with North Carolina and not the crown of England. Either the relative newcomer Collins had once held public office or he was ambitious to do so. Perhaps he took the oath in public to make sure that his peers recognized his commitment to become a man of public importance in North Carolina.[28]

From 1777 until his death in 1819, Josiah Collins, or as he was frequently referred to, "Captain Collins," lived in Edenton where he amassed economic wealth and social status sufficient for acceptance by the status-conscious Edenton elite.²⁹ Josiah Collins was nothing if not the personification of a mercantile capitalist. Judging from the degree of wealth he attained and the alacrity with which he achieved it upon his arrival in a new home, Collins very likely reached American shores with sufficient capital to set himself up in business. His initial economic base derived from extensive mercantile activities between 1777 and 1785 as a senior partner in the firm of Collins, Stewart, and Muir. During that period he acquired a rope walk which produced large quantities of rigging and other naval necessities for the developing federal navy.

As late as 1800 Collins' rope walk was still supplying rope, or cordage, to the United States Navy. Naval goods necessary to shipbuilding and operation were in bountiful supply in North Carolina, but in the raw state. Cotton, timber, and pine rosin were all products available to commercial capitalists like Collins, if they had enough labor to turn them into cordage, planking, and tar for ships. As a letter written by Jacob Blount in Edenton to John Gray Blount in Washington indicates, supply could not keep up with demand and government contracts were too important for Collins to ignore:

Edenton Jan. 21st 1800

Dear sir
    Your letter respecting twine never came to hand, and at this time the demands for that article is [sic] so great that it won't be possible to get it until next week when Mr. Millin says I shall have that quantity if Possible, ...J. Collins having made a contract to the U. States with 40 Tons Cordage by a certain time is obliged to brake off some of His twine Spinners and put them to spinning Rope Yarns,...³⁰

Capt. Collins, never reluctant to seize the main chance, enriched himself when opportunity appeared and sought opportunity when it did not. Nor had he been reluctant to accept the honor and responsibility inherent in holding public office, such as the judgeship of the admiralty in 1779. In spite of having been a "nonparticipating Whig" during the Revolutionary War who eschewed military participation, Collins did serve on "commissions for cannon, coast navigation, magazines and other projects." Holding those offices did not take so much time away from his shipping business and manufacture of rope that he suffered financially. In fact, his wealth continued to grow.[31]

One of the new directions in which Collins ventured his investments was land speculation. After turning operation of the rope walk over to his son in 1783, Capt. Collins entered into a new business alliance in 1784 which ultimately proved successful enough to provide a foundation for the wealth of two more generations. Collins entered into a partnership with Nathaniel Allen and Dr. Samuel Dickinson to take advantage of the legislature's previous authorization allowing a land company to drain nearby Lake Phelps. The original company failed to act on the authorization, so Collins and his partners formed the Lake Company to carry out the drainage and development. However, they did not drain the seventeen-hundred acre lake, but took the company in another direction and bought slaves - a venture which enriched at least one of the three partners.[32]

Collins was well set up to oversee the acquisition of new slaves as cheaply as possible by voyaging directly to Africa and underwriting the voyage through use of his ships and commercial holdings. He financed the risky venture of going directly to Africa for new slaves by sailing a cargo to Boston on his ship _Alliance_, followed by another cargo aboard the _Camden_ bound for Philadelphia, Boston, and Cape Francois. The cost of the African voyage would be paid from the cargo of the _Alliance_. It would be the _Camden,_ thus re-fitted from its previous cargo to accommodate a human one, that would bring back the new slaves. The _Camden_ would off-load its first cargo of barrels of pork, hogsheads of tobacco, and other merchandise in Philadelphia, turn toward Boston with the remaining load of turpentine, tobacco, and rice from North Carolina. The ship's lading for Cape Francois was not indicated and it may have been off-loaded temporarily in Boston while the ship was re-fitted. Presumably, the _Camden_ then sailed for Africa to obtain slaves for the Lake Company which, by 1800, was no longer a partnership but had become the personal property of Josiah Collins.[33]

The _Camden_ arrived with its cargo of "80 New Negroes" and was logged into port records on 10 June, 1786 as having paid import duties at the Port of Roanoke (Edenton).[34] Although these Africans had been imported specifically for the Lake Company, Collins routinely engaged ship captains for his own private mercantile business and underwrote other commercial voyages where the cargo was not slaves. In September, 1788, two years after the African voyage, the <u>Alliance</u> entered the port of Roanoke at Edenton laden with thirty-five barrels of sugar, forty cases of gin, and three hogs of rum from Guadaloupe.[35] The ship's master, Edward Preble, employed by Josiah Collins on that voyage eventually gave up such routine rum-runs to represent the United States Navy as a commodore in the Barbary War.[36]

Capt. Collins gained economic wealth and social standing in his new nation too quickly to have entered its ports as a poor man. He probably brought capital or credit with him when he left England for what were still her colonies in 1773. Perhaps he had been successful as a merchant in London and had the experience necessary to take chances with mercantile capitalism in a society which needed great quantities of capital and labor. With capital or credit, he could acquire the other necessary commodity of labor by buying slaves.[37]

Certain private personal decisions made by Josiah Collins also had public consequences for the financial well-being of his children and grandchildren. He chose to leave his younger daughter Elizabeth behind when he immigrated to North America. She was reared in England and never lived with her father or siblings in North Carolina. Elizabeth married an English lawyer named Cook and had at least five children. Through his will Collins left lifetime annual incomes to his daughter Elizabeth and her five children, but no land or slaves. When he died, his real and chattel property in the United States remained intact for the two children he had brought with him from England. His grandchildren who were the children of Collins' older daughter Ann inherited joint ownership of a tract of land five miles from Edenton called the Holly Grove Tract. However, the bulk of his wealthy estate eventually went to the children of his son, Josiah Collins II.[38]

Collins made another decision which had long lasting consequences by not marrying a second wife and creating a second family of children to split his wealth. The children of his only son inherited most of his estate. Collins settled on his son's children without granting ownership of Somerset Plantation at the lake to his son. His will stipulated that Josiah Collins II would receive "during his lifetime the land on Lake Phelps with all improvements. Also all the negroes, upwards of one hundred in number for his lifetime." Collins left only management, not the ownership of his plantation property to his son. Josiah II was only to manage, protect, and pass to his children the wealth that had been accumulated by their grandfather. Josiah Collins willed a tract of land to Josiah II, but the land and slaves at the lake were to perpetuate his fortune and achievements for his son's children: Ann Daves; Mary Matilda; Josiah III; i-Henrietta Elizabeth; Hugh Williamson; John Daves; and Louisa McKinlay Collins.[39]

Josiah Collins II was neither a man of distinguished public service nor the daring venture capitalist his father had been. Young Josiah's strengths inhered in the ability to maintain what his father created, marry well, and perpetuate an American branch of the family, Perhaps being the only son of Capt. Collins was too daunting a life for the younger man to accomplish more. From a description taken from a letter written in 1784 to the Rev. C. Pettigrew by James H. Thomson, young Collins lacked his father's acquisitive talent and aggressive nature:

> Rev. & Dr. Sr.,
> ...What induces me at present to write is, to ask the favour of you to accept Dr. Blair's lectures upon Rhetoric & the Belles Letters... I have also to request that you will engage young Mr. Collins' attention to peruse it. He has genius & a fondness for literary exercises, & nothing can prevent his making a respectable figure, if everything great & noble in him be not swept away by the rapid torrent of dissipation in the place where he lives.[40]

The place where "young Mr. Collins" was living may not have meant Edenton, but possibly a university. Perhaps Mr. Thomson shared the same fear (the dangers of educating young men away from home) which prompted the Rev. Pettigrew to remove his own sons from the new university at Chapel Hill.[41]

Another fact of young Collins' life that suggests a studious and passive personality was the age at which he married and the youth of his bride. Collins was forty years old when he and the scarcely-eighteen-year old beauty Rebecca Ann Daves of New Bern married in 1803.[42] Regardless of his age; he fathered a family of eight children with her between 1804 and 1824. His preference for solitude and quiet was noticed by at least one of his lakeside neighbors. In the first quarter of the nineteenth century, the plantation at Lake Phelps was not the primary residence of Josiah Collins, II and his family. They lived at "the Homestead" in Edenton and occasionally visited the lake where Josiah had constructed a small two-storied, four-roomed building called the Colony House.

His presence at this property which lay next to the Pettigrew plantation of Bonarva elicited the following observation from Ann Pettigrew in a letter to her friend in October, 1828:

> Mr. Collins has been on the Lake the greater part of this year without his family, they have not yet returned from their northern visit, he seems to enjoy the loneliness of the place-such is the effect of age, he is very unlike his family—they are gay and fond of the world, ...[43]

Ann Blount Pettigrew attributed Collins' reticent behavior to his age, but nothing in his public or private life indicates that he was a man who sought public office or acclaim. Collins was a man of good breeding, family, and stature within his own community who seems to have been satisfied to live in quiet luxury and refinement. In all the productive relations of his life, he benefited from the labor of others; his wife produced eight children, his land excellent corn, and his slaves numerous off-spring. Josiah Collins II controlled an estate which gave him great rewards from the ambitious merchant capitalism of his father, the fertility of his women, and labor of his slaves.

The work with which Capt. Collins had made his wealth and the care he took to protect it paid off for his granddaughters and the men they married. And the patriarchal authority with which the third-generation male scion of the Collins family passed judgment on his sisters' suitors acted to guarantee a careful selection of husbands. When Louisa wed Thomas Harrison in December, 1842 all of the slaves and land which had been her inheritance passed from her ownership to her husband's total possession. In July, 1843 Harrison delegated a power-of-attorney to his brother-in-law Josiah Collins III to act on his behalf in matters regarding property which had belonged to Louisa Collins Harrison prior to their marriage. Harrison requested that Collins do the following:

...to cause to be surveyed any or all of the lands devised to my wife, (lately Louisa M. Collins) by her Grandfather Josiah Collins, Sr., as well as all other lands owned by, or being in the possession of my said wife at the time of her marriage,...[44]

This request may have served more than one purpose for Harrison. Undoubtedly he was aware of Collins' earlier disapproval of his courting Louisa, so he may have wished both to have someone close to the land watch over it and to flatter an egotistical man.

By marrying Louisa, Thomas Harrison was assured of acquiring much of what he needed to establish his own plantation and enter the upper echelon of a hierarchical society. Through marriage he gained a labor force for cotton production, land that could be sold or borrowed against, access to loans and credit endorsements from the men of her family, and the social legitimacy which marriage conferred upon a man in a patriarchal social order.

Charity Paine and her family were also part of Louisa's inherited wealth. At the time of Louisa's marriage to Harrison Charity Paine was a thirteen-year old slave living with her family at the Somerset Plantation at Lake Phelps. As Harrison made preparations to leave North Carolina for his new land in Alabama, the large community of African-Americans who made up the slave community at Somerset had to be evaluated so that Louisa's share could be removed. Division of Somerset slaves into seven shares resulted from Josiah Collins' will which left each of his son's children an equal portion of is wealth. In order to divide the wealth inherent in the slaves, each one had to be evaluated to assure that their owner's part was equitable. One group was valued at $5,907.14 and another at $12,670.75. Each heir had to receive an equally valued group of slaves.[45] The Collins' family practice of keeping families intact prevailed, but must have complicated the sorting out of inherited shares of the estate as the Collins sisters and brothers balanced market value against family ties. In many cases, they paid each other the monetary differences between various slaves and their babies to compensate for financial loss. When planters grouped slaves together into their conception of who constituted a slave family and permitted them to remain together, they did so out of good business sense rather than merely to respect the integrity of slave families.[46]

If Dr. Harrison practiced benefolent paternalism regarding his slaves, it is not a matter of record. However, treatment of Somerset slaves by Louisa's brother Josiah Collins III was observed and noted by the ever-watchful Pettigrews. Many remarks critical of Collins' personality and behavior were made by some of the residents of the neighboring plantation. Ebenezer Pettigrew criticized and disapproved of much about Josiah Collins III. Pettigrew disliked his arrogance, his pride, his advocacy of "preaching to negroes," and his apparent (to Pettigrew) harshness with the work animals at Somerset. He regarded Collins as an absentee landlord who looked down on the Pettigrews for residing on their lake-side plantation.[47] Even Collins' physician of many years included a critical assessment of him in a book published many years after Collins had died. Dr. Edward Warren was an exceptionally well-trained medical doctor who treated Josiah Collins and had opportunity to observe the patriarch in familia. Dr. Warren limned Josiah Collins HI in these less than flattering terms:

> ...the predominating trait in his character was pride. The senior member of the family, and having imbibed his father's English ideas and convictions, he regarded himself as the representative of every excellence which appertained to it. He esteemed his blood the bluest, his opinions the wisest, his tastes the truest and everything identified with him the most perfect that the world contained. He was an autocrat with a will as imperious and a sway as absolute as the Czar himself;[48]

Josiah Collins III lived by aristocratic ideals that were as much a part of his grandfathers' legacy as the material goods so carefully amassed by the older man for his heirs. His grandfather had set an early example of the degree of largess in entertainment incumbent upon a man of aristocratic aspirations in July, 1790. Collins' way of celebrating the national holiday of his adopted land was to host a gala event on his yet undeveloped estate of Somerset on 4 July, 1790. A jousting tournament complete with colored costumes for the competitors and bright flags was hosted by Collins at the plantation in honor of the anniversary of the birth of the new nation. The day's events began as the queen of the tournament approached the plantation on a barge which was drawn along the slave-dug canal that served as a link to the nearest river. Temporary viewing stands had been set up for guests to watch the competitions and pageantry before eating the large meal served. In spite of the celebratory nature of the day, at least one young "knight" died while taking part in an event. Wild hogs had been herded into the jousting arena where mounted men were to spear the hogs. Falling from his horse and into the melee, a would-be knight was gored and trampled to death. According to a contemporary account, even his death could not squelch the rest of the celebration.[49]

No finer example of the southern patriarch in all his power and arrogance may be found than Josiah Collins III. He stood at the apex of a society where only a combination of material wealth, an overweening sense of personal honor, absolute sway over a large body of subordinate persons, which included his wife and children, made the man. These were the three generations of Collins' men who helped create the world in which Louisa lived and set the standard of her expectations.[50]

When the defeat of the Confederate armies brought an end to racial slavery and institutions derived from it that benefited the slaveholding minority, elite women such as Louisa Collins Harrison faced a society deeply altered for them. Prolonged absences of the men upon whom most elite women depended and their eventual loss of slaves certainly had an impact upon them, both materially and psychologically. As a group, elite southern women suffered serious material and psychological disturbances and loss as the economic base of their privileged position was swept away at slavery's demise. It has also been argued that while they did lose much in a short term analysis, they gained in the longer view of advance for white southern women as a group. By coping from necessity with what their men would have shielded them from had they not been away at war, elite women laid the groundwork for social changes to be realized more for their daughters and granddaughters than themselves.[51]

Louisa Collins Harrison was thoroughly acquainted with the pain and loneliness of losing dear family members long before the war touched her life. By the time her first husband died in 1858, she was bereft of both parents, two sisters, two brothers, and at least two young nephews. And Harrison's death itself was reflective of the constant sense of impending loss of life or health which emerges from the letters of nineteenth-century rural Southerners. Harrison was fatally injured leaving a social evening he had attended at a neighbor's home near Faunsdale. Thrown from his carriage, he was taken to his own home and died without regaining consciousness.[52]

Brother Josiah made preparations to go to his sister's side and offer his aid. He explained that he must again leave home after just returning and would be unavailable to carry out some intended business with the letter's recipient:

> ...and [I] am now obliged as suddenly to leave home for Alabama having heard of the decease of my brother in law Dr. Harrison who was thrown violently from his vehicle and died after lingering a few days. My sister therefore with a single child is left alone and I feel myself compelled to join her as soon as possible.[53]

Of course, Louisa may have requested his presence, but Josiah Collins III was not a man to wait for any woman to give him permission to act.

At Harrison's death, his widow was left to manage the operations of Faunsdale plantation in Alabama as well the one he had recently gone deeply in debt to purchase in Louisiana. For five years Louisa was alone and the guardian of her daughter Louise. She was also responsible for making decisions about the sale of the land and slaves in Louisiana.[54] This was a heavy burden of responsibility for a woman of her time whose married state had prevented her from even owing land. As he had in the past, Josiah probably tried to make decisions for her. Knowing her brother and desiring to avoid his criticism may have impelled Louisa to hesitate in telling Josiah when she decided to remarry.

Louisa's marriage in 1863 to the Rev. William Stickney elicited a rather disapproving response from some of her male relatives. Josiah's eldest son, Josiah IV, expressed his reservations regarding her choice in a letter to his father, dated 14 January, 1863:

> Well, they are all going to Alabama to see another wedding there. My reflections on which have not improved my opinion of it. If poor Louisa does not have to pay a pretty high price for her generosity, I shall be agreeably disappointed. But I do not mean to be bitter as the thing is inevitable.[55]

The letter sheds no further insight into the reason for his poor opinion of his aunt's choice of a husband, but the issues which usually concerned the Collins' men were money and status, both lacking from the possession and position of a country priest. Louisa's brother had also disapproved of her first husband and had actually forbidden the marriage of another of his sisters to the man she wished to wed; she obeyed her brother and ended that relationship. Perhaps his thirty-two year old son had taken his lead from the family patriarch and judged Louisa's second choice deficient also. The current of family disapproval was distinctly male and may have derived from their suspicion that the new husband would rely upon her generosity (economic support), create a second family, and divert the wealth away from her kin. If those were their fears, they were never realized for under Stickney's hand the plantation remained productive and self- supporting into the twentieth century. Ironically, when Louisa's imperious brother Josiah died in 1863, his death revealed actions which brought an allegation of fiduciary laxity and even deliberate wrongdoing as trustee of the estate of a young ward; nephew Josiah proved incapable of keeping his own estate of Somerset which he lost in those lean postwar years.[56]

Brother Josiah had not been privy to her decision to marry her priest, nor was he told until she confided in those members of her family who were her emotional mainstays—her sisters. When sister Henrietta Collins Page received a letter from William Stickney in which he told her that he and her sister Louisa were to be married, she immediately responded in a positive vein. Henrietta wrote to her younger sister Louisa, expressing her love for her and approval of Stickney. Yet within the sentiments of congratulations and wishes for happiness from the female kin, another message emerged as well. The message was that the women of the family kept much between themselves and away from "Brother's" oversight. Although Henrietta admitted her absorption with her sister's news, this sudden turn of events did not cause her to forget discretion:

> I am so taken up with this one thought, as almost to have forgotten the war. An matters are to be consummated in January? If you cannot write, which I can believe let Annie (Henrietta's daughter], & I shall keep the letter to myself. I wish to get to you, but I am dependent

upon brother [Josiah]. as you know... [h]e knows nothing of the contents of Wm. Stickney's letter..."[57]

Henrietta assured Louisa that she had not revealed the letter's contents to "Brother," but only to a female cousin and their sister Alethea. The adult women of the family shared a warm and supportive emotional network, but the opinions of the men still carried the weight of authority within the family just as they did within the community. After slavery ended, Southern patriarchs were left with precious few subordinates as they were forced to grapple with ideals sheared from reality. Men such as Josiah Collins, Thomas Harrison, and William Stickney with their arrogance and need for control over their "family black and white," faced life in a society full of black women and men who could no longer be owned. At the same time they were living on most intimate terms with white women whose dependence upon and confidence in the patriarchal superiority of white Southern men must have been deeply challenged.[58]

As the summer of 1865 wore on at Faunsdale plantation and William Stickney was made increasingly aware that the violent coercion of slavery was no longer his to employ, he learned to rely more and more upon the new methods at hand. Stickney had presented his servants with their first labor contract in June, 1865 as he simultaneously relied upon tying, whipping, and denying rations to his workers. Quickly disabused of his idea that he could continue to treat free black workers as he had when they were slaves, Stickney adapted. Subtle changes were taking place within and around the old master as his "servants" became "hands" and finally "hired hands." Against his need to maintain the absolute and undivided authority of a white male slave owning patriarch, planter William Stickney entered into market relations with free labor made manifest in a written contract. If any single act or material object essentially stood for the profound alteration from patriarch to employer, it was the labor contract. The market relations of northern capitalism had finally penetrated the old patriarchal relationship between master and slave and rendered it obsolete. Deep consolation must have been taken by the ex-masters from the strength, loyalty, and dependence of their own women.[59]

By mid-June Stickney had drawn up a contract and presented it to the ex-slaves of Faunsdale. He excluded five, possibly the four men who had "run off to

Uniontown" to complain and the wife of one of them. As soon as he was satisfied that they would comply with his rules, one that "[d]isrespect to authority,...or other misdemeanor, [was) to be punished by dismissal & forfeiture of wages," he re-instated all five.[60] The first contract carried the names of one hundred and six persons, representing almost the entire group of adults or near-adult children who had been slaves at Faunsdale. Stickney reported in January, 1865 to the Confederate government that his number of slaves totaled one hundred and seventy-eight men, women, and children. Of that total, fifty-four were aged ten years to a few months of age and thus too young to have been considered as laborers. Of the remaining one hundred and twenty-four, one hundred and six names were carried on the first contract.[61] During the fall harvest months of 1865, the make-up of the labor force varied somewhat from the initial group who first signed in June, but most signers of the first contract remained at least until December's end.[62]

The labor contract William Stickney offered to his new class of laborers was scarcely one of reciprocity. It simply restated that the old relations between master and slaves would be the way business was done at Faunsdale. The workers would acknowledge Stickney's total authority and he conceded nothing. How quickly he adopted use of such a market device as a contract probably bore a direct relationship to the proximity of Union forces. However, officers of the enemy camp were not the only voices warning him and the men of his class that the old relations of slavery were as dead as that institution and must be buried. Among his personal correspondence William Stickney kept a letter from James Speed addressed to his neighboring planter, Mr. R. H. Adams. Speed's signature does not identify his position, but internal evidence within the letter suggests that he was the same James Speed who was the United States Attorney General in 1865.[63] Although the letter was not addressed to Stickney, the message it bore for Mr. Adams had equal significance for any man of his class and bore the same weight for any white ex-master:

> As to confiscation, I am sure that you need not fear it, if you will make up your mind to fall in with the new order of things, viz, <u>instant obliteration of slavery</u>. We are issuing pardons..., but all are upon the

condition that the offender <u>emancipate all of his slaves & that he never will hereafter own a slave or make use of slave labor.</u>[64]

Speed's letter to Adams opened with references to Adam's son and other prisoners of war, but the letter was also his advice, his admonition against the possible recalcitrance of planters in accepting the patent fact of slavery's end. His response reveals a degree of the pressure that was being applied from one federal of/ice against the hard-headed planters to relinquish old ideals and habits of autocratic authority. Speed's manner of addressing Adams suggests that they were once close or had known each other well. Perhaps Mr. Speed was a southern man with Unionist leaning who recognized how difficult it was going to be for men like Mr. Adams to accept the new order:

> I have thus my dear Sir, talked plainly and without apology as to an old and esteemed friend. It has been your fortune to live in an age when it becomes a necessity for you to change the habits & convictions of your life. That it will not only be inconvenient but painful to you I can well see. But some generation had to meet & live through such pain, and as it has fallen to our lot, let us bear & overcome it bravely.[65]

In spite of Mr. Speed's obvious commitment from his level of office to the theory of protecting the freedom of black women and men in the South, the practice at local levels was not always what he might have desired. After the initial upheaval and "dissolution" of the months of May and June, the labor force remained remarkably stable at Faunsdale throughout the first six months of freedom. One very strong reason had to have been the force available to white land owners from federal soldiers posted in various sections of the state. Units of the United States Army were stationed in near-by Uniontown and more distant Selma. Neither the federal troops nor agents of the new Freedmen's Bureau demonstrated consistency in their commitment to the freed men and women of Alabama. They represented the only protection against trepidations from former masters, or any white men; if they did not provide that protection, there was none. In many parts of the state, officers established pleasant relations with the elite men and women which compromised their objectivity.[66]

The measles epidemic which swept through the quarters in June and July would certainly have contributed to the persistence of so many black women and men at Faunsdale. Stickney first mentioned the illness in his diary entry of May, 31. Two house servants, William and Jane, and another male referred to as Henry were the first to show evidence of the illness. Stickney's note in the back of his diary for 1865 lays blame for the outbreak as having spread to his place "thro' Capt. O'N[eal]'s boy Henry." The illness reached epidemic proportions at Faunsdale. By the 5th of July, Stickney recorded "only 13 hands in [the] field. Measles still raging."[67] Thirteen hands of one hundred and six who had signed the contract, or had it signed for them three weeks before, were too ill to work. And very likely too ill to care about walking away either. Some may have been less ill than they reported to Stickney, but having very ill children or adult family members would preclude leaving at that point. Between 5 July and 23 August, Stickney noted the death of eight persons. Of the eight, six were infants or children and he attributed the deaths of three to measles. The remaining two were old and he did not remark on the possible cause of their deaths.[68]

Another probable reason for the persistence of most of the freed people was a cluster of issues related to family concerns among them. Under slavery it had been Collins family policy to keep slave families intact. The slaves of Louisa Collins Harrison Stickney probably suffered less of the agony of seeing dear family members taken away than slaves whose children or marriage partner were sold.[69] Of the seminal group of slaves brought to Faunsdale from Somerset in 1843, almost all (of those yet living) were still part of the slave community of Faunsdale in 1865. Upon emancipation some returned to North Carolina while some remained in the vicinity of Faunsdale, but were too old and tired to work.

Age took precedence among the freed slaves as they determined who would remain active workers in those first days of freedom. Family ties remained strong and the old African ways persisted in many familial duties as the younger workers provided for their older relatives. From the December, 1864 list of those that Stickney noted as too old to work (Tom Mutton, Miles, Moses, Delpha, Hannah Paine, Celia, Tamar), only one ever worked for the old master again. Only Betsy signed the contract in 1867, the same year that her husband Tom Mutton died, to work for the old master. Most of the old ex-slaves had adult children with whom they could spend the few years left before death claimed them, as it did

Tom Mutton in 1867, Delpha in 1868, and Hannah Paine in 1870. Two of the elders who lacked any adult family members to take care of them, Celia and Miles, were fed and housed for a while by the old master.

Several of the older workers who chose to leave the toil of field labor also chose to live close to the plantation, although they no longer worked for Stickney nor lived on the plantation. Some still had children and grandchildren working for the old master who would leave their work long enough to visit with the elders, but Stickney was not a man to give workers time off. He would permit them to leave their field work for a day or a half day to visit relatives, then charge the time against their account. When Cassius or Albert or Lavinia wanted a day or two to visit their mother, they had to pay for it. Many of the freedwomen and men valued their elder family members enough to pay the costs.

On the tax list complied in December, 1864 Stickney listed the names of sixty-two females who were old enough to work. Their ages ranged from eleven to seventy-five years, with eleven over age forty-five. By January, 1866, not one of the eleven eldest was working for him, although seven had signed the first contract in 1865. And they did not necessarily leave the area—at least six were still living in the Faunsdale beat when it was enumerated for the 1870 Census. The same was true for the seven eldest males who, in 1864, ranged in age from fifty-three to sixty-eight. In 1866 not one of them had signed the contract to work for Stickney, although three had earlier in June, 1865. Two of them were also carried on the 1870 Census. by 1870 eight were still living in the area but not working for Stickney, three had died, two had left the area but visited occasionally and the other five are unaccounted for. For the younger generation, Faunsdale remained their home for a longer time.[70]

Nelson and Catherine provide a good example of the generational differences within one family. Nelson never signed a contract at all and probably left Faunsdale as soon as possible. His wife Catherine remained and signed for herself and three of their eight children: Eliza 19; Aggy 17; and Merinda 15. The names of the two youngest, Jerry 11 and Sam 8, were not on the contract. No evidence emerges from the records to answer the question of why Nelson left while Catherine remained until her death in 1867. One cause may be found in a letter Stickney wrote in 1870 to Louisa in which he referred to Nelson in very derogatory terms. Perhaps Nelson was driven away, but his name does surface one last time in the Faunsdale records when Stickney included in his diary entry for 8 July, 1865 that "Old Nelson came for a visit of 2 or 3 days." That was the last of Nelson as far as any recorded personal appearances. However, that was not the case for the younger generation of Nelson's and Catherine's union (Lavinia, Manuel, and Molly) who remained about Faunsdale for several years, playing their parts in much that occurred there.[71]

Within the cluster of family-related reasons for staying put for a few months may have been the pregnancy of several of the women. One of the first actions taken by the newly-freed black women of Faunsdale, free <u>pregnant</u> black women, was to retire from the hard labor of the fields until they chose to return. Stickney began recording the time lost by each worker as soon as they went to work under contract. He noted who was missing time in the field and for what reason. On the first time sheet, he remarked that "Hannah, Adeline, Eliza, Henrietta, [and] Lavinia [are] really doing nothing-pregnant." Throughout all the years that Stickney carefully kept up with the absences of each worker and noted every woman's pregnancy, recording which day she first left the fields and what day she returned after the baby's birth, he never included any provision in the contracts for pregnancy.[72]

Pregnancy provided the female field hands a legitimate time out from field work during the first season of freedom when men like Stickney were still unconvinced that they could no longer use the old methods of whipping or corporal punishment against black workers. Besides being pregnant, the common factor among the six women of the first group to leave field work in 1865 was their marital status; all were married.

If having a husband to continue providing her support allowed Henrietta, Adeline, Lavinia, Eliza, Adele, or Hannah to rest from field work in that first season of freedom, it did not continue to be a prerequisite condition in their future. Hannah and Adele were soon off the contracts, with Hannah separating from her husband Solomon and Adele and husband Robert leaving the plantation. Herietta and Adeline remained married to the men to whom they were married at the time of their pregnancies in 1865, both working occasionally for Stickney and having other pregnancies. Lavinia and Eliza were soon single mothers who also gave birth to children, thereby receiving Stickney's acerbic remarks about their bastard children - but he did not fire them because of that.

The most likely conclusion that may be drawn is that the decision to cease working at field labor during a period of pregnancy rested with the woman rather than her man or her employer. Had her employer at Faunsdale had any control over the decision, he would have kept the women at work and forbade them to produce children outside any other relationship than one that had been sanctioned as legal marriage. Nothing in his contracts indicated that pregnancy was to be respected or insured a period of rest and recuperation for the female field hands. Rather, the context of familial responsibility recognized by the old master within the contracts was to direct the men of his work force to be responsible for controlling their "dependents." If he could not be their master, then another man must.

Stickney moved early into the role of master of the household and head of the family because it was a position created by the overall system of a patriarchal control of society. If the particular man, like Josiah Collins III, also possessed the individual personality that aided in his carrying out his role as pater familias, such traits attributed to his father, Josiah II, as pride, arrogance, autocratic, strong-willed, and demanding, then his systemic position of power and authority was reinforced. When William Stickney begin to see that he could no longer rely on the social and economic system of slavery to exert the same degree of control over all those he saw as his dependents, over the freed ex-slaves, he did not simply give up his ability to wield power over them any more than his social antecedent Collins would have. Stickney found another existing social structure to work through and a new way to exert old authority.

# END NOTES

1. This quotation is a portion of the 21st verse, 18th chapter of the book of Exodus, King James Version, <u>Holy Bible</u>. William Stickney's sermon based on the verse, "How to rule the masses, & hold the negro to us," dated 17th S. of T.U.T. '66; Stickney Family folder, Inventories Box, FPP, BPL. For a complete text of the sermon, see Appendix A.

2. John Demos, <u>A Little Commonwealth: Family Life in Plymouth Colony,</u> Oxford, 1970

3. A body of literature addressing the history and culture of the Creek Indian nation grows steadily with such work as Michael D. Green's <u>The Politics of Indian Removal Greek Government and Society in Crisis,</u> University of Nebraska Press, 1982 enrich the history of the South.

4. Biographical information on William A. Stickney may be found in Inventories Box, Stickney Family, FPP, BPL; "Alabama Historical Quarterly," winter 1947, pp. 604-605, reprint of John Witherspoon, <u>Chronicles of the Canebrake 1817-1860.</u> The term commonly associated with the five southwestern counties of Alabama which make up part of the "Black Belt" is a recent one of the twentieth-century. In 1865 the same area of Alabama in which Marengo County lies was called the "Canebrake."

5. The present owner of Faunsdale is the great-great-granddaughter of Louisa Collins Harrison Stickney and is the fifth generation of Women to own it.

6. Op. cit., King James Bible

7. William A. Stickney, "How to rule the masses and hold the negro to us," Stickney Family folder, Inventories Box, FPP, BPL

8. Ibid.

9. Ibid.

10. Ibid.

11. Walter L. Fleming, <u>Civil War and Reconstruction in Alabama</u> Peter Smith, Glouster, MA, 1949, p. 72

12. John B. Myers, "Black Human Capital: The Freedmen and Reconstruction of Labor in Alabama, 1860-1880" (Ph.D. Dissertation, Florida State University, 1974)p.17

13. Stickney diary, 4 April, 1865, folder 80, Stickney box BI, FPP, BPL

14. On the "masters' mentality," three excellent sources are; James L. Roark, <u>Masters Without Slaves: Southern Planters in the Civil War and Reconstruction</u>. New York, 197T; Bertram Wyatt-Brown, <u>Southern Honor: Ethics and Behavior in the Old South</u> New York, 1982; Gerald D. Jaynes, <u>Branches Without Roots: Genesis of the Black Working Class the American South, 1862-1882,</u> New York, 1986.

15. Force and violence, or the implied threat of it, had been the planters method of propelling slaves and maintaining slavery. For more on their inability to let go of it after slavery ended, see Jaynes, op. cit., chapters 6, 7, and 8, esp. pp. 106-108, 112, 114, 128-135.

16. Although Stickney's diary for 1865 does not reveal anger, many planters had publicly expressed their anger toward the Confederate government because of the impressment of slaves and general interference with the business of growing cotton.

17. Stickney diary, 12 May - 30 May, 1865

18. For more on the relationship between labor and the Freedmen's Bureau in Alabama, see Elizabeth Bethel, "The Freedmen's Bureau in Alabama," <u>journal of Southern History</u>, XIV (1948), pp. 49-92; Peter Kolchin, <u>First Freedom: The Response of Alabama's Blacks to Emancipation and</u>

Reconstruction, Westport, 1972. On relations between labor and planters in general, see Willie Lee Rose, Rehearsal for Reconstruction: The Port Royal Experiment, London, 1964; Jaynes, Branches Without Roots,; Eric Foner, Reconstruction: America's Unfinished Revolution, 1863-1877, New York, 1988.

19. For the polar positions on the question of federal agents and their relationships with white Alabama planters, see Fleming, esp. pp. 315, 384, 428- 429, and Jonathan M. Wiener, Social Origins of the New South, Alabama 1860- 1885, Baton Rouge, 1981 esp. pp. 50-56. For a more synthesized view, see Bethel, "The Freedmen's Bureau in Alabama," and Kenneth White, "Wager Swayne: Racist or Realist?" Alabama Review, XXXI (April, 1978), pp. 92-109.

20. Stickney diary, 2 June - 15 June, 1865

21. Lt. Col. W. B. Britain to Mr. Stickney, Head Quarters US Forces, Uniontown Ala June 15/65, folder 52, Stickney box II, FPP, BPL

22. Bethel, "The Freedmen's Bureau in Alabama," p.57 made this observation about Gen. Wager Swayne who was the Bureau Assistant Commissioner for the state of Alabama from late July, 1865 until late 1868. Swayne's approach to administering social justice to freed women and men has been both praised and damned.

23. Stickney diary, last page of 1865, lists the names of his ex-slaves from Faunsdale who had gone to the federal military forces garrisoned in Uniontown. Stickney wrote their names under the heading "Beginning of dissolution."

> Old Sal, Christopher, Austin, Barney, up to U'town 1/2 Friday June 9th, to complain.
>
> Cassius, Edward, Tom, Anderson, London, Peter, Howitt, up to U'town 1/4 Saturday 10th on mules out of field.
>
> Cassius, Edward, Wilson, Tom, London up all Monday 12th.

24. On the economic consequences of emancipation see Roger L. Ransom and Richard Sutch, One Kind of Freedom: The Consequences of Emancipation, Cambridge, 1977; Eric Foner, Nothing But Freedom: Emancipation and Its Legacy, Baton Rouge, 1983; Gerald D. Jaynes, Branches Without Roots: Genesis Of the Black Working Class in the American South, 1862-1882, Gavin Wright, Old South, New South: Revolutions in the Southern Economy Since the Civil War, New York, 1986. Some examples of books which deal with the political and more general social responses of Emancipation and Reconstruction are W.E.B. DuBois, Black Reconstruction in America, 1860-1880, New York, 1935; Leon Litwak, Been In the Storm So Long: The Aftermath of Slavery, New York, 1980; Howard Rabinowitz, Race Relations in the Urban South, 1865-1890, Urbana, 1980; Joel Williamson, The Crucible of Race: Black-White Relations in the American South Since Emancipation. New York, 1984; Jacqueline Jones, Labor of Love, Labor of Sorrow: Black Women, Work and the Family from Slavery to the Present (chapters 2,3, and 4), New York, 1985. However, none of these address the attitude of male superiority among freed black men or their expectations that their women would conform to their domestic desires as exampled by the often quoted Laura Towne, which may be found in full in chapter [6].

25. In her recent book Within the Plantation Household: Black and White Women of the Old South Chapel Hill, 1988, Elizabeth Fox-Genovese denies the legitimacy of the term of patriarch as applied to white slave-holding southern males. Her position is grounded on the point that these men lacked the legal authority to kill their wives and children, a right which she sees as crucial to correct application of the term to that class of white southern males. However, since this was frequently their own choice of terms for themselves and because I do not agree with the argument put forward by Fox-Genovese that all turned upon the right to kill family members, I use it only in reference to white slave- owning Southern men.

26. On gender, see Joan W. Scott <u>Gender and the Politics of History</u>, New York, 1988 (esp. ch. 2 "Gender: A Useful Category of Historical Analysis" pp. 28-50).

27. William S. Powell, ed. Dictionary of North Carolina Biography, vol. a AC, Chapel Hill, 1950, pp. 404-405

28. Don Higginbotham, ed. <u>The Papers of James Iredell, Volume I, 1773-1778a</u> Raleigh, 1976, pp. 454-455

29. According to the <u>WPA Guide to the Old North States</u> Edenton quickly became the unofficial colonial capital. Not only were its male citizens leaders in commercial, political, and social activities, but the twon's elite ladies organized the "Edenton tea party" to demonstrate their patriotism.

30. William H. Masterson, ed. <u>The John Gray Blount Papers volume III 1796-1802a</u> Raleigh, 1965, p. 338. Jacob Blount was the clerk in Collins' rope walk and his son-in-law as well. He had married Nancy, Josiah's daughter.

31. Powell, op. cit., p. 404

32. Ibid. pp. 404-405

33. I am deeply indebted to Mr. George Stevenson, Division of Archives and History, Department of Cultural Resources, Raleigh, North Carolina for his assistance in deciphering both the ledger books of the Lake Company's business and their implications. The information regarding the cargoes and destinations of the two ships may be found in the "Treasurer's and Comptroller's Papers, Ports, Port of Roanoke, Accounts of Imports and Duties Received," 1786-1787, 1788-1789; Collins Papers, Private Collections, (CPPC) the State Archives, Raleigh, North Carolina (SARNC).

34. Ibid., "Port of Roanoke, Account of Imports and Duties Received," 10 June, 1786

35. Ibid., 20 August, 1788

36. Ibid., "24 September, 1788 Alliances master Edw. Preble, Brig, 70 tons, 6 men (presumably crew size), North Carolina [registry], Edenton (built), Josiah Collins [owner], Guadaloupe (sailed from), 35 barrels sugar, 40 cases gin, 3 hogs rum For more on Edward Prebles' later naval career, see Fletcher Pratt, Preble's Boys Commodore Preble and the Birth of American Sea Power, New York, 1950.

    For more on the problems facing such men as Josiah Collins in their efforts to carry on trade in the relative absence of specie, see Alan D. Watson Money and Monetary Problems in Early North Carolina, Raleigh, 1980.

37. For more on the problems facing such men as Josiah Collins in their efforts to carry on trade in the relative absence of specie, see Alan D. Watson Money and Monetary Problems in Early North Carolina, Raleigh, 1980.

38. A copy of the will of Josiah Collins, Sr. may be found in the Chowan County Will Book C, pp. 73-76. For a summary of the will, see CPPC, SARNC.

39. Collins' will lists the names of seven children of his son Josiah because the eighth, Alethea, had not yet been born.

40. James H. Thomason to Charles Pettigrew, 18 May, 1784, Sarah McCulloh Lemmon, ed. The Pettigrew Papers, Volume I 1685-1818, Raleigh, 1971, p. 27

41. Ibid., xvii

42. At the time of their marriage, Collins was forty years old and Rebecca Ann Daves was no more than eighteen. From the portrait of Ann Daves Collins which still hangs in the "Colony House" at Somerset Plantation, she was a beautiful woman.

43. Ann Blount Pettigrew to Mary Williams Bryan, 20 October, 1828, Sarah McCulloh Lemmon, ed. The Pettigrew Papers, Volume II 1819 1832 Raleigh, 1988 p. 103.

44. See folder P.C. 417.11, Harrison, Louisa (Mrs. Thomas) "Heirs of Josiah Collins, I" CPPC, SARNC.

45. For more information on the lists of slaves and their evaluations to be divided into equal shares among the eight grandchildren, see P.C. 417.8, Slave Records, 1720-1865, CPPC, SARNC.

46. See P.C. 417.8 "Slave Records", CPPC, SARNC. Collins, or someone in his employ, kept careful account of the slave women and their children. Five lists among the slave records are revealing of family connections among the Somerset slaves: "List of Women and their Children at Lake Phelps" and "List of Male & Female negroes at Lake Phelps (belonging to Josiah Collins in his own right) the 1st January 1829;" "List of Negroes at Lake Phelps July 1st 1839" [a fifteen-page document divided by sex which lists first name, age, wife/husband, mother, no. of children, and names of children. Nowhere on the document is a father's name carried]; "List of Negroes at Edenton belonging to the Estate of the Late Josiah Collins Deed (valued by Commissioner April 1st 1840)" [carries each slave's name, age, and value); and "list of Families taken 1843" [lists every cabin by number and all occupants of each].

47. Lemmon, Vol. II, op cit., pp. xx, 103, 376-378

48. Dr. Edward Warren A Doctor's Experiences in Three Continents Baltimore, 1885, p. 81. According to the National Cyclopedia of American Biography, James T. White Company, 1947, Volume XXXIII, pp. 169-170, Waren was a highly trained physician who was a pioneer in innovative medical practices. While working on the Poor Ward in a Philadelphia hospital in 1850, 'he conceived the idea of using morphia hypodermically-that is, injecting a solution of morphia under the skin with a lancet puncture and an Anel's syringe." He practiced medicine for a few years in Edenton with his father, also named Edward Warren, and it is possible that both men treated Collins who suffered from headaches and "moodiness."

49. John Darden, "The Story of Washington County," v.2, pp. 2-6. Somerset Plantation, Creswell, North Carolina.

50. In her book The Creation of Patriarchy, op. cit., pp. 238-239, Gerda Lerner deconstructs the word "patriarchy," in order to make it more responsive to use in writing history and less tainted by narrowly defined meanings.

51. For more on the opening up of opportunities for the post-war generation of elite white southern women, see Ann Firor Scott The Southern Lady from Pedestal to Politics 1830-1930, Chicago, 1970; and LeeAnn Whites War, Industrialization, and Gender Reform: The Process of Feminization in the new South, Augusta, Georgia, 1860-1900, (forthcoming).

52. The explanation that Dr. Harrison's accident resulted from a social evening and drunkenness was related to me by the great-great-granddaughter of Louisa and Thomas Harrison.

53. Josiah Collins III to "My Dear Sir" 15 September, 1858, Letterbook, p. 105, CPPC, SARNC

54. Ironically, after ignoring Louisa's earlier suggestions in 1843 he at least look at land further west before deciding on a plantation in Alabama, Harrison went deeply in debt to buy another plantation in Louisiana. On his 1857 land-hunting trip, he visited his sister who had married a Dr. Balfour and lived in Vicksburg. Her letters to Louisa subsequent to Harrison's purchase were full of happiness that her brother and sister-in-law would be closer to her since she had no family close by. After Harrison's death, Louisa was saddled with land that would not sell and the problem haunted her for years.

55. Josiah Collins IV to Josiah Collins III, 14 January, 1863, P.C. 417.1, "Correspondence" CPPC, SARNC

56. An extremely rich source of historical information regarding Somerset Plantation may be found in William S. Tarlton's MS, "Somerset Place and

it Restoration," Division of State Parks, North Carolina Department of Conservation and Development, 1 August, 1954.

57. Henrietta E. (Collins) Page to "My own dear Lou" (Louisa Collins Harrison), 29 December, 1862, folder 18 (1860 - 1862), Harrison box 1, FPP, BPL

58. According to Whites, loss of the labor power of men from their households was experienced by white women of the South in distinct class terms. With their men away or incapacitated, elite women were empowered by their domestic war efforts while lower class women were left vulnerable and unable to obtain even basic necessities for living. White men of the South could no longer live up to their "patriarchal claims to cover and protect all women."

59. Ibid. esp. chapters 3 and 4. Whites also see creation of Southern war memorial associations as compensatory movements arising largely through the efforts of the wives, daughters, and mothers of the elite men who had lost so much.

60. Point 2. Of the first labor contract, 17 June, 1865 stated that "[d]isrespect to authority, as well as gross moral, or other misdemeanors, to be punished by dismission & forfeiture of wages." A copy of the 1865 contract may be found in folder 15, Stickney box VII, FPP, BPL.

61. "St. Winifred's Family & Day School and Slave Register," pp. 11-19, entitled "Ages of Negroes rendered to Confe3derate Tax assessor, Dec. 13th 1864," folder 55, Stickney box V, FPP, BPL.

62. "Crop & Labor" records, 1865-1869, folder 54, Stickney box V, FPP, BLP

63. According to the typewritten summary (which identifies the families whose papers are included in the Faunsdale Plantation Papers) in folder "Family History," Inventory Box, FTT, BPL, entitled "Bradford, Thomasene Lock McCorcle Papers," R.H. Adams was not known to be kin to Harrison or

anyone at Faunsdale. However, there was a long relationship between the Harrisons and Adams and much Adams family material is in the Faunsdale collection.

64. "My dear Sir" [R.H. Adams from James Speed, July 1, 1865, folder 52, Stickney box II

65. Ibid. Speed is also referred to by Foner in <u>Reconstructions</u> op. cit., p. 182.

66. Although I have used the term "remarkably stable," it could be misleading if not qualified. More precisely, I do not mean to imply that all of the men and women who had been slaves at Faunsdale passively remained there. Rather, I can say with a good amount of certainty that almost everyone who <u>did</u> work there was a member of the young adult generation who either came there as an infant or was born at Faunsdale. There was no mass exodus from the place.

67. Stickney diary, 1865, op. cit.

68. Some information on the deaths of ex-slaves who continued to work at Faunsdale was entered into the "St. Winifred' Register" long after they were free people.

69. Again, reference the careful records kept by Collins and Stickney, the family ties across time and place may be made.

70. "St. Winifred's Register," op. cit.,; "Labor Contracts, 1865, 1866, 1867," op. cit.,; "Crop & Labor Records, 1865-1869," op. cit.; and 1870 Federal Census for Marengo County, Alabama.

71. Ibid.; William A. Stickney to Louisa Collins Stickney, 27 February, 1867 and 13 January, 1870

72. "Crop & Labor Records, 1865, 1866" op. cit.; "Plantation Day Book 1867," folder 8, Stickney box VII, FTT, BPL

CHAPTER THREE

# "Remember me to Adeline and tell her I saw her mother..."[1]

When Louisa Collins Harrison left her home in Edenton, North Carolina for Marengo County, Alabama, she left a family of loving kin and a community of friends. It was the place of her birth, childhood, and where her family lived in well-tended comfort. She was the seventh-born in a family of three sons and five daughters with only sister Alethia younger. Eighteen-year old "Letha" wrote a poignant account of their leave-taking:

> Dearest Sister, I felt so sad the day I bad [sic] you adieu that I cried almost the whole day and cried myself to sleep at night. I have looked at your beautiful vinaigrette over and over again, and can but feel that I ought not have taken so handsome a piece of jewelry from you. Brother looked at it the night after you left and admired it very much, and spoke of your having worn it.[2]

While young Alethia wrote letters of admiration and longing for the sister closest to her in age, letters from their older sisters were directed more toward offering advice and moral support for Louisa. Henrietta and Ann Daves (Mary, the fifth sister, died in 1837) reassured Louisa that she had the ability and the trained domestic slaves to allow her to meet the challenges of running a household. Sisters "Henrie" and "Nancy" were able to offer advice based on their knowledge of the black women who would be assisting their sister. If the frequency with which her name was invoked by Henrie and Nancy accurately reflected her skills, slave Adeline was an excellent housekeeper upon whom they told Louisa to rely for household management.

Communications between the four Collins sisters included more than advice about housekeeping problems; they wrote of what they would have shared in conversation had they been together, and they wrote about what mattered to them as members of the same family. Throughout the first year following her move to Alabama Louisa received letters of local Edenton news, genteel gossip, and expressions of affection from her sisters. Through letters, the three women in North Carolina shared community news and the activities of "members of our society" with their isolated sister. They wrote of births, engagements, broken romances, marriages, church conventions, occasionally about the bishop's health and frequently about their own. Most of their letters also included a request that Louisa "remember me to the servants."

The literate white mistresses of Somerset and Faunsdale also played amanuenses for their slaves.[3] Communications crossed the color line when Henrietta, Alethia, or Nancy queried Louisa about some favorite ex-Somerset slave who had moved to Louisa's Alabama household. The North Carolina sisters passed messages to Louisa from Charlotte, the free black woman who had reared them. Yet as often as the Collins sisters mentioned favored slaves, they seemed to have done so without awareness or sensitivity that the slaves were also suffering the pain of being separated from home, friends, and kin.

Communications crossed the color line, but little else could in spite of the similarity of circumstances for the black and white women who made the move to Faunsdale. Just as Louisa had to leave the family and community of her birth, her church and friends, so did the black women who were part of the slave community of Somerset plantation and the Homeplace in Edenton when they were taken from there as her newly-acquired inheritance in 1843. Just as Louisa was to be separated from her family of birth by her choice of husbands, that decision would bring about a separation between their families for many of the slaves who accompanied her to Alabama with the new master. Old women like Hannah Paine who would have been allowed to "retire" had she remained at

Somerset had to take up a new job as cook in the new household of her mistress and master; Hannah Paine also left some of her own kin. Young women left their mothers and fathers and sisters and brothers, but they lacked the freedom of movement to ever travel freely and visit their families in North Carolina as their young white mistress could, provided her husband would permit it and she had a proper escort.[4]

Family ties and affectionate relationships had as great a meaning, or perhaps even stronger since they had so little else, to enslaved women and men as to their masters and mistresses. Unfree black women and men were part of the dense webs of kinship ties just as free white women and men were, but the African base of their culture had provided different examples of marriage and family structures than those to which most white Anglo-Americans living in the southern slave states adhered. The experience of slavery had made race the great divide, the line that could not be crossed (for white women and men) that came between members of a family. Family was the primary unifying social structure for whites only if everyone in the family was white. Race took precedence over familial solidarity and obligations.

For slaves, kinship made the family. Since the earliest establishment of racial slavery in the Cheasapeake, the condition of the child followed that of the mother if she were a slave. No matter who the father was or what his race, if the mother was black and a slave, then her child was as well. For enslaved women and men, family took precedence over race. However, until they were free, freer than while slaves, they lacked the chance to shape their families as they wished. With emancipation black women and men would finally be able to act with more of their own needs in mind. So if Adeline, the excellent mulatto housekeeper upon whom Louisa would depend for so many years, left a white father behind in Edenton or Somerset, she might have been leaving only half of her family when she went to Alabama to work for her new mistress. Even if she were Louisa's half-sister, that biological kinship could not make her part of the white family. The best she could hope for was a good position within the white household.[5]

Once Louisa married Harrison and moved to Alabama, she was the mistress of the white household from which all relations intrinsic to the economy of the plantation flowed. It was, after all, only after marrying her that Harrison was financially able to put a labor force onto the plantation that he had bought on credit. It was only from her inheritance of slaves and money that he could follow his preferred profession as a planter and not have to rely upon establishing a medical practice. He needed the marriage to establish his economic base and he needed a wife and family to legitimate his social status among other planter families; the household formed the core of his life as a planter. Louisa, as his wife and the mother of his child, created their household; but it was sustained by the labor of domestic slave women that they depended on to run the household and field hands to work the plantation.[6]

Harrison was dependent upon Louisa and what she had brought to the marriage and household to make him a master. What she contributed to the household in economic terms was a work force and a set of familial connections that were based on a trust in her family which in turn gave Harrison greater access to credit and promissory notes; what she brought as the practical means that were necessary to the establishment and function of a household were the laborers for food preparation, making or buying clothes, child care, nursing the sick, and providing support for all of the social activities that were part of their class obligations to their peers. And just as Harrison was dependent upon his wife to make him a master, she was dependent upon slaves, especially her female domestic slaves, to make her a mistress.

The slaves that Louisa and Thomas brought to Alabama were those who had been inherited by Louisa Collins at the time of her father's death. They were part of the estate amassed by Josiah Collins I, her grandfather, and at his instruction, held by his only son in stewardship for the eventual dispersal among all his grandchildren. Before leaving North Carolina, each slave had to be evaluated to guarantee that all heirs of the estate received an equal share of the wealth.[7] After evaluating each slave and some trading among the heirs was accomplished, a list of names was drawn of the slaves who were to go to Alabama. The names on the list were not haphazardly arranged, but grouped by families. It was a Collins' policy to keep slave families together as much as possible.[8]

The list of fifty-nine names was arranged into eleven units based on familial and marital relationships among the slaves:

| | | | | |
|---|---|---|---|---|
| (I) | Milton<br>Linda and child Albert | | (V) | Lewis<br>Judy<br>Alfred |
| (II) | Fed (Blacksmith)<br>Nancy Paine<br>Charity Paine<br>Sal Parsons<br>Becky Parsons<br>Cassius<br>Wilson<br>Charlotte Paine<br>Adeline (black) | | | Hester<br>Jupiter<br>Dunkey<br>Malvina |
| | | | (VI) | Sam Hostler<br>Tamar<br>Joanna<br>Lank<br>Stephen Tamar |
| (II) | Jack Kit<br>Sylvia | | | Ruth<br>Noah<br>Oppha<br>Ashberry |
| (III) | Nelson<br>Catherine<br>Lavinia<br>Manuel | | (VII) | Allen<br>Mary Newbern<br>Robert |
| (II) | Ben<br>Esther Paine | | (VIII) | Mack |
| | Austin<br>Shadrack<br>Scotty<br>Airey | | | Penelope<br>Hanna Paine |
| | | | (IX) | Fanny<br>Philip |
| (IV) | Delphi<br>Joan Haughton<br>Willis<br>Teresa<br>Rosette<br>Shepherd<br>Lucy | | (X) | Sampson<br>Edy<br>Tom Mutton<br>John Iredell[9] |

A second, smaller group of slaves was included in the one to go to Alabama that was made up of slaves who were at Somerset. The second list of names were those slaves who were to be taken from other residences belonging to the estate. Combined, the two lists represent the core of the slave labor force at Faunsdale in 1844, many of whose children and grandchildren remained after emancipation as sharecroppers:

| | | | |
|---|---|---|---|
| Moses Murdaugh | (1797) | Barbara | (1788) |
| Ned Taylor | (1785) | Cyrus | (1824) |
| Margaret Wills | (1824) | Providence | (1829) |
| Nancy Wills(twins) | (1824) | Milly | (1824) |
| Adeline(house) | (1819) | Katy | (1818) |

| | | | |
|---|---|---|---|
| Celia | (1791) | Emily | (1828) |
| Easter | (1829) | Miles | (1796) |
| Quough | (1831) | Caroline | (1819) |
| Granville | (1823) | Betsy | (1819) |
| Calista | (1819) | Oliver | (1817) [10] |

The twenty names were taken from a longer, alphabetized list of all slaves at the Edenton residence, the Homestead. Slaves' names on Collins' list of 1843 and Harrison's of 1848 and 1857 were always grouped in the same pattern which indicated who the master assumed to be a family. Had the slaves been asked, they may have disagreed and had different ideas about who belonged to which family, but neither Josiah Collins nor Thomas Harrison ever thought to ask before imposing his own concept of what made up a family on the slaves. The only slave taken to Alabama with the Harrisons that came from some location other than the Collins' holdings was Oliver. Oliver may have been the only slave that Harrison owned before he married Louisa. In all of the postwar records for which Oliver gave a family name, he used Harrison. Apparently he had a sense of kinship or familial association with the Harrison name since he could have used any name he chose.[11]

Familial and marital kinship bound nineteenth-century members of the white planter class tightly together. Even racial slavery was often referred to euphemistically in familial terms and regarded as an extension of paternal rights and duties of elite white males. Whether slave-owners respected the integrity of slave families or not, they recognized the value of marital and familial stability in reproducing both their labor force and their crops. If permitting slaves a relatively stable family life would aid in diminishing or preventing unruly or runaway behavior from them or keep cotton production up, pragmatic planters would adhere to the practice.[12]

The restraints of slavery, however, profoundly altered the nature of marriage and family for enslaved Africans transplanted to the new world, but black families survived its viciousness. Had African women and men had the freedom to re-create their cultural patterns in North America, they probably would have structured their families along the (for them) familiar lines of an African corporate family and polygamous marriage.

For the Somerset slaves, moving to Alabama may have undermined some of their remaining African cultural traits, but the move did not lessen the deep importance of family ties and kin relations. Kinship formed the most basic relationships of their society and could not be destroyed just by separating family members. Old Hannah Paine's move to Alabama neither robbed her of knowledge of her adult child in North Carolina nor did it change her understanding of what made a family. What she and every slave knew about family went with them in their trek to a new home and would remain part of their mental cultural template for how to create a family even if masters prevented the manifestation. of those patterns. In the past, newly imported Africans had clung to the memory of the old ways and old home. Some of Somersets' slaves died in desperate and grief-driven attempts to go back to Africa. One overseer remembered how early Africans brought to dig the canals for Somerset in 1786 continued to long for Africa:

> At night they would begin to sing their native songs, and in a short while would become so wrought up that, utterly oblivious to the danger involved, they would grasp their bundles of personal effects, swing them over their shoulders, and setting their faces toward Africa, march down the water [of the lake] singing as they marched till recalled to their senses only by the drowning of some of the party. The owners lost a number of them that way, and finally had to stop the evening singing.[13]

Collins did not wish to lose his investment and labor force before they had produced his wealth, so he stopped them form the singing of home, but he could not control their ideas. He had no way of altering what they knew, but he did have the power to prevent any realization of those ideas. The type of marriage and family and other core institutions necessary to replicate African cultures could not be re-created in the new world as it had been in their old one, but they remembered the old ways.

It is ironic that the oppressive institution of slavery as it was generally practiced in North America reinforced one of the old ways of African society such as the arrangement within a polygamous marriage where each wife lived separate from her husband, but with her children. The form of this arrangement was reproduced by slavery, but not the inherent meaning of the social structure. What was true for some African cultures was neither true for all nor did the custom necessarily persist throughout all slave states. The point is what was typical or "normal" African family structure or living arrangement for African societies of the eighteenth- and nineteenth-century was probably based on the wide-spread practice of polygamous marriage with separate living quarters for each wife or multi-generational corporate families. What was most uncommon was a nuclear family of the biological mother, father, and child living together in one dwelling that was typical for nineteenth-century white families.[14]

Polygamous marriage based upon a corporate family structure rather than the monogamous nuclear family was common to most societies in eighteenth-century Africa. In her work on contemporary sources of oppression among African women, Italian sociologist Maria Rosa Cutrufelli notes that the modern nuclear family structure within African societies "does not stem from the evolution of pre-existing family structures but from the forced integration of traditional societies into a capitalist economy." She further notes the older traditional family structures intrinsic to African cultures were usually of a corporate nature that placed great importance on the kinship ties of a large extended family. These corporate family structures often included married couples residing separately from each other with child rearing responsibilities falling to the mother.[15]

While Cutrufelli's main interest lies in exposing present manifestations of the oppression of African women, the work of historians Deborah Grey White and Allan Kulikoff examines some of the same social structures among African and African-American slaves in eighteenth- and nineteenth-century North America. Kulikoff points out difficulties experienced by newly-arrived African males when they encountered slaves who were settled into slave communities in the eighteenth-century Chesapeake. Between 1700 and 1740, slavery brought fifty-four thousand blacks into the Chesapeake, creating a steady influx of African cultures into the area. Kulikoff refers to the Chesapeake area of Virginia and of Maryland, but the north-eastern portion of North Carolina in which Somerset plantation lies is geographically part of the same area receiving Africans.[16]

Kulikoff recognizes that African cultural experiences had an impact on newly arrived male slaves and the communities receiving them. He does not argue that polygamous marriage was the prevailing marital arrangement in a place with uneven sex ratios which existed in eighteenth-century Chesapeake communities. But he recognizes the continuing importance of African patterns of kin and marital social structures and that "the origins of their culture were less important than its autonomy." To hold onto what was African was to hold onto some degree of control in a life that sought to deny all such rights.[17]

White draws attention to the similarity, to "some imperfect analogs in the African experience..." and cultural elements usually attributed as typical to American slavery. On large plantations, the typical spatial arrangement where married slave women and men often did not live together and the primacy of the mother-child bond were echoes of African practices. Further, although they were enslaved and separated from their cultural foundations, African women clung to known familial and child rearing patterns.[18]

Kulikoff and White agree that the most likely marital arrangements among late eighteenth-century slaves reflected both African and Africans-American influences. White sees childbirth rather than marriage as the rite of passage from girlhood into full adult status for young African women. Kulikoff is in agreement that significant African cultural elements persisted among enslaved African men and women and that African woman probably remained with their birth family after their first child was born.

One thing lost to transplanted Africans was the autonomy derived from being an integral part of a culture. The loss of the culture equated a loss of autonomy for African males who were stripped of the material conditions and social systems that upheld their status. Male slaves had nothing left upon which to base any claim for autonomy except their sex, by the gender privileges and authority for African men did not apply to slaves. Once the African males were enslaved, their gendered authority was sheared from its base, cut off from the supporting culture, and they were made dependent upon a master. It was a necessary planter imperative to regard male slaves as less than men, to negate and disregard their male-based authority.

Regarding female slaves as dependent upon their masters was less of a problem for men of the planter class since they were accustomed to female dependency. Dependency was one of the defining characteristics of the female gender just as independence and the right to own one's body and labor was part of the gender definition of maleness. Enslaving a male feminized him by taking from him authority and autonomy, but since dependency and restriction were part of the gendered role of women, enslavement served to magnify that condition. One basic African cultural element remained intact with African women; the mother-child bond. It was the primary bond upon which a family could be built when they were slaves and remained a powerful one for black women after emancipation.[19]

Importing eighty slaves directly from Africa to Somerset plantation in 1786 also imported their African concepts of family and marriage. Somerset's 1843 slave population had grown from the original core of eighty "new Africans" and those later acquired gradually in small local purchases. By 1843, two generations of African-Americans had lived on the isolated site, retaining much of their original cultures. Dr. Edward Warren, Josiah Collins III's physician, called on Collins often enough during the 1840s and 1850s to be familiar with plantation routines. There, around the time of Christmas, Warren witnessed slaves re-enacting an African ceremony called "John Kunering" or "John Canoe." Warren also noted that many of Collins' slaves spoke a common, but (to him), unintelligible language and thought it confined to the "Guinea negroes" on the plantation.[20]

The ritual described by Warren was North African in origin and not unknown to other locations in North Carolina. In his analysis of the entire ritual, historian Sterling Stuckey points out that the deeply held African beliefs of the slaves must have been especially relevant (and frustrating) to Collins and the Episcopal priest who attempted to teach their own religion to the Africans. In spite of being provided with a priest and place of Christian worship, Collins' slaves kept their own religious and temporal belief systems - which Warren described as including belief in "evil genii, philters, metempsychosis, [and they]...habitually indulged in an infinitude of cabalistic rites and ceremonies."[21] The women and men who left Somerset carried the African teachings of their parents and grandparents to the isolations of Faunsdale plantation, Marengo County, Alabama.

Stolen from the material conditions of Africa which nourished their indigenous cultures, stripped of all supporting social and personal relations in a forced immigration to North Carolina, pushed by circumstances into unions with native-born African-Americans, the children and grandchildren of the eighty "new Africans" finally walked hundreds of miles away from their established community and arrived in Alabama with little to sustain them psychologically except each other. Bonds of kinship must have strengthened among the slaves of Faunsdale. Even bondage could not dissolve their own ideas of who was family and how they were regarded. Masters had the ultimate power to create or destroy the outward structure of a slave family or marriage, but even their authority could not direct the slaves' most intimate sense of marital and familial commitment. In examining the scattered fragments of data from the last twenty years of slavery lived out by the men and women whose names appeared on the 1843 lists, one may find echoes of an African past and an emerging pattern of an African-American future. Although some slave family groups followed the same structural pattern as the common nuclear triad of the biological father, mother and child, some continued to live as they might have in Africa. For many slaves, the experience of a mother living with her children and separate from their biological father was the norm. A third alternative of living arrangements did not derive from Africa, but from the specific experience of Africans in North American slavery when domestic slaves resided within the white household rather than living in slave quarters with their own kin.

Three family groups have been selected as examples of the different patterns of marriage and family structures in which all of the slaves of Faunsdale lived. Echoes of the African patterns of polygamy and the corporate family resonate in the examples of Linda and the large family of Fed Blacksmith, but the example of Adeline indicates a third one that would also increase in future living arrangement for many freed black women. The three family groups chosen as examples from the entire slave population of the Faunsdale plantation also give evidence of the pervasive and primary commitment to family that characterized freedwomen and men in the postwar South.

## I MILTON - LINDA

Linda's small family group presents a good example of the way slavery reinforced the primacy of the mother-child bond over the man-woman marital one. Her family structure echoes the polygamous marital arrangements of Africa in which women lived apart from their husbands and reared their own children. Milton was listed as Linda's husband, but his name was not on any of the Somerset plantation slave lists as the father of her child Albert. Linda was effectively the only parent to both her sons, Albert (born 1842) and Peter (born 1847) for twenty years. Her experience was also a very common one on smaller plantations where the farmer might own only one or two slaves, and those were usually a woman and her child.

Milton's name appeared first on the list of those slaves to be taken to Alabama in 1843 with Linda and her son Albert. Four years earlier, Milton's name had been on the "List of Negroes at Lake Phelps July 1 1839" where he was noted as being thirty years old, with a wife named Linda who was the mother of a child Daphne. Milton may have been a Collins' slave as early as 1829 since a "Milton" was included in another inventory of taxable slaves at Lake Phelps which indicated the slave's age as twenty, the same as Linda's husband Milton. Because his name appeared on the 1843 list of slaves belonging to Louisa Collins Harrison, Milton was intended to be taken to Alabama. However, neither Milton's name nor the child Daphne's ever appeared in any subsequent Faunsdale records. Linda and Albert, the child born between the time and the two lists were drawn, did reach the new plantation where she remained until her death in 1864 and where her son Albert also lived at least until 1874.[22]

The records are silent on the fate of Milton. If he died before arriving in Alabama, it must have vexed Harrison because Milton was valued at seven hundred dollars and the loss of a field hand that valuable would have disappointed any owner.[23] What became of Milton will probably never be known, but there were many in the past who cared about him and mentioned his name when exchanging greetings and news of home. One of Alethia's letters written to Louisa in 1848 included this message from the slave Maria to her relatives in Alabama:

Maria, Willi's nurse, sends a great deal of love to you and says she hopes she may see you this winter. She says please remember her to all the servants and tell Adeline to bring news of all the servants, especially her sister-in-law, the wife of Milton, and her child.[24]

The exact nature of Maria's kinship ties to Milton and his wife are not clear, but she was not his sister. Maria was to become especially important to Willi since he was so recently bereft of his own mother, Nanny Collins Shepard, who died in early spring, 1848 soon after the birth of another child.

Harrison's first cotton crop in Alabama was picked in the summer and fall of 1844. During the final quarter of the year he listed the names of 28 women and 20 men as field hands. Milton's name was not one of them, but Linda's was. Harrison kept a daily account of the amount of cotton picked by each hand. Linda, who was twenty-eight years old, was a prime hand. In August Linda picked 2,294 pounds of cotton. The average among the other women was 1,370; she picked 4,625 in September, when the average for the others was 2,832; 4,303 in October when the other women averaged 2,135. Only at the end of the season in November was her total of 1,038 about the same as the female group average.

Beginning in August, 1845 Linda again appeared to be a strong worker who consistently picked large amounts of cotton until 7 October when the entire labor force lost five days to rain. Linda did less than a week's labor for the remainder of the year. Harrison failed to record amounts picked by individual workers during 1846 and 1847, keeping them again in 1848. Linda was back at work in 1848 when, at age thirty-two, she picked 2,708 pounds in August, 541 in September, and was not on the list at all for the rest of the year. The absence of her name from the list of field hands for part of 1848 may not be taken as prima facie evidence that she was absent from the plantation, since her name was on the 1848 slave inventory. Harrison may have drawn up the list in anticipation of buying another plantation and needed to account for all slaves. His 1848 inventory showed the names and ages, again in family groups, of all the slaves. By then Linda had two children, eight-year old Albert and Peter, age one. No man's name was listed as her husband or as the father of the new baby.[25]

The last data recorded on Linda, Albert, and Peter before Harrison's death in 1858 was the 1857 inventory which he did in anticipation of moving them to the new Louisiana plantation that he had purchased. Harrison moved some slaves from Faunsdale onto the new land, but his death halted the move and all slaves were eventually returned to Faunsdale.[26] Linda and her sons were at Faunsdale in January, 1864 when Louisa's second husband, the Rev. William A. Stickney, compiled a register of slaves in which their names were grouped both by family units and individually listed by age. Linda's name was part of a family where the first name was George Washington, 31, followed by Linda's who was 48, and after her name was her son Peter's, age 17. Linda's name dropped from the register of slaves after her death from pneumonia in April 1864.[27]

Early in 1865 Peter showed signs of discontent. In February, he worked away from the plantation at a salt work. He was one of the six slaves referred to by Stickney in his diary for 23 January, 1865.

> Wrote to B. M. Worlsey (saltworks) by 6 sv'ts sent for 3 mons. to make salt. Took them down to Demopolis - no boat yet for them. Left them & returned by cars.[28]

Stickney did not clarify if he had willingly hired out the slaves or if they had been impressed by the Confederate government to work at one of several saltworks in Alabama.[29] Peter ran away from the saltwork. But he did not run to the Union army or the distant North; he ran back to Faunsdale:

> 16th Thursday. Boy Peter came up - 2nd runaway from saltworks. Whipped him well & started him back to Demopolis with him on cars.[30]

After emancipation, Peter again demonstrated dissatisfaction with conditions at home and a willingness to act to change his life. He was one of eighteen freedmen and one woman who left the fields in June, 1865 and headed for Uniontown to register complaints with federal soldiers garrisoned there. In spite of his dissatisfaction, Peter remained with what was left of his family until his death in 1868. Stickney noted in the plantation day book for 24 June that Albert had lost a full day of work because he was "...in with Peter (died early)."

The next day Stickney wrote in his personal diary that he had "buried Peter, S'vt, before Breakfast."[31]

Albert, Peter's older brother or half-brother, left North Carolina as a three-year old child in 1843, was listed on both of Harrison's inventories in 1848 and 1857, and listed again in Stickney's register of slave families in a section titled "New families, formed in 1865." The Rev. Stickney officiated at the marriage of Albert and Eliza while both were still slaves in January, 1865. Eliza bore an infant in July who died soon after birth. Eliza, the eighteen-year-old daughter of Catherine and Nelson, did not remain with Albert after 1865. If they had followed the African tradition of marriage based upon the birth of a child, then after it died Eliza may have chosen to remain with her parents. Or perhaps the "marriage" of Albert and Eliza had been at Stickney's insistence to appease his sense of morality.[32] Whatever the reason, Albert and Eliza ended the union soon after the death of the infant and by 1867 Albert had a new wife named Anne Maria with whom he had several children while he continued to work at Faunsdale. Eliza signed the first contract in 1865, but disappeared from the records after that.[33]

Many of the slave families that left Somerset for Alabama persisted and produced two generations there, but for Linda's family, only Albert remained. The absence of Milton's name from Faunsdale records while his North Carolina relatives continued to mention his name and address greetings to this wife points to the enduring strength of kinship ties among the African-Americans of Somerset and Faunsdale. For young Peter who ran away from the Confederate saltwork and back to his small family at Faunsdale, the affectionate ties of his brother and friends may have been all that sustained him.

## II CHLOE PAINE - FED BLACKSMITH

A very different family, much along the structure of a large and extended corporate one was that of Chloe Paine and her husband, Fed Blacksmith. When Fed Blacksmith's name showed up on the 1843 list for slaves bound for Alabama, he was approaching old age for a slave who had worked at the physically punishing job of smithing.[34] Fed and his mother Nan were living on the plantation at Lake Phelps in 1803 when Josiah Collins I and his family still resided in Edenton. In 1786, Nan would have been about twenty years old and may have been among the group of African brought to the plantation that year on the ship <u>Camden</u> and of whom the overseer wrote about their deep grief for Africa that led them to drown in the lake as they sang of home and mourned their loss.[35]

If among them, she survived the initial years of labor and the grief of being bereft of her home while still rearing her children. By 1803 Nan had three children, but no husband's name listed: Dunbar (1785); Fed (1789); and George (1794). Nan was one of the Lake Company slaves belonging to "Mess's Collins, Allen and Dickinson," slaves who were owned by the three men jointly and not the personal property of either Josiah Collins, Nathaniel Allen, or Dr. Samuel Dickinson. A later slave register for Lake Phelps (Somerset) showed that in July, 1839, seventy-one year old Nan had become the personal property of Collins, was the wife of another slave named Jupiter and noted only Fed and George as her children.[36]

When at Somerset, Fed, Chloe, and family lived together on what Edmund Ruffin described in his <u>Farmer's Register</u> in 1839 as a model of Southern agriculture which consisted, among the total household, of a community of more than 200 workers. Of the entire population of 299 persons living at the plantation in 1840, 281 were slaves. They lived in twenty-five cabins faced toward the shore of the lake and led away from the main house, toward the Pettigrew plantation. Fed Blacksmith, Chloe Paine, and their children lived in one of the cabins along the avenue.[37]

Of the twenty-five, three measured 20 by 20 feet and had a second story, which the rest of the cabins lacked. The larger cabins also had a fireplace at each end with hearths of brick laid over a stabilizing foundation of cypress planks. The rest of the twenty-two cabins were of a slightly smaller dimension, 18 by 18 feet, and one-story in height. The number of slaves who were quartered in the twenty-two one-story cabins and three large two-story ones was 285. The cabins were occupied along lines of kin. Thus the number of persons in each cabin varied and was not necessarily evenly distributed according to space. According to the "List of Families Taken 1843," the occupants of number 20, which was one of the smaller, one-storied cabins, numbered 15 and were related to each other through the woman Chloe Paine.[38] The relationships between the occupants of cabin 20:

| No. 20 | Old Fed | Chloe's husband |
|---|---|---|
| | Ben | married to dau. Easter |
| | Jack | Chloe's son |
| | Easter | Chloe's dau. |
| | Charlotte | Chloe's dau. |
| | Becky | Chloe's dau. |
| | Nancy | Fed & Chloe's dau. |
| | Charity | Fed & Chloe's dau. |
| | Scotty | grandchild (Ben & Easter) |
| | Adeline | grandchild (Charlotte) Chloe Paine |
| | Shadrack | grandchild (Ben & Easter) |
| | Austin | grandchild (Ben & Easter) |
| | Wilson | grandchild (Becky's) |
| | Cashus | grandchild (Becky's) [39] |

Chloe's eldest daughter Sat Parsons was not an occupant of that cabin since she lived in Edenton. her name was usually listed with that of old Moses Murdaugh and she may have been his wife.

Old Fed and Chloe were a married couple and everyone living in the cabin with them was related in some way, but most of the children were not from that union: only Chloe and Fed's twins Nancy and Charity were theirs; Chloe's four other children (Easter, Jack, Charlotte, Becky) and Chloe's six grandchildren (Scotty, Adeline, Shadrack, Austin, Wilson, Cassius) also lived there. Easter and her husband Ben, parents of Scotty, Shadrack, and Austin, also lived there. Chloe's granddaughter Adeline was Charlotte's daughter, and her grandsons Wilson and Cassius were the children of Becky. Only Fed and Ben were not related by blood to Chloe.[40]

The bias of the person recording the information, whether it was a clerk, the overseer, or even Collins himself, was reflected in the manner in which the occupant's names were listed. It was the usual pattern for the name of the eldest male in each cabin to be listed first - filling the position as if he were the head of the household - unless there were no adult male living there. Fed's name was at the top of the list, although it was a family of Chloe's kin. The same men who denied the rights derived from male authority to the black men who were the husbands and fathers of families routinely noted their names at the head of each group as though they were the acknowledged heads of the households.

How names were listed may be taken as a reflection of the master's ideology; who lived in the cabin as members of the same family reveals more of the slaves' values. Harrison's pattern of listing the same slaves' names followed the one used by Collins. If there was an adult male in the group, his name was listed first, but it was to their mother's quarters that so many of the young women brought their husband and child. The Somerset register of slave families for my, 1839 shows a generally matrifocal arrangement for Somerset (and by a logical extension, for those who went to Faunsdale). The typical spatial arrangement within the slave quarters at Somerset was for married daughters and their husbands to live in the mother's cabin regardless of the size of the cabin or of the number of family members. Chloe's daughter Easter married Ben at Somerset and in 1843, at age thirty-four, Ben was living with Easter in her mother's cabin. Chloe's cabin was not a large one and it had a very large number of occupants while Ben's mother Suckey lived in one of the larger ones with only five grandchildren sharing it with her.[41]

Somerset slave records identified the parents of slave children with enough consistency to be trusted. Fathers of slave children were usually identified whether married to the child's mother or not. Fed had another child named Charles listed as his who was not the child or Fed's wife Chloe and she had several children for whom Fed's name was not noted as father. It appears that the master of Somerset, or his agent, was aware of the paternity of slave children and made record of it if they man belonged to him. While they might record the biological father's name, it was inconsequential to the master otherwise, since he was the social master of all his female slaves and as slaves, they had no need of another father's authority in their cabins. What mattered to Collins and men of his class was the productive and reproductive powers of their slaves, not a replication of black male authority in the quarters.[42]

Chloe Paine's name was not on the list of slaves taken to Alabama, although the names of her husband and all their children (except Providence) were. Taking into consideration that she had been valued at only seventy-five dollars immediately prior to the departure, Chloe must have been ill or incapacitated and did not survive long enough to make the journey.[43] If Fed retained much of his African heritage, the lack of respect for elderly slaves and forced abandonment of the graves of their dead pained him deeply.[44] Without wife Chloe or mother Nan, Fed and his large family arrived in Alabama in late December to live in the existing slave quarters on the plantation. In May, 1844 Tom and Louisa were both living on the plantation where he could then oversee the labor of making a good stand of cotton on poorly treated soil. Harrison recorded the total amounts of raw, baled cotton for 1844 and commented that his first crop was not as good as he wanted because of the poor condition of the plantation.[45]

Harrison's concern over the condition of the land may have compelled him to ignore the practice of permitting older slaves to eschew demanding field work and "retire" at fifty-five. His utilization of old and domestic slaves in field work suggests that he drove his slaves hard to produce as large a crop as possible. During 1844 Harrison kept older, less productive men like Fed at the same field work as much younger hands. In spite of Harrison's efforts to wring more labor from the old man, Fed was absent from the field so often that his name was not carried as a field hand after 1844.[46]

The children of Chloe and Fed who had been taken to Alabama—Sal Parsons, Becky Parsons, Easter Paine, Charlotte Paine, Jack Kit, and twins Charity and Nancy Paine-experienced relative stability as a family since they all remained on the same plantation for twenty-two years, until emancipation. Although bound by the restraints of slavery, Fed and Chloe's succeeding generations of children and grandchildren lived in the midst of a large family. Unlike the experiences of Linda and Milton, Fed and Chloe's family was large and persisted.

While slaves, most of the adult members of Fed and Chloe's family attended the Episcopal chapel built for slave worship at Faunsdale. Louisa followed her brother Josiah's example of how to inculcate slaves with those aspects of Anglican theology which shored up patriarchy and encouraged obedience. In a letter to Louisa which Alethia wrote for Josiah in 1844 (his inflamed eyes kept him from writing), Alethia addressed his concern to Louisa:

Brother has desired me to write particularly to request you to remember both sister Mary, himself, and the children to the servants, especially the communicants and the children who attended the Catechetical [sic] instructions... Both Brother and sister Mary [his wife) are very anxious that you should do it personally.[47]

Louisa took Brother's advice to heart and instructed the slaves. She went even further and had an Episcopal chapel built at Faunsdale in 1861 for the slaves' use.[48] She kept a chapel register intended as a record for "Baptisms, Confirmations, Marriages, Communicants" within the slave community, but recorded only the baptism of infant slaves and occasionally an adult slave was baptized. Stickney kept it current throughout the 1870s and into the 1880s, listing the names of children baptized, their parents, and the sponsors of every baptized child. Among those communicants whom he still considered to be in good enough standing with the church to fulfill the responsibility of sponsoring new members were several from the family of Fed and Chloe.[49]

When William Stickney made up the register of slave families in 1864, he listed Sal Parsons and Old Moses as a family. Sal and sister Easter Paine were "cooking [and working at] half task spinning, & washing for Mrs. Knox." Sat had no children to be concerned about while spinning, washing, or cooking. Easter and Ben had four children who traveled to Alabama with them: Scotty (1833); Airey (1836); Shadrack (1840); and Austin (1842). After moving to Alabama, Easter had at least five more children: Adele (1844); Cheshire (1846); Julia (1848); Johnson (1850); and Jordan (1854). By 1864 Scotty, Airey, and Adele were no longer listed as part of their parent's family. Each daughter's name was then carried as a separate family - not because each was married, but each woman had a child or children. Adele, Airey, and Scotty had achieved adult status with the birth of a child and were recognized as adults. Scotty, Airey, Adele, and Cheshire remained at or near Faunsdale after their parents left.[50]

Of all Scotty and Oliver's many children, only daughter Ella remained closely associated with the white household for very long after emancipation. In 1869 "Young Miss Lou" wed her cousin Willie Shepard and returned to North Carolina with him. Scotty's fourteen-year-old daughter went with Miss Lou as a personal maid. Louise's letters describe her feelings at the parting:

> (Petersburg, Feb. 1st, 1869)
> I could not help having a hearty cry after the carriage left the door; I looked back & dear old Faunsdale seemed so quiet & peaceful in the calm bright moon-light that I can never forget the picture.[51]

Her descriptions of Ella's responses were probably based more on how Louise preferred to interpret Ella's behavior rather a deep understanding of what the young girl was actually experiencing:

> Tell Scotty little Ella is getting on nicely, says she is perfectly contented to stay with me and asked me to send "all her love" to her Mother...I kept her in the cars with me all but one day & night; on the Ga. & Tenn. road they would not let her come into the Ladies' car, so Oliver took her under his care...Strange to say, she was not at all satisfied with her Father, but cried & got right home sick, & said "if she was with Miss Lou...she would not get homesick."...Tell Scotty not to be troubled about her, that I will take good care of her.[52]

Ever-dependent upon black hands for assistance, Louise relied on Oliver, who was traveling with her, to help collect her many bundles and pillows from the train when it was delayed in Petersburg because of an accident on the track. Their checked baggage remained on the train, but once the track was cleared, they resumed the journey. Perhaps Louis's realization that the old moon-lit home and childhood had been left behind made her a little more aware of Ella and prompted her to reassure Ella's mother that she was being cared for.

As her mother had done years before, Louise Harrison Shepherd relied on black women to aid her in domestic labor. Twelve days later Louise wrote another letter to "darling Mother" which echoed the same concerns of another young wife a generation before. Louise feared that her skill and authority in management of her household were inadequate. In choosing Ella as her maid, Louise continued to mesh the lives of yet another generation of white and black women:

> (Edenton -- Feb. 12,'69)
> I have been intending to write you a good long letter ever since I reached this place...I sent Ella over with the cake for Aunt Lethe,...I fear I don't know how to keep house as I ought to do. It is so different here from the way you do. In the first place, carrying the keys myself, there is so much for me to attend to that Mammy does at home, and I have no idea how much of different things ought to be given out.[53]

Although Louise's letter sought assurance from her mother that she could manage her domestic responsibilities, she also included two messages to Scotty:

> I enclose two cartes Oliver had taken in Petersburg for Scotty & asked me to send...Ella is well & perfectly satisfied.[54]

Possibly Scotty was less than joyful over the message that her daughter was "perfectly satisfied" with her Young Miss Lou and not at home with her own family.

Oliver's regard for family ties seemed to have stretched no further than what would cover his own interests. He objected to the removal of his daughter Ella to another state only after he had been fired by Stickney a year later. Oliver had been the carpenter at Faunsdale when a slave and then was the general overseer for five years after emancipation. Although Stickney hired Oliver to represent him and act on his behalf, Oliver took the opportunity to act as an independent labor agent who first rounded up all the unattached young workers for his own squad and then went out to solicit other black workers to work for another planter.[55] When Stickney re-organized Faunsdale's labor force from gangs to squads in march, 1867, he made Oliver a head man for the third squad. Stickney appointed each man to head a squad and then allowed him to fill the squad with members of his choosing. The first two squads were comprised of relatives and in-laws of that squad's head man, but most of Oliver's were older adolescent sons and daughters of past Faunsdale slaves who lacked any family of their own with whom to work - Oliver claimed to be the father of some of his squad members, although they were not children of his wife. Oliver used the strength of family ties to his own advantage rather than having been bound by them.

Stickney had depended heavily upon Oliver, but finally fired him after discovering that, among other acts of self-interest, he had been bilking fellow workers of money. By the time Stickney fired him, Oliver had consolidated considerable authority among the plantation work force. His offenses might have seemed less deplorable and punishment less swift had he not challenged the authority of the old master. Oliver's wife remained with him and both were in the Faunsdale beat in 1870 when she was listed as a member of Oliver's household by the census taker.[56]

No single black family had a monopoly on the domestic skills for the white household. Although Oliver was the carpenter and his wife Scotty was the seamstress, her sisters were field hands. Airey was a field hand when a slave and remained when freed. Her weekly averages for cotton picked in September and October 1860 and 1861 were usually higher than those of any other hand on the plantation. Her weekly averages for four weeks in 1860 were 312, 348, 365, and 338 pounds per week from mid-September through mid-October. During a comparable time period for 1861, averages for all hands were lower; Airey's were still highest at 238, 206, 290, 274, and 283.[57]

When presented with the contract in June, 1865, Airey made an assenting mark for herself and son Herbert. No man signed for her or committed the labor of her eleven-year old son to work for the old master. Since almost every healthy freedwoman and man at Faunsdale in June, 1865 also made their marks on the first contract, Airey's actions were not unusual.[58] However, the absence of her name from later contracts should serve as a red flag of attention and raise the question of why the most productive female hand did not remain at field work at Faunsdale. Ostensibly Airey was able to provide for herself and her son. Unlike Scotty who had several children, Airey had only one to care for and unlike the older female field hands, she was young enough to continue the hard work at which she was so proficient. If Airey had a husband on another plantation, she probably would have gone there as soon as she was free to leave Stickney, or simply signed with a neighboring planter. Whatever took, or drove, Airey away in 1866, she returned home for the last time in 1877:

5 Oct. 1877 Brought the body of Airey, wife of John Norcum cold; used full service.[59]

Cheshire, Scotty and Airey's brother, disappeared from Faunsdale records after 1865, reappearing again only in 1876 when his body was also brought to Faunsdale for burial. Sister Adele and her husband Robert had been noted by Stickney as one of the "new families" in 1864. She was a field hand and Robert was working in a Confederate saltwork. As slaves and as freed persons, neither demonstrated the traits of tractability, deference, and requisite cheerful obedience Stickney required of his workers. Excerpts from Stickney's diary for 1865 illuminate Adele and Robert's refusal to acquiesce to his control:

> 14 Feb. London came home from saltwork-ran away. At night went over & whipped him, Robt, & Sam.
>
> 23 March Laughan out see Adele.
>
> 6 June Punished Sv't Robt for disobedience to Ben [who was Robert's wife's father].
>
> 8 June Whipped Sv't Adele at night.
>
> 13 July Settled with boy Rob't by commuting dismissal to whipping.
>
> 18 December all day getting back a stolen pistol...Traced it to our boy Rob't as rouge. Got him thro' Sq. Bos(?)'s court fi have authority to commit him to jail.[60]

By the end of 1865, Adele's baby was dead, her husband jailed, and her parents and brothers Shadrack and Austin were gone from Faunsdale. With no family to hold her in the area, Adele left and her name also disappeared from Stickney's records.

In spite of suffering the loss of family members, all three of the children of another of Chloe's daughters, Becky Parsons, remained as field hands after emancipation. In 1864 two of the, Cassius (26) and Edward (20), were field hands while Wilson (23), had been hired out to the Central Railroad for $20.00 a year. While still a slave, Cassius worked for the railroad while his wife Hester (tiger) picked cotton on a part-time basis and was also a spinner. Hester (tiger) had at least three children, Jim (born 1859), Wellington (born 1862), and Henderson (born 1864). The two younger boys had already died when the measles epidemic which swept through the quarters in July, 1865 killed their ill and weakened mother Hester, who had been "long lingering." Of the children of Cassius and Hester (tiger), only Jim survived, leaving Cassius facing freedom bereft of his wife and two other children.[61]

Wilson and his family did not stay together following their freedom from slavery. He had been listed in the 1864 register in a family which consisted of himself (23), Lavinia (24), Josiah (8), Boston (6), Catherine (3), Gabriel (1), and Becky (no age given). The children were Lavinia's, and Becky was probably his mother. The 1870 census of Marengo County listed Lavinia Bennett (3), as head of a household and her occupation as "keeping house" rather than "field Laborer." Members of her household and their ages were Josiah 14, Boston 13, Rebecca 3, and Catherine 9. Wilson was no longer part of her household. It is unlikely that he was the father of Josiah and Boston since his name was not recorded in the chapel register and he did not claim the right to direct their labor once all were freed. The union between Lavinia and Wilson may have been Stickney's attempt to create familial ties that would militate against his running away again as he did in 1861. In the 1870 census Wilson's name, Wilson Holloway, was included in the household of his brother, Cassius. In the 1880 census Wilson Holloway was the head of his own household, which consisted of wife Delia, age 23 (field laborer), children Emily 8, Jake 6, Henrietta 2, and mother Becky (Parsons) 61. In 1864 Stickney had identified Wilson, Lavinia, and her children as a family, but in the next few years Lavinia and Wilson reconstructed their lives and families according to their own concepts.[62]

Most of Chloe's children remained in the Faunsdale beat for at least a few years after freedom, but her son Jack Kit and his wife Sylvia did not. When Josiah Collins had directed that the inventory be taken of his slaves at Somerset in 1843, Jack lived in his mother's cabin 20, but Sylvia was not an occupant. Since she was pregnant at the time she left for Alabama and her name was carried on the list of those departing for the new plantation, she must have been following the matrifocal living arrangement that permitted her to live in her own mother's cabin until her child was born. The child with whom she was pregnant on the journey was born in April, 1844 and named Christopher. Hessie, their daughter, was born at Faunsdale in 1852.[63]

Jack Kit had been valued at seven hundred dollars, an amount that indicated he was a first-class field hand in good physical condition.[64] Of twenty male slaves who were field hands at the Alabama plantation during September, 1844 Jack Kit picked the greatest amount of cotton for the month. The total amount picked by each man that month ranged in weight from a low of 752 pounds picked by forty-eight-year old Miles to the high of 5,042 pounds by twenty-five-year old Jack. The men whose totals for September came closest to that of Jack's were John Iredell (22) with 4,879; Granville (21) with 4,528; Cyrus (20) with 4,255; and Lank (30) with 4,133. Each of them had also been valued as highly as Jack Kit.[65]

As good as Jack Kit was, the hand whose totals beat his was his female cousin Airey. The greatest amount of cotton picked on the plantation for September, 1861 was 5,560 pounds picked by twenty-five-year old Airey, daughter of Esther Paine and Ben, and the granddaughter of Chloe. The least amount of cotton picked by one male for the month was 2,015 pounds by ten-year-old Lafayette and the greatest was 5,145 pounds by twenty-year-old Manuel. Close to Manuel's total for September were Philip (20) with a total of 4,925; Edward (17) with 4,800; Robert (18) with 4,755; Rubin (16) with 4,455; and Austin (19) with 4,305. By 1861 Jack Kit was 40 years old and could no longer keep up with his younger workers. However, both he and his cousin were good enough field hands to be very valuable to their master.[66]

Jack Kit and Sylvia were field hands for the twenty-two years that they were at Faunsdale except for a short time in 1864 when Jack worked for the railroad. Their son Christopher, who at twenty would have been a prime field hand, was also sent from field work to a saltwork. He did not care for it any more than young London and Peter had, for he too, ran away. However, Christopher's luck did not hold; instead of making it back to the plantation, he was jailed. When recording the event in his personal diary, Stickney marked only the day of Christopher's return, saying nothing of how long he had been in jail. Christopher was returned from jail to the plantation in April, 1665 but was soon joining with his aunt Sal and two freedmen in an abortive effort to find allies among federal soldiers:

9 June, Friday First sign of Yankee poison among the Negroes - 4 ran off to Union Town & returned by noon. A Yankee captain out to investigate, [the 4 must have said] "No complaint to make." [67]

Stickney repeated his report of the incident on the last page of his diary. His choice of words for the heading revealed concern that the social fabric, in general, and his authority, specifically, were about to unravel. He named each offender:

"Beginning of dissolution"
Old Sal, Christopher, Austin, Barney [went] up to Union Town 1/2 [of] Friday June 9th to complain.

Cassius, Edward, Tom, Anderson, London, Peter, Howitt, up to Union Town 1/4 [of] Saturday 10th on mules [taken] out of field.

Cassius, Edward, Wilson, Tom, London [went] up (to town) all Monday 12th [of June].[68]

Christopher, as well as several other hands, was dissatisfied with life as a "free" worker at Faunsdale and was making efforts to get the attention and aid from Yankee soldiers. Still, his name appeared on the first labor contract that was signed in June, 1865 and was in effect until December along with the names of his parents Sylvia and Jack Kit. In December the contracted time was up so Jack, Sylvia, Christopher, and Hessie left. Their names also vanished from Stickney's records.

The living arrangements of another of Chloe's daughters in 1843 suggests the multi-generational nature of the corporate family structure when Charlotte Paine, at age 27, and her child, still lived in her mother's cabin with her mother, various other relatives, but no husband. She was still part of the family unit with Chloe and Fed in October, 1843 when the list was compiled of those slaves bound for Alabama.[69] The family formed when she married Lank demonstrated the unshakably strong memories of loved family members and kin ties among slaves in spite of separations. The parents of Lank, Sam Hostler and Tamar, had eight children named Grace, Lank, Stephen, Ruth, Noah, Oppha (Orpha), Ashbury, and Joanna. Following a naming pattern that was common among members of Somerset and Faunsdale's slave communities, one of Tamar's daughters named her daughter for a sister from whom she had been separated.[70] Tamar's daughter Ruth had a daughter in Alabama in 1847 that she named Grace, the name of her eldest sister who remained at Somerset. The sister Grace who remained in North Carolina named two of her children the same names as her brother Lank in Alabama gave two of his children. Grace had a daughter in 1839 whom she named Henrietta and a son in 1840 named Barney, while Lank and Charlotte named their first two children Henrietta (1844) and Barney (1847). The last child born to Lank and Charlotte while at Faunsdale they named Providence, the name of Charlotte's older brother in North Carolina.[71]

Charlotte Paine and Lank Tamar made their marks on the 1865 labor contract, but soon ran against Stickney's ideology of control:

18th Monday Early off for Linden [the county seat] on Fanny [a saddle horse. About the court house to hear Judge's charge, Home after dark—almost sick with heavy cold... Dismissed sv't Lank—refusing to work Sat. afternoon. [72]

And a week later in the midst of a physically stressful week in which he returned to the county seat on horseback to address legal problems, Stickney made another diary entry:

25th Monday Note to Mr. Brooke at Linden by Carolina & Wm., sv'ts—down to court...to U'town to see Yankee official... Note to Capt. Pluss by Philip. Sent away sv't Charlotte. Arrested Yankee with 2 negroes & wagon trying to steal cotton. [73]

The diary neither explained why he fired Charlotte, nor why she had remained for a week after her husband's dismissal.

Kinship between Ruth, Cyrus, Willis, Grace, and Augustus has been difficult to sort out with certainty. In spite of the difficulty in establishing precise marital and kinship ties, they require as close a reading as possible because much that freedwomen did grew directly from such social structures. Ruth was born in 1822 to Tamar and Sam and traveled to Alabama with them in 1843, giving birth to her own child Grace there in 1847. Only Ruth's name was listed in the chapel register under the heading of "Parents" with no name for the father. On the 1848 slave inventory, their names were carried as part of Ruth's birth family, still without a husband's name included; by the time of the 1857 inventory list, Willis' name had been added to those of Ruth and Grace, indicating that they were a separate family. Seven years later in Stickney's 1864 tax list in the "families" section, Willis, Ruth, and Grace were still noted as a family, but Ruth's death in April altered living arrangements for Grace.[74]

Acting as the head of a family which, by 1865, now consisted of himself, Adeline (black), and Grace, Willis signed a labor contract for all of them. Stickney recognized and accepted the right of a black freedman to commit the labor of those considered to be his dependents, i.e., wife, child, younger sibling, niece, to a contract. A woman could sign for herself if not living with a husband or father and could also commit the labor of children or young relatives, but never her own husband. Grace was eighteen years old, unmarried, and apparently lacking a father, thus could have signed for herself; instead, her labor was directed and her name committed to a contract by a man whose only patent claim to authority in her life was having been married to her mother. In 1866 and 1867 Grace's name was not listed under that of Willis, but under those of Cyrus and wife Fanny. The 1869 contract stated that Cyrus signed for "himself and his daughter, Grace." Why he was considered her father is not clear since Cyrus had long been considered as Fanny's husband and noted as the father only of Fanny's younger children born between 1850 and 1863 at Faunsdale. He was identified neither as the father of her eldest child Philip born in 1841, nor had Cyrus ever been identified as Grace's father. However, once free of a master's control over their own labor and that of their dependents, some of the men who had been slaves on the plantation made claims on the labor of children based upon less-than-apparent grounds.[75]

Any resident plantation owner or manager could easily have known who the mother of a child was, but identity of the father would be less obvious. Often slave owners failed to acknowledge (in writing) biological fathers of slave children for different reasons; one reason was that if the father was not the property of the master, there was not reason to recognize him. The actions of many freedmen following emancipation show that they were keenly aware of kinship ties and relied upon them when seeking to reconstitute a fragmented family or claim the right to direct the labor of their children. Even though Louisa Harrison had recorded birth dates and parent's names of slave children in the chapel register, the women and men to whom those children were born knew their kinship ties better than their mistress could.

The most obvious conflict between what the mistress thought constituted a family and what the African-American men and women involved thought about it can be seen in the example of the two couples: Cyrus and Fanny; Willis and Ruth. According to Louisa's recorded chapel data for slaves, Cyrus and Fanny were married and parents of just one child, Augustus. Willis and Ruth were also a married pair with only Ruth's daughter Grace noted as their child. However, after emancipation, Willis and Cyrus claimed the right, as the fathers, to commit the labor of several children other than those listed as theirs in the chapel register. Oliver, another married slave whose children by his wife were listed in the register, also claimed a parental right to other children after freedom.[76]

When Cyrus signed Grace's name to the 1869 contract as her father he also placed an implicit claim on the right to direct her labor and receive her wages just as Willis did with Augustus. Oliver also claimed the right to commit the labor of two young boys named John Harrison and Isaac Black in 1869, identifying Isaac as his ward and John as his son. Not only did Oliver have the right to sign a contract committing the labor of the boys, neither of whom was a child of his marriage to Scotty, but he was also held liable for their fines and received their wages. Young John (Harrison/Wills) was the son of Nancy Wills and Oliver was his father.[77]

Questions immediately arise: upon what grounds did these three men base their concept of fatherhood? did they know themselves to be the biological fathers of children mis-identified by a master or mistress too far removed from field hands to know details of their lives? Were the fathers responding to elements of earlier African social structures which recognized parental authority based upon some claim other than biology? If they were adapting the dominant culture's patriarchal right to commit the labor of their wives and children, then being the father of a healthy teen-aged boy or girl could add more to the dinner table than just another hungry person wanting to be fed.[78]

As slaves, African-American men and women lacked the same socially recognized and legitimated marital and parental authority which accrued to free white persons.[79] As slaves, black women did not receive either the protection or privileges which usually accrued to white women and were often the only acknowledged parent of a child. Male slaves were denied the same authority over and right to the fruits of womens' production and reproduction exercised by white males as husbands and fathers. But once free, black women and men faced conflicts among themselves and between themselves and ex-masters over gender relations and parental authority of black children. And if a couple who had children while slaves separated when free, both claiming the right to direct the labor of their child/ren (esp. if the man's relationship to the child/ren was unclear to white authorities), how were the conflicts to be resolved? To whom would socially legitimate parental and marital authority adhere? What kind of freedom would African-American women find with the end of racial slavery within the context of kin structures and marital arrangements?

The interpretation of a black household by a census taker in 1870 serves as a precis for the direction in which black families were headed, or being pushed. In enumerating the household of Nancy Wills, a single mother of maturity who had worked for years at slave labor, the census taker considered her sixteen-year-old son as the head of the household despite his recognition that two women over forty (one was the boy's mother) also lived in the same household with the young man. The boy's name was listed as John Harrison, but was the same person known to William Stickney as John Wills and for whom he had been appointed legal guardian. John Wills/Harrison was also one of the young field hands for whom Oliver (Harrison) had claimed to be the father.[80] The names listed after John Wills/Harrison's on the census form to show who else resided with the head of that household were Nancy Wills, Charity Paine, and the names of Charity's children. In the eyes of the man taking the census count, a proper head of the household was a male, even when he was the teenaged son of an adult woman who lived in the house. In spite of the opinion of a white male census taker, neither was the boy the head of their household nor was either woman his dependent. Instead, the white male census taker adhered to his own cultural pattern of family hierarchy.

## III HANNAH PAINE, MACK, AND PENELOPE

Hannah Paine's family structure was one which was the least like an African corporate family or a polygamous arrangement. It was one in which the individual members as well as the group as a whole social unit had adapted away from either type. Hannah and her grandchildren were an African- American family with domestic skills that would enable the women to earn cash wages rather than work for shares on a family-based farm. This advantage, the relative freedom of movement afforded by being paid in cash, could allow them the relative freedom of movement and a greater access to the economy of the city. The children of Hannah Paine, a black slave woman, also differed from most of the other slave families of Faunsdale because they had a white father. In census records Hannah was always denoted as Black while her children were listed as Mulatto and in older slave records, no man's name had ever been given as the father of her children. African women and men forced to adapt to North America became African-Americans and that forced adaptation also carried an added burden for so many black women who accepted the children of men that they had not chosen, especially when the men were their white masters or overseers. Most slave mothers nurtured their children, holding to the primacy of the mother-child bond without regard of the race of the father. Such a child was Adeline, housekeeper and member of the household at Faunsdale from 1844 until her death in 1896. Adeline and her sister Penelope were children with only one openly acknowledged parent, their mother Hannah Paine. Although she may have lacked a father, Penelope found a husband old enough to have been her father.

Mack was past fifty when he, his second wife Penelope, and their daughter Hannah Paine left North Carolina for Alabama. As a carpenter, Mack's value was listed as $400.00 and would have been higher had he been younger. Penelope was half his age and valued at $450.00 while her infant was worth only $50.00. The three slaves belonged to Ann Daves (Nancy) Collins and were swapped for another slave who was twenty-four and valued at $740.00. Louisa and Nancy traded the slaves, with Louisa adding $150.00 to equal out the value of their exchange. Thus the small family remained intact and moved together to Faunsdale.[81]

The few bits of data relevant to Mack's family life reveal a close adherence to African naming patters and the use of some African names. [82] He had two wives and at least one child who was born at Somerset in 1828 while he was a slave there. Hannah Sally, the first wife, died seven days after the birth of their child and until her death, had been the eldest surviving child of one of Somerset's earliest slave couples, Cuff and Sally. Sally (born UI) and Cuff (age not known) had several children: Hannah in 1789; Betty in 1798; Murriah in 1800; Nica in 1803; and Cuff in 1807. In the exploration of her own genealogy, Dorothy Redford posits that Cuff was a native African because she interprets his name not as the common slave name Cuff[ee], but an Akan day-name Kofi. Redford also assumes that the name of Cuff and Sally's youngest daughter that was written in plantation records as Nicey was an Anglicized version of the Akan name Nsia. Cuff and Sally would have been about the right age for capture as slaves in Africa if they were part of the 1786 cargo of 80 slaves brought from Africa to somerset and would have been predisposed to give their children African names.[83]

Mack's first wife was called Sally's Hannah, or Hannah Sally after the custom at Somerset to attach the mother's name to the name of her child to distinguish those children who bore the same first name, creating a female version of a patronymic. Several women in Mack's life were named Hannah, but each name was modified either by a matronymic name or descriptive word. His second wife's mother was Hannah Paine and that wife's first child was called Young Hannah Paine. Penelope and Mack's child named Hannah Paine was born in 1841 and taken with her parents and her grandmother, Old Hannah Paine, to Alabama in 1843. It was Old Hannah Paine to whom Louisa's Sister Nancy referred in a letter to Louisa soon after the departure for Alabama in which Nancy complimented her sister on her wise choice of a household staff:

> I was so pleased to find you were working out so well in the way of house servants. Hannah, I recall, used to be considered an excellent cook, but she had been so long in the shades of retirement at the Plantation that I had forgotten her genius lay in the culinary line...with

Adeline at the <u>helm</u> & Margaret's devotion & Jupiter's promise, you cannot fail my dear...[84]

Old Hannah Paine was Louisa's cook, Hannah's daughter Penelope was a seamstress, and daughter Adeline was the housekeeper.

Perhaps Old Hannah Paine's mother Sally had taught her what she could remember about cooking African food. Sally was still living at Somerset in 1843 when her name was listed on the "List of Families [sic] taken 1843." The list was not a partial one meant to include only those to be taken from Somerset, but was a full inventory of all slaves living in the quarters on the plantation and the inhabitants of each cabin. Sally occupied no. 13 with Linda, Minton [Milton], who was Linda's husband, Linda's child Albert, Sally's grandchild Edy, and a man named Tom Mutton. Tom Mutton may have been kin to Edy because he was part of the removal group taken to Alabama and his name was usually grouped with Edy's in the same pattern as cohesive family units. Of the slaves who occupied cabin 13 when the inventory was taken in 1843, only Old Sally was left behind at Somerset, separated from all her kin who had lived in her cabin with her.[85]

Slave kinship was important to the masters and was documented by them only for living slaves. Once a slave died and was not longer useful to the master, there was not need to keep their names current in plantation records. Mack had two slave children by his first wife at Somerset, but once she died, her name was no longer listed for them. The names and ages of Mack's two older children, Peter and Linda, were carried in the same slave book that listed Mack as their father. Fifteen years later Mack, wife Penelope, baby daughter Hannah (young), daughter Linda, her husband Milton, and Mack's wife's mother Hannah Paine were all taken to Alabama, leaving Peter behind. Linda named her second son Peter for her brother from whom she was parted.

Soon after settling down at Faunsdale, the slave was subject to Thomas Harrison's anxious concern to get his plantation in good working order and to start producing cotton. The first picking season witnessed Harrison's use of domestic and aged slaves in field work. Although fifty-five years old, Mack was still listed as a field hand. And like old Fed, he was also listed as being absent from work almost every day. After the fall months of 1844, Mack continued receiving food and clothing from Harrison, but did not return to field work.[86]

Hannah Sally's death would not necessarily have severed Mack's ties with her kin, especially since there were two living children from the union. But his marriage to Penelope pulled him into a new circle of kin and into the orbit of the household in which his wife's family worked. Through marriage, Mack became a link between his first family who were all field hands and his second one which was made up of domestic slaves. With the birth of Penelope's child Hannah in 1841, Mack was a middle generation between the Africa of his parent's generation and the America of his own child. It also brought him into a close association with one of the domestic slaves who had some influence with the master and mistress, Penelope's sister Adeline.

Adeline was a valuable slave in both categories of capital investment and personal regard. Her monetary value in 1840 when she was twenty-one was $450.00 and put her in the high-cost bracket for female slaves owned by the Collins' estate.[87] However, the high regard with which she was held by her "families both white and black" speaks more to her true worth. She went with her new mistress on a trip in the spring of 1843, after Louisa's marriage in December. Louisa corresponded with her sisters in North Carolina as she traveled and visited. While in South Carolina with her cousin Martha, Louisa received several letters from Nancy, Henrie, and Letha. Of Adeline in a letter to Louisa, Nancy wrote:

> Remember me to Adeline of whom I am happy to receive back good accounts.[88]

Nancy was the eldest of the four sisters and felt responsible for the training and behavior of the domestic slaves from the Homestead in Edenton.

Responsibility for Adeline was not what motivated Louisa's younger sister Alethia, whose letters were cheery and full of family news:

> Tell Adeline, with Charlotte's love, that she received "the things and change" all safely...My remembrance to Adeline. Charlotte sends hers to you.[89]

Charlotte Cabarrus was the free black servant who had been the nurse to the children of Josiah Collins II and probably continued to tend to the children of Josiah III, Louisa's brother.[90]

After Harrison completed the necessary movement of slaves, goods, and furniture to Faunsdale in the winter of 1843-44, he and Louisa settled there in the spring. Louisa's pregnancy had made him especially anxious to get her moved from North Carolina before it was too advanced for her to travel. As in the year before, letters flowed between Louisa and her sisters and as before, they remembered Adeline. In March, 184 Alethia asked that Louisa

> Tell Adeline with my remembrances, good bye for me, and say to her I am sorry, I did not see her...[91]

Henrie wrote in May that

> [o]ur servants were charmed to hear from you & Adeline. They send you many affectionate messages with much love to Adeline. Remember me particularly to her & Margaret.[92]

Even Cousin Martha Pride in South Carolina remembered two of Louisa's slaves, referring to them as "your two Lieutenants Adeline and Oliver.[93]

The longest message sent through the white mistress for one of the slaves came as a congratulatory one from Charlotte and was conveyed to Adeline in a letter from Letha written in July, 1844 after the birth of Louisa's daughter Louise in the previous month:

> Charlotte says, I must give her best love to you and tell you, that she cannot find words to express her feelings toward you or to tell you half that she should like to say... Charlotte sends her love to Adeline and Jupiter. She said she intends to write them when she gets a chance... I expect Adeline has her hands full now. Emily sends her love to Adeline and all the rest.[94]

Although a great favorite and strongly depended on by those who thought they owned her, their attention and praise could not diminish Adeline's commitment to her own family. After emancipation, Adeline .often acted in the place of a parent for the children of Penelope by signing contracts for them and receiving their year-end wages. Penelope and her children did not follow mother Hannah Paine's or aunt Adeline's domestic occupations; they were field hands. Many ex-slaves were too old or feeble to work and were dependent on someone for support. Without families, women like old Hannah Paine or crippled Penelope had few options, although in the case of Faunsdale's aged ex-slaves, William Stickney provided for several. Although married to "old man Gregory," Penelope required aid from another quarter. Her sister Adeline assumed responsibility for Penelope and her children, paying their fines and bills, buying them shoes and clothing, and taking care that her sister, nieces, nephew, and even Penelope's "old man Gregory Cox" received support.[95]

Adeline and her husband Jupiter had no children and after his death in 1864, Adeline remained unmarried and lived in the house with Louisa and William Stickney. Louisa relied on Adeline for aid in what must have been the most severe loss of her life when her only child, her daughter Louise Harrison Shepard, died in March, 1872 shortly after the birth of her own daughter. Accompanying Louise's body on the final journey back to Faunsdale where her husband Willi Shepard and the baby who then remained at Faunsdale to be reared by her grandmother, Louisa Collins Stickney. Adeline became her nurse.[96]

Mack, Penelope, and Hannah. At first glance, this trio of names appears to represent a typical triad of father, mother, and child. However, deeper investigation peels back the obscuring anonymity to reveal a complex set of social relations in which the immutable biological absolutes of sex and race became justifications for mutable systems of social control based on an asymmetrical gender system and class superiority based on race. Mack connected two different slave families in a dense web of kinship ties which spanned four generations an ocean. His sister-in-law Adeline linked three generations of her own enslaved black family of laborers to three generations of the white planter-class family with whom she lived and performed the most intimate and trusted domestic duties. As brief as the history of Adeline and her family is, it is an intrinsic part of the primary social and psychological structures of a household in the nineteen-century Cotton South and reveals how central women were to those structures.

Adeline left what had been her home with her mistress Louisa in 1843 and they remained together until death. It was Adeline to whom the sisters of mistress Louisa always asked to be remembered; it was Adeline to whom the slaves in North Carolina passed messages through the letters of the Collins' sisters; it was Adeline upon whom Louisa depended when she established her own separate household; and it was Adeline who faithfully supported her own sister Penelope and Penelope's children. Adeline passed from her life into death January, 1896 and Louisa followed in November. Whether Louisa or Adeline ever fully comprehended their life-long relationship or not, their lives had been as bound together as if sisters.

What bound Adeline to the white household for her entire life did not act to bind the freed field hands to Faunsdale's cotton fields after emancipation. In June, 1865 the Rev. William Stickney presented something to the ex-slaves which would be the new basis of their employment; he had drawn up a contract for the hired laborers to have read to them, then make their marks upon so that he could get on with the business of making a profit from cotton. Just how much market relations and relying on the legal structures of contracts would change the lives of Faunsdale's household remained to be seen.

# END NOTES

1. Nancy (Ann) Daves Collins [during the course of this period of correspondence, 1842-1848 she married William Biddle Shepard] to Louisa Collins Harrison, March 9, 1843, Harrison box 1, folder HI (Correspondence), FPP, BPL.

2. Alethia Collins [during this period of correspondence she married Dr. Thomas Davis Warren] to Louisa Collins Harrison, "Somerset Place" March 28, 1844, Harrison box 1, folder 2 (Correspondence), FPP. BLP.

3. In his 1937 oral recollection of life as a Somerset slave, Uriah Bennett said that "Negro children had to go to school every day, and Sunday too." Also, throughout the correspondence between Louisa and her kin, are indications that letters from one slave to another were being enclosed. Uriah Bennett's testimony may be found reprinted by Dorothy Spruill Redford in "Somerset Slave Community: An Antebellum Genealogical Study," pp. BH-B14, printed and distributed by the author, 1986. Redford's work is a genealogical study of her own family, descendants of some of the Somerset slaves, and she is presently a project manager for the historic site of Somerset Plantation.

4. In addition to slaves, Louisa McKinlay Collins inherited land and silver bullion (and possibly stock in a New York bank) at her father's death.

5. For a look at the terrors endured by a runaway slave mother to both remain near her children yet shield them from knowledge of her presence, see Harriet A. Jacobs, Incidents in the Life of A Slave Girl, ed. Jean Fagan Yellin (Harvard University Press, 1987).

6. In one of his letters to Louisa prior to their marriage, Harrison sought to impress upon her how little he wished to practice medicine and how central to his plans were her slaves.

7. "List of Negroes for October 1843 Receipt [sic] of Dr. Harrison for the within named Negroes" Collins Papers, Private Collections (CPPC), Heirs of Josiah Collins I, folder P.C. 417.11 North Carolina State Archives, Raleigh (NCSA).

8. See Redford, op. cit., p. B-8 for an example where the policy was followed.

9. "List of Negroes at Edenton belonging to the Estate of the Late Josiah Collins Deed...April 1st 1840," CPPC, NCSA.

10. Op. cit. "List of Negroes for October 1843 Receipt of Dr. Harrison"

11. For the Harrison's slave lists for 1848 and 1857, see Faunsdale Plantation Papers, Box 1, folder 4, BPL.

12. John B. Boles Black Southerners 1619-1869a (University of Kentucky Press, 1984) makes the point of the pragmatism of allowing slaves to establish families and that planters also saw their familial stability as a hedge against serious rebellion.

13. See Peter Wood, "Digging Black History," Southern Exposure (March/April) 1983, pp. 62-65.

14. For more on the statistics of slave marriages, see Herbert Gutman The Black Family in Slavery and Freedom: 1750 1925 (Vintage Books, New York, 1976).

15. Maria Rosa Cutrufelli, Women of Africa of Oppression, (Zed Press, London, 1983; translated by Nicolas Romano), chapter 2., esp. pp. 41-42, 53-61.

16. Allan Kulikoff, Tobacco and Slaves: The Development of Southern Cultures in the Chesapeake, 1680-1800 (University of North Carolina Press, Chapel Hill, 1986), pp. 320-321.

17. Kulikoff, p. 354.

18. Deborah Gray White, Ar'n't I a Woman? Female Slaves in the Plantation South (W. W. Norton, New York, 1987), pp. 65-66.

19. See Orlando Patterson Slavery and Social Deaths (Harvard University Press, 1982).

20. Dr. Edward Warren's book, A Doctor's Experiences on Three Continents (Baltimore, Cushings and Baily, 1885), as quoted by Sterling Stuckey in Slave Culture: Nationalist Theory & The Foundation of Black America (Oxford University press, New York, 1987) pp. 70-73 also includes a lengthy description of the "John Koonering." For another first-hand description of the same Christmas-time celebration, called there "Johnkannaus festival," see Harriet A. Jacobs Incidents in the Life of a Slave Girl Written by Herself, (Harvard University Press, Cambridge, 1987, ed. Jean Fagan Yellin) pp. 118-120.

21. Ibid., Stuckey, p. 72

22. Data on Milton, Linda, and Albert were drawn from several documents: "List of taxable Negroes at Lake Phelps belong to Josiah Collins in his own right, on the 1st April 1829;" "List of Negroes at Lake Phelps July 1st 1839;" CPPC, NCSA. Information about Linda and Albert after arriving in Alabama may be found in the slave register, Stickney box V, folder 55, and squad books from 1867- 1877, Stickney box VII, folders 8, 9, 10, FPP, BPL.

23. Milton's value reflected an 1843 estimate. In the slave papers of the Collins Collection in the North Carolina State Archives is an 1846 estimate stating that "...negro men between the ages of 18 and 25 years old are worth from $600 to $650 and girls from 14 to 20 years old are worth from $400 to $450 if these negroes are sound..." The estimate was signed by Malachi Haughton who was otherwise unidentified. Milton's value was taken from the privately owned slave papers still in the possession of the present owner of Faunsdale.

24. Alethia Collins to Louisa Collins Harrison, "Edenton, October 31st 1848," Harrison box I, folder 6 (Correspondence of Louisa Collins Harrison), FPP, BPL.

25. The daily amounts of cotton picked by individual slaves and their field presence or absence for the picking seasons for the years 1844 through 1848 are in "Thomas A. Harrison's Account Book," Harrison box 1, folder H27a, FPP, BPL; slaves present at the plantation in 1848 are listed on the "List of Negroes for 1848," Faunsdale box 1, folder 4, FPP, BPL.

26. Harrison purchased a plantation in Louisiana in 1857 and apparently moved some of the Faunsdale slaves to work it, but his death a year later ended the venture. No inventory specifies which slaves went to Louisiana or how long they remained before returning to Alabama.

27. Louisa's second husband, William A. Stickney, prepared a register in 1864 that, in part, listed all of the slaves at Faunsdale as grouped into families. Birth and death dates were noted for most of the names. Linda's name was listed with that of a male slave called George Washington.

28. William A. Stickney 1g65 diary, 23 Jan., Monday, Stickney box III, folder 80, FPP, BPL.

29. For more on Alabama's salt works from 1861 to 1865, see Walter L. Fleming Civil War and Reconstruction in Alabama (Peter Smith, Gloucester, Mass., 1949), pp. 158-162.

30. Op. cit., Stickney diary, 16 February, 1865.

31. Ibid., 9-30 June, 1865; 24, 25 June, 1868.

32. Form more on Stickney's disgust with the black women who conceived children by any man other than one to whom they were wed, see his remarks on the baptismal records. John Witherspoon DuBose, "Chronicles of the Canebrake: 1817-1860" published in Alabama Historical Quarterly (Winter, 1947). On page 604 DuBose suggested that as a young and

unmarried priest, William Stickney "exhorted and preached celibacy for the clergy."

33. Harrison's "List of Negroes for 1848" and "List of Negroes for 1857," Faunsdale box 1, folder 4; Stickney's bound register (containing sections titled "Families 1st Jan. 1864," pp. 1-8, "New Families, formed in 1865," pp. 8-9, "Ages of Negroes rendered to Confed'te Tax assessor, Dec. 13, 1864," pp. 11-17, "Mortality of the year 1864," p. 19, "Non-producers in the year 1864," pp. 21-23"), Stickney box V, folder 55; Stickney diaries for 1865 and 1867, Stickney box IH, folder 80, FPP, BPL.

34. ..

35. Fed (Blacksmith) was a blacksmith, as noted by Peter Wood, op. cit.

36. "A List of the Negroes at Lake Phelps belonging to Mssr's Collins, Allen, and Dickenson, 10th November, 1803;" "list of Negroes at Lake Phelps July 1, 1839;" CPPC, NCSA.

37. Op. cit., Wood, pp. 62-65; "List of Families taken 1843," CPPC, NCSA.

38. Ibid., Wood

39. Op. cit., "List of Families taken 1843"

40. Slave records used are "A List of the Negroes at Lake Phelps belonging to Mss' Collins, Allen, and Dickinson, 10 November, 1803;" "List of Births at Lake Phelps, 1828;" "List of Male and Female Negroes at Lake Phelps (belonging to Josiah Collins in his own right) 1st January, 1829;" "List of women and their children at Lake Phelps, 1829;" "List of Negroes belonging to Josiah Collins in the town of Edenton and County of Chowan, 1 August, 1838;" "List of Negroes at Lake Phelps July 1, 1839;" "List of Negroes at Edenton belonging to the late Josiah Collins, 1840;" "List of Families taken 1843;" and the last list which was the one indicating which slaves were leaving Lake Phelps and going to Alabama. All above records are located in the North Carolina State Archives, Raleigh, North Carolina.

41. The spatial arrangement for each cabin in terms of the size of each one and how many persons occupied each cabin comes from two sources: the "List of slaves taken, 1843" which is really a census for each cabin and the published report of archaeological findings by Peter Wood, op. cit.

42. Op. cit., slave records

43. Chloe's value may be found on the list "Negroes belonging to the Estate of the <u>Late</u> Josiah Collins, Deed valued at $101,420. Each share amounting to 12,678.75." The original is in the possession of Gertrude Shepard Sims at Faunsdale with a copy held by the author.

44. On the material culture and persistence of African burial and beliefs regarding death, see John Michael Vlach, The Afro-American Tradition in Decorative Arts, (Cleveland, Cleveland Museum of Art, 1978).

45. Thomas A. Harrison's account book 1844-1857, Harrison box 1, folder H27a, FPP, BPL.

46. Ibid.

47. Alethia Collins to Louisa Collins Harrison, "Somerset Place March 28th 1844" Harrison box 1 (Correspondence), folder 2, FPP, BPL.

48. See Minnie Clare Boyd <u>Alabama in the Fifties: A Social</u> Study (AMS Press, Inc., New York, 1966) and John Witherspoon Dubose, "Chronicles of the Canebrake," Alabama Historical Quarterly Winter, 1947.

49. The preface written into the slave chapel register reads in part "The request of Mrs. Louisa M. Harrison for the Consecration of Faunsdale Chapel. The undersigned,..., having the ability wherewith God blessed her, erected a Church or Chapel for the worship of His Holy Name, and for the spiritual instruction of her slaves. Witness my hand and seal this 30th day of June, in the year of our Lord 1861—being the fifth Sunday after Trinity." Faunsdale plantation box 1, folder 7; "Baptisms," Stickney box V, Folder 51, FPP, BPL.

50. Birth data for the (acknowledged) children of Oliver and Scotty may be found in the Faunsdale chapel register and baptism records kept by William Stickney.

51. Louise Harrison Shepard to Louisa Collins Stickney, Stickney box I, folder 2(Correspondence 1868-1869), FPP, BPL.

52. Ibid.

53. Ibid.

54. Ibid.

55. Oliver's activities were detailed in two letters from W. A. Stickney to Louisa Stickney, dated 13 January and 23 February, 1870, Stickney box I, folder 3, FPP, BPL.

56. Ibid.

57. Faunsdale Plantation Papers, Inventory, 1860-1861 Cotton Totals, FPP, BPL.

58. For the complete text of the first contract, see Stickney box VII, folder 15, contract 1865, FPP, BPL.

59. Op. cit., William Stickney diary, 5 Oct, 18Z7. For more on the association between Collins and Norcoms of Edenton, see Harriet Jacobs <u>Incidents in the Life of a Slave Girl Written By Herself</u>. An uncle of Harriet Jacobs was owned by Josiah Collins III, who was an Edenton Neighbor to Dr. James Norcom. While Norcom lived in town, his son owned Auburn, a near-by plantation, and field slaves.

60. Op. Cit., William Stickney diary, 1865.

61. In the case of two slaves having the same name, a modifier was attached to each name (in written records) to differentiate between the slaves, thus

Hester (big) and Hester (tiger). Op. cit., William Stickney's 1864 slave family register; 1865 diary; Louisa Harrison's (Stickney) 1861 slave chapel register.

62. Op. cit., Stickney 1864 slave family register; 1870 Federal census for Marengo County, Alabama; 1870 squad book.

63. Op. cit., "List of Negroes at Lake Phelps July 1 1839;" "List of Families taken 1843;" "List of Negroes" CPPC, NCSA; Louisa Harrison's (Stickney) 1861 slave chapel register.

64. The original evaluation of Somerset slaves for exchanges among heirs of the Josiah Collins II estate is in the possession of Gertrude Sims, Faunsdale, Alabama with copies held by author.

65. Op. cit., Thomas A. Harrison's account book 1844-57.

66. Op. Cit,, Faunsdale 1860-1861 cotton totals.

67. Op. cit., William Stickney diary, June, 1865.

68. Ibid., end page 1865 diary, "beginning of dissolution."

69. White, <u>Aren't I a Woman?</u> pp. 105-108; "List of negroes at Lake Phelps July 1 1839;" "List of Families taken 1843;" "List of Negroes;" CPPC, NCSA

70. Ibid.

71. For a list of all of Tamar's and Grace's children by 1839, see the "List of Negroes at Lake Phelps July 1 1839." The "List of Families taken 1843" shows that Tamar and Sam's daughter Grace lived in cabin #33 with several children. For the names of Chloe's children, also see the July 1, 1839 list of families, CPPC, NCSA. For the birth dates of Charlotte and Lank's two children named Barney and Henrietta, see the slave chapel register of Louisa Harrison (Stickney).

72. Op. cit., William Stickney diary 1865.

73. Ibid.

74. Op. cit., "List of Negroes at Lake Phelps July 1 1839;" "List of Negroes;" Louisa Harrison's (Stickney) slave chapel register; Thomas Harrison's 1848 and 1857 slave inventories; and William Stickney's 1864 bound register of slave families; Stickney's 1864 register; 1865 contract; cotton picked by individual name, "Crop and Labor Accounts, 1865-1869," Stickney box V, folder 54, FPP, BPL; for the full text of the 1869 contract, Faunsdale Plantation Inventory box; on birth and parents, Louisa Harrison (Stickney) slave chapel register, Faunsdale Plantation box 1, folder 7, FPP, BPL. For those family groups taken from Somerset to Faunsdale, see "List of Negroes," CPPC, NCSA.

75. Op. cit., 1869 contract between Stickney and laborers.

76. Philip, Augustus, and Cyrus formed one family; Willis, Ruth, and her daughter Grace were another. Willis may have been Grace's biological father, but he was not so identified in the chapel register. About a year after Ruth died in 1864, Willis and Adeline (black) were noted as a "new family" with infant Rosa. Rosa did not live long, but her parents remained together and two more children were born to Adeline in 1867 and 1869 for whom Willis was acknowledged the father. Margaret and Henderson were the two added to Adeline's family of three older children of Milford (1854), Joyce (1856), and Richard (1859). Adeline had also given birth to a child named Amanda who lived four years before dying in the measles epidemic in 1865. If Willis were the father of any one of the older four children, he had not been identified by Louisa or Harrison.

77. See Rebecca Scott, "The Battle over the Child: Child Apprenticeship and the Freedmen's Bureau in North Carolina," Prologue, 10 (Summer 1978), 101-113 for a discussion on some of the efforts of white and black adults to exert parental authority over black children.

78. For more on the creation of stepfamilies and acceptance of "outside children" into a marriage among post-war black families, see Jo Ann Manfra and Robert R. Dykstra, "Serial Marriage and the Origins of the Black Stepfamily," Journal of American History, Vol. 72, no. 1 (June, 1985), pp. 18-44.

79. Op. cit., Patterson Slavery and Social Death: A Comparative Study

80. John Wills was the son of Nancy Wills, one of the original slaves from Somerset who remained at Faunsdale into the 1880s. Over a forty-plus year period, she was described as insane. In February, 1872, Stickney noted in his diary that he had several of Nancy's family "to unite with her in petitioning the Probate Judge to make me Guardian over her boy John." John Wills/Harrison was sixteen years old in 1872.

81. Op. cit., 1865 contract; 1866 contract; 1867-1878 squad books; 1870 Federal census. The name Jack Jones showed up in the records of Faunsdale only after emancipation.

82. Redford, "Somerset Slave community" pp. C20-21. For the authoritative work on the pattern and significance in how slaves named their children, see Herbert G. Gutman, op. cit.

83. Op. cit., "List of Negroes taken;" "List of Negroes;" Harrison's 1848 and 1857 slave inventories.

84. See letter addressed to "Mrs. Thomas A. Harrison, Faunsdale P.O., and Marengo County, Alabama" and dated May 21/44. The signature, written vertically and almost totally hidden on the first page, is "affectionate sister A.D.S." (Ann Daves Shepherd). The letter may be found in Harrison Box 1, folder 2, FPP, BPL.

85. Op. cit., "List of Negroes taken"

86. Op. cit., Harrison's 1844-1848 cotton records.

87. Op. cit., 1843 evaluation of slaves-Adeline.

88. Nancy Collins to Louisa Collins Harrison, 9 March, 1843, Harrison box 1, folder 2, (Correspondence) FPP, BPL.

89. Op. cit., Alethia to Louisa, 29 may, 1843

90. Charlotte Cabarrus was a free black woman who lived in the plantation house at Somerset and was paid a wage, according to Redford, pp. C3-C5.

91. Op. cit., Alethia Collins to Louisa Collins Harrison, 28 March, 1844.

92. Op. cit., Henrietta Collins [during the course of this correspondence, she married Mathew Page] to Louisa C. Harrison, 21 May, 1844.

93. Op. cit., Martha Pride to Louisa Collins Harrison, "Wyoming [Pride plantation in South Carolina] March 30th, 1844 Old Green Lake."

94. Op. cit., Alethia Collins to Louisa Collins Harrison, 4 July, 1844

95. For an example of Adeline's responsibility toward the children of Penelope, esp. Amy and Jackson, see the 1869 labor contract; for the feeble condition of Penelope, see the 1880 Federal census for Marengo County, Alabama.

96. More on Louise's death and burial, as well as Adeline as the nurse for Louise's infant daughter may be found in William Stickney's diary for 1872.

CHAPTER FOUR

# "A Contract-for Carrying on the Faunsdale Plantation"[1]

William Stickney's assumption that his authority remained unalloyed after emancipation speaks through his initial labor contract drawn up in June, 1865. the efforts of freed black women—sometimes successful, often not—to wrench concessions from old masters while redefining gender relations with their own men may be read in subsequent contracts. Stickney's initial assumption was that he could carry on business as usual by giving it a different name while keeping the old structure in place. He assumed further that he could rely upon the men who contracted with him to act as his agents in keeping order among the women and children. He realized greater success with the second assumption than the first.

For men such as William Stickney, a labor contract between themselves and black field workers was little more than a device to satisfy federal men while continuing to bully and intimidate a people lacking experience with written agreements. Not that most white planters had much experience with contracting for labor, for in their society white slave-holding planters seldom used a contract to achieve their goals. Planters accustomed to meeting the exigencies of their social order depended on controlled violence and personal autocracy when dealing with interiors and a code of honor among peers. [2]

However, as an Episcopal priest who had earned a Bachelor of Arts degree from the University of Alabama and attended seminary in New York, William Augustus Stickney was somewhat an anomaly in his own class; he was a well-educated, literate man comfortable with books and written information.[3] Perhaps this long reliance on literary sources explains the alacrity with which he wrote a labor contract two months before General Wager Swayne required the use of contracts in Alabama. The use of contracts was a mean to achieve the end of extracting labor from reluctant workers. In his first contract of June, 1865, Stickney adapted his old slave master style of control while keeping the content unaltered. He did admit one exception to the old way; members of the now-free labor force (all of whom had been slaves at Faunsdale a month before) were now to be paid

> for carrying on the Faunsdale Plantation, the balance of the year… The entire expenses of the place (plantation, white & black families) to be defrayed out of the growing corn crop. The wages of Employees to be one third of the net surplus of said crop after deducting the above expenses.[4]

The freedwomen of Faunsdale may have seen the contract for what it really was and wanted something vastly different. What none yet knew were the ways of free labor for free women (or free men) and William Stickney was not inclined to teach such lessons.[5]

By not specifying in detail just what he would provide, Stickney revealed his faith in the prevailing belief among white planters that black men and women could not manage their own lives and needed the kind, but firm, hand of a wise white father. His concession to pay wages in kind rather than cash was almost certainly not what the laboring women and men would have chosen, but was what the master thought best for them. Since he lacked a large amount of cash, it certainly was best for him. According to the contract, they would be paid more than just the privilege of living. Stickney paid them 466 and 2/3 bushels of corn on 27 December, 1865, an average of approximately 4 bushels per worker. Perhaps he thought that be still had the upper hand with all his previous power intact. The habit and language of the master slipped out in a phrase of the contract stipulating that "eggs & chickens (were) to be sold to the master only,..." He had not relinquished his old ideology.[6]

His 1865 contract addressed six areas for agreement between himself and the hired hands. Later contracts were more specific with greater attention paid to wages, housing, rations, tools, farm stock, and finable offenses. But the first one reveals the Rev. Stickney's continuing reliance upon tire relationship which had existed under slavery. Workers' dissatisfaction with the terms of the first contract soon intruded into their working and social relations with him, showing up as changes in later contracts. However, in 1865 Stickney itemized those areas in which he would hold complete authority and require compliance from the contracting workers: (1) authority over field work; (2) conduct and attitudes of Workers; (3) stealing; (4) raising and selling chickens; (5) how Sundays were to be spent, (6) and recognition of the essential mutual benefits of a contract for all contracting parties. A document brief in specifics and deep in assumptions, it was attached to a two-page list of names (or marks) of one hundred and six ostensibly free contracting black men and women, three white male witnesses, and the endorsement of a Freedmen's Bureau agent.[7]

After stating what the wages were, Stickney laid down rules and penalties with attention going first to his most immediate concerns:

1. The kind R degree of field work to be directed by the foreman under the instructions of the Employer. Penalty for refusing to work as so directed to be a forfeiture of one half of the year's wage for the first offence; dismission with forfeiture of the whole for the second.

2. Disrespect to authority, as well as gross moral, or other misdemeanors, to be punished by dismission & forfeiture of wages.[8]

Field work was the first topic addressed, but the embedded worry was how to maintain an accustomed level of authority and productivity. Under slavery, work had been organized in gangs overseen by drivers who took orders from an overseer who had his instructions from the owner; and Stickney expected this method to work with hired men and women. As had been the custom during slavery, only men were chosen for positions as overseers. From the first provision of the contract it is clear that Stickney had assumed total authority for decisions over field work with no regard for the experience of his hired hands. He also failed to specify what he meant by "work" when explicating the penalty for not doing it. "Refusing to work as directed" was an ambiguous phrase that could cover any job he chose. Retaining command over the hired laborers and producing a good crops were concerns so bound together for William Stickney that the two were conflated, just as his first contract illustrates. Solutions for these two problem areas had to be found if he was to remain a successful planter while maintaining control over dependents.[9]

The second contractual rule was to straightforwardly written to doubt its meaning, but conflation of the two separate issues of productivity and authority within the first rule of the contract leaves questions unanswered; had the field hands demanded a part in making decisions relative to growing the crops which prompted Stickney's initial assertion of authority? Was he just making a formulate statement to remind them that he was still in charge or had some of the more ambitious black workers sought the responsibility of making decisions about what would be planted? Had they badgered him for land or autonomy in the cultivation of sub-divisions of Faunsdale? They certainly caused more than one disturbance, or in his words, "a fuss" about something. They made enough of a fuss that some were dismissed just as his rule stipulated in 1865:

13 July    Settled with boy Robt. by commuting dismissal to whipping. The same with Tom.

29 July    Long talk with the negroes gathered & read the Rules again.

14 August    Dismissed Hiram for refusing to work Sat. afternoon & refusing to make it up.

15 August    Sv't begged back.

18 August    Dismissed Sv't Lank for refusing to work Sat. Afternoon.

21 August    Short talk with negroes.

22 August    Left Wil S. to have some of the negroes removed. Fuss ensued.

23 August    Wil S. told me of negro fuss-must go at it week.

25 August    Sent away sv't Charlotte (wife of Lank].[10]

Charlotte did not automatically leave when her husband Lank was dismissed a week prior to her being "sent away." Stickney made several observations in letters to his wife or in other private records that he had dismissed a man or boy in order to get rid of a particular woman, but no evidence connects the two of them to the fuss or indicates what caused it. However, something was flaring up between Stickney and his workers.

For the initial contractual period between June and December of *1865,* the antebellum hierarchy of order and authority remained in place with the employer (master) in command, instructing the foreman (overseer) who then ordered the employees (slaves). Stickney returned immediately to gang labor and did not parcel the plantation land into separate lots of land or farms for the women and men of Faunsdale. Letting go was not going to be done willingly by a man who had reiterated the customs of slavery on paper and called it a contract. Changes would be made, but the impetus for them was not being generated by "employers." Many acts of defiance, passive as well as aggressive, would have to be committed by "employees" to enlighten their "employers."

One small, subtle act of defiance was cleverly masked as an act of sympathy for the master and family. Louisa's niece had been on an extended visit at Faunsdale when she died there. Anne Page died on 22 June, 1865 and was buried two days later in the white family burial ground in a plot near the grave of Louisa's first husband:

24 June    Put up a beautiful cross over Anne made by Oliver.[11]

Even in death the old order was observed when a white member of the household was laid to eternal stillness within the wrought iron fence while black household members were buried close to those they had served in life, but still on the other side of the fence.¹² However, it was the living black members of the household who turned the moment to their advantage:

> 25 June    Negroes too upset to offer their services in their place.¹³

With respect to the kindness of those who had known Anne, it is more likely that Stickney misunderstood their act of subtle defiance, seeing it instead as grief for the loss of a member of the mistress's family. He allowed them time away from the fields when Anne died, but was less considerate of their loss later in the summer when eight of their own children and old people died and he failed to grant them free time for burials or grieving.¹⁴

Stickney's third rule addressed the racial prejudice common to men of his class that blacks were inherently dishonest and as likely to steal after emancipation as before. This was the same assumption which led him to hid family treasures as the Yankees approached without letting the house slaves know of the hiding place and dictated including a rule against theft in the contract:

> 3. A forfeiture of two fold the value of the thing stolen, the penalty for stealing.¹⁵

Including the rule and penalty might also have reflected a need to reclaim his seigniorial right to mete out justice which had passed from his bailiwick into that of the Yankee officers at Uniontown.

In May, scarcely a week after the garrisoning of federal troops in Uniontown, Stickney was at their headquarters over a theft committed by one of the ex-slaves. Seizing an opportunity, house servant George left Faunsdale and took a mule with him. Rather than apply his proposed penalty for stealing, Stickney had George tied and delivered to the Yankee soldiers. A county official advised Stickney to act as he did since "U.S. forces do not recognize...the existence of our courts," thus local courts could not be depended on as a remedy to bring George to justice:

> I understand...that the Officers in command propose to hold all guilty negroes subject to punishment for larceny of animals, & yesterday

committed several to jail for running off with their Master's (J. N. Shadrack) mule...[16]

Whether Stickney was more concerned about returning George for justice or retrieving the stolen animal is not clear. But George was confined to jail to wait a trial.[17]

Stickney's adherence to his patriarchal ideology and his failure to comprehend that his hired laborers were no longer his property to command speaks through the contract's fourth rule. It he put it into practice, Stickney was introducing capitalistic market relations with the same persons over whom he wanted to maintain the old mastery:

> 4. Raising chickens a conditional license: eggs & chickens to be sold to the master only, at one third less than market value: For violations, license to be withdrawn, & a forfeiture of half the value of stock.[18]

According to the contract, he would allow only one economic activity to take place on the plantation by hired workers, and it was one that had traditionally been exercised by female slaves. Of all the animals raised in 1864 for use by the household, only poultry were tended by a female. Two adult males, Nelson and Cyrus and eight teenaged boys, Ryus, Isaac, Tom, Armstead, Joe, twins Hugh and Parker, and Lafayette minded the hogs, sheep, and cows. However, neither the sale of those animals nor their products were considered in the contract. Perhaps Stickney did not regard such female husbandry as raising and selling chickens and eggs as a threat to his authority.[19]

Religion was another device for exerting social control for the man who was both a priest and a planter. Stickney was a man who combined Christian ideology with the practice of slavery apparently without conflict. He accepted the inherent sexism of the church because his entire identity and value system rested on the concept of a social hierarchy with women of his own class as his subordinates. Superiority as a propertied white male and religious righteousness resonated in this rule:

4. No leaving the place on Sundays but by permission. Prompt attendance in the Church on the place whenever opened for Service. For each neglect, forfeiture of a Saturday afternoon. [20]

His last rule may have devolved from his need to mystify reality and make it conform to his ideology. Or it may have been just an expedient intended to satisfy the Bureau agent:

5. Any of the above penalties may be commuted by mutual agreement between the contracting parties.[21]

Embedded within this simple statement was all of the hidden sham, deception, and sheer inappropriateness of a southern application of the Republican" free labor" ideology of the North.[22]

Postwar labor contracts between white ex-masters and black ex-slaves were a material manifestation of the Republican party ideology. Rooted in the capitalistic society of the North, Republican ideology reflected the concepts of a society antagonistic to the slavery-based political economy of the South. In their attempt to remake the postwar South in their own image, men in the federal government and positions of local authority in the South advocated using written labor contracts. But even the most enthusiastic supporters of capitalism had to admit the obvious: labor contracts could not guarantee the rights of black farm workers. Since federal armies, Congress, President Johnson, and agents of the Freedmen's Bureau had, in effect, colluded with ex-masters to keep black workers on plantations through contracts, ex-slaves hardly constituted a free labor force.

The free labor ideology that failed to regulate social relations between owners and workers in an truly open market exchange of wages for labor power in the postwar South was a sham long before its southern application. It was a failure in postwar southern. social relations because that society continued to be divided into racially determined classes which did not allow for blacks to rise to their full economic potential. However, the free labor ideology had never been relevant to women whether working for wages or as unpaid domestic labor, North or South. This ideology drew in part upon the belief that value was derived from labor and that labor was one of the quintessential definers of masculinity.[23]

Whenever the benefits of free labor (the right of a <u>man</u> to rise above his original condition through his own labor) were extolled, racial slavery was excoriated as the exemplar of unfree labor. But those espousing free labor were blind to the unfree condition into which women were born. A man could rise via labor and accumulation of property; a woman rose by marrying that man. Thus her condition, rise or fall, was determined not by her own labor but by that of the man she married. Most who opposed slavery recognized that men forced to labor without gaining its rewards because of their immutable condition of race could never be free to remake themselves as Republican party ideology touted. The biological fact of sex was also a condition that could not be risen above, but this was not part of free labor's ideological armory in the antebellum war of words.

That the free labor ideology as represented in contracts failed to aid recently freed black women and men in achieving real freedom soon became obvious; that it never addressed the needs of black women, or any women, did not. When northern exponents of free labor such as Samuel Gridley Howe publicly preached its virtues and made statements like "[i]t emasculates people to be protected in this way. Let them be used to protecting themselves," he was not including women as part of the free labor force. Much of the underlying meaning contained in such statements derived from the subordination of women in a permanently unfree condition which such phrases as "free soil for free men" strikingly revealed. Or when such an important Republican as Abraham Lincoln declared

> It was not the fault of the system [when a man did not rise above the position of wage earner] but because of either a dependent nature which prefers it, or improvidence, folly, or singular misfortune,...[24]

One is led to wonder if that "singular misfortune" might cover the dependent condition which derived from being born female. If Easter, Charity, Lavinia, Charlotte, or any of the women of the plantations across the South were to find freedom, it would be made in their own terms and in spite of great opposition.

Stickney's contract was no real contract at all. He would probably have tried any means to keep land in cotton production once he saw that slavery was absolutely denied him as a method of organizing labor. In his attempt to meet his economic needs while abiding by the regulation of society by the military powers representing civil authority in Alabama, Stickney created a document that he called a contract. While white men in power upheld the farce of having illiterate workers sign agreements which did guarantee the workers very little, few offered terms of equality. When Stickney wrote in his contract of 1865 that "any of the penalties may be commuted by mutual agreement," he meant that the owner, not the workers, could make changes.

Not every single black adult who had been a slave at Faunsdale during slavery's last month's made a consenting mark or was represented on the first contract. A few names which were carried on the December, 1864 Confederate tax list as slaves at Faunsdale were not on the contract written by Stickney six months later. From the 1864 total of one hundred and seventy-seven names on the tax list, one hundred and six were on the contract. Sixty names can be accounted for by age-they were either too old or too young to be productive. The seven listed on the tax list as too old to work were also excluded from the contract: Delpha 68; Miles 68; Tom Mutton 63; Moses 67; Hannah Paine 75; Celia 74; and Tamar 70. Neither the too-elderly seven nor the too-young fifty-three appeared on the contract. [25]

Three from the 1864 list of one hundred and seventy-seven, Edie, Jupiter, or Ashbury, died before they ever saw freedom or were faced with the decision of signing a contract. Of the remaining one hundred and fourteen men and women who were all but eight signed. The names and ages of the eight not Signing were Nelson 55, Cyrus 40, Margaret's George 24, Shadrack 24, Lavinia's Joe 18, Becky 51, Adele 20, and Mela 13. Some of the eight did show up from time to time in some of Stickney's records and some were noted in the 1870 Census of Marengo County. [26]

A contract was a useful and immediate device by which Stickney could wield social control over those freed persons who had been so much as his command as slaves. he did not use the contracts provided by the Freedmen's Bureau or rely on Bureau agents to write his, but drew up his own and read it aloud to the hired hands who then made their marks on it. The first contract made was witnessed by three white men who were kin or indebted in some fashion to Stickney. T. W. Hall, C. Badenhausen, and W. B. Shepard witnessed the signing before the contract was certified by a Bureau agent in Demopolis, Alabama in September, 1865.[27] The gap between custom and law can be as great as the one so often observed to separate theory from practice. What was written on paper and pressed upon freedmen and women to agree to was not necessarily what they did. But words on paper might have given temporary reassurance to a man accustomed to trusting the power of written words.

This particular contract may be read as the beginning of an on-going dialogue between workers at Faunsdale and William Stickney during the first few years after emancipation. In spite of receiving initial assurance of the freedmen and women's agreement in the form of marks on the contract, Stickney soon witnessed the departure of Lank and Charlotte with three of their children: Barney, Armstead, and Ryus. Broad pen strokes were drawn through the adult's names on the contract.

The old master had assumed too much as he put names on paper. As a priest, much of his faith flowed from his trust in the power and veracity of the Christian Bible as the source of truth. Perhaps his dependence on written documents flowed as a natural consequence of that faith and written expectations for workers seemed the formula for success. Obversely, marking through the names of recalcitrant workers perhaps revealed his desire to be rid of the person as easily as he was rid of the names. For Lank and Charlotte, illiterate and accustomed to an oral cultural, action was more important than all the words written on any paper—so they acted.[28]

Refusing to follow the old master's order was an overt act of asserting one's right to autonomy even though it usually was interpreted by Stickney as defiance. In August Lank decided that Saturday afternoons did not belong to the boss and would not work on them. Stickney fired him for refusing. Earlier in the summer Stickney had dismissed Robert for being disrespectful to the foreman, then took him back with a punishment of whipping instead. Hiram and Tom were also fired for refusing to work on Saturday afternoons, but Hiram was reinstated by "begging back." Lank was either too proud or self-confident to put on a show of remorse and beg back. A week later his wife Charlotte was also fired. Neither was ever employed again at Faunsdale and their names were not in the 1870 census for the Faunsdale beat. [29]

Some who would not turn out for field labor were too ill to do it during the first summer of freedom. The measles epidemic took a heavy toll in the quarters, taking the lives of very young and old. Between 6 July and 4 August, Mary's child Amelia, two unnamed infants, Orpah's child Mills, and Rose, infant daughter of Adele and Robert died. Cassius' wife Hester died on 11 July and their new-born baby ten days later. On 23 August Ol Milly had died by daylight. Her death received more attention from the Rev. Stickney because she had been a communicant for whom Holy Communion had been given two weeks before her death. At one time in July all hands except thirteen were too ill (or so they told the old master) for work. Hannah, Henrietta, Eliza, Adeline, and Lavinia decided in June that being pregnant allowed them to "do nothing" and did nothing for the remaining six months of the year in spite of having their names on the recent labor contract.[30]

January, 1866 in the Canebrake was cold and wet. It was time for the confrontation between owners adamantly set against giving land to freed slaves and workers who expected to receive it. [31] Stickney took the offensive in the campaign:

Jan. 2    Ordered all the Quarters cleared by tomorrow morning. Point gained & contracting began at night.

Jan. 3    Quite a stir among the negroes—some moving off others contracting. Busy all day on the business till after tea. [32]

The contract mentioned in his diary is not extant, so terms for 1865 and 1866 cannot be compared. But based on diary entries and a summary of plantation expenses for 1866, Stickney apparently paid the workers cash wages monthly:

Feb. 23    Up till late hour...on books & Acc'ts for negroes to pay up end of month.

Apr. 30   Settled with negroes at night month's wages.

June 29   All day busy on getting ready for negroes monthly Settlement.³³

Although the 1866 contract between Stickney and the hands did not survive, another contract of sorts did. U disgruntled assessments of the work and personal behavior of free black workers by discomfited white men of the planter class could be taken at face value, one could believe in the accuracy of Stickney's reason for the contract of June, 1866. He wrote "...at noon [I] made [a] contract with the <u>drones</u> for self-protection."³⁴ He objected to uncontracted persons living on the place and sought a way to extend his control over those renegade scofflaws. The contract between "W. A. Stickney and certain Persons for the protection of his interests, allowed to reside on his place during the year 1866" opened with this declaration of purpose:

> On my part, I have consented to permit Said persons—former servants on the Faunsdale plantation, Marengo County, Alabama— to remain free of charge on the same place the balance of the year fi to live among their relatives & friends, under this written promise sustained by security, that they will comply with the following conditions to which their own names & the names of their securities are signed & pledged: 35

Four conditional terms for uncontracted persons were stipulated: (1) to attend all church services; (2) to recognize Stickney's authority over relatives "cheerfully & unmurmeringly;" (3) to not treat his property as "a commons from which any desired materials could be scavenged;" (4) to obey his wishes "respectfully & orderly" and to conduct themselves respectfully toward each other. He also attached a fine to each possible breach of order.³⁶

Of the nine persons named in the agreement who were to be allowed to live at Faunsdale without having signed a contract, three had been called too old to work two years before. Delpha (70 and his wife Joan (60) were parents of Shepard, who stood as their security and the venerable Hannah Paine (78) must have been so much a part of Faunsdale that she was allowed to stay without anyone as her security. Becky Parsons (56), daughter of Chloe Paine, was vouched for by her son Cassius. Penelope (49), physically disabled, was secured by sister Adeline. The remaining four persons, Mary Newbern (50), Hester Iredell (42), Nancy Paine (37), and Murriah (18) were young and healthy enough to have worked, yet each was secured by a man. Mary Newbern's husband Allen guaranteed her behavior and Hester's husband John stood for hers. Both men had been slaves at Faunsdale, but the men who signed for Nancy Paine and Murriah had not. Jack Jones secured Nancy Paine's right to live at Faunsdale and Jim Flood secured a residence for Murriah. Theirs were new names in the records of the Collins-Harrison-Stickney family.[37] If the old master could not exert direct authority over this group of women, then he expected their men to do it for him.

Stickney's itemized assessment for family and business expenses for the year of 1866 reveals his relative financial success and indicates that he had some cash to pay his workers:

1866 Summary of Expenses - Plantation:

| | |
|---|---|
| To Money Wages field hands | $3,697.70 |
| To Meat rations | 1,626.00 |
| To Money Wages Carpenter Jim Flood | 192.77 |
| To Meat | 35.70 |
| To Money Wages Reported over hoe hands | 50.00 |
| To Money Wages General Supervision (Oliver) | 500.00 |
| To Meat | 35.70 |
| To Money, Meat & Clothing, corn shelling, ac | 58.80 |
| To Tools, Nails, Salt, Plough lines, Taxes, Bagging & Ties | 1,022.77 |
| To Mules lost (5-3 died, 2 stolen) | 1,000.00 |
| Total Expenses | $8,235.40 |

He showed his net income for 1866 to have been $12,350.14. A note at the bottom of the page added that he had cotton on hand from a former year's growth which he had sold that year, but had not included above.[38]

In 1867 something caused a new set of terms between "Master & Hired Servants" that was reflected in new contractual terms for the organization of labor and form of payment. Since 1866 was a profitable year, why did he change what had worked so well? Money wages for field labor were not uncommon in 1866 since many hired workers preferred to be paid that way, if they were not going to get their own land, and William Stickney was not giving away his wife's plantation. He probably had not intended to alter the method of payment for a third time either, but that is what happened the next year.

The changes may not have been desired by the master but were required of him. That he did not wish to make them was plainly expressed in a letter to Louisa in 1867:

> I had hoped to plant corn the end of tilts week. Before then is a big job on me: setting off the land to their [hands] respective parties—"Squads"—& settling those parties in proper shape. I dread the work.[39]

Early in January, 1867, William had taken Louisa to the Collins' home in Edenton to stay with her daughter Louise who continued to suffer from a seriously debilitating illness. Louisa remained there into the spring.[40] Although Stickney noted in January that he had drawn up a contract with new terms what he wrote to Louisa suggests that she contributed nothing to the management of the plantation beyond directing the gardener.[41] In a letter of 13 March, 1867, he wrote to Louisa at length on the same topic and again used the expression of dreading the division of land and reorganization of the labor to work it in what he saw just "[a]nother load...yet on me."[42]

Why did William Stickney alter a proven system of labor and payment which brought him a handsome profit? One strong reason must have been dissatisfaction, the fusses, among his workers. Their resistance concerned him enough that he noted he would have to "go at it" to restore order and compliance among them. He kept the plantation profitable during a generally poor year for cotton-growers while keeping sufficient labor then changed to one which he dreaded and perceived as a burden. He also wrote to Louisa that the hired hands were very excited over the prospect of working in squads. In order to keep the level of production and requisite labor force, Stickney assessed the situation and made changes which he incorporated in the 1867 contract.

If the first labor contract of 1865 was one short on detail and long on assumption, 1867's was the reverse. Stickney called the first section "Conjoint obligations" to indicate mutuality of interests being represented, but it reflected only his concerns and interests about religion, dissolution (of the contract), disagreements (among the workers), time lost, fines, and mutual expenses (bagging and bailing). Each topic was adequately addressed and sufficiently detailed to clarify his expectations, but none were radical or challenging changes. The first term of the contract addressed an issue always close to Stickney's heart:

> 1st-of Religion We acknowledge Almighty God as our Ruler & Provider. And we will set apart to Him all Sundays, certain week days—Fasts & Festivals of the Church—to be devoted to His worship, by ourselves & families assembled, decently clad, in His Holy Temple on the place whenever open for Service.[43]

Months before he wrote that "negro indifference to the soul" made him feel "crushed to think on negro apathy," revealing his deep disappointment over the hired hands seeking their own religious expression rather than accepting his, but it did not cause him to suspend attempts to force his beliefs on the field hands. He simply incorporated his expectations into the labor contracts.

The obsessive attention to detail and order in Stickney's contracts, especially the finable offenses, were part of his need to control and maintain order in his life. The first part of the 1867 contract dealt with the joint obligations of what he called the Partnership and the second with "Individual Obligations of The Master" which began with a classic statement of a man dedicated to the inherent rightness and righteousness of a social system which accustomed men to controlling others as a masters, fathers, and husbands:

>...as Master, I will be uniformly kind to my Hired Servants, & considerate of their temporal & spiritual condition: furnishing them, free of charge, with house room, fire wood, medicine, & half their meal rations when engaged in actual labor for me; with Religion Services in the public [sic] chapel on certain week days & Sundays; & with coffins & interment of the dead.[44]

He must have thought that his persistent offer of coffins was one of generosity calculated to be the final inducement which would sway his ex-slaves to remain with him.

He reserved for himself authority to make all decisions on the quantity of land planted and how to work it. His second stated obligation was to furnish the land and all requirements needed to farm it, including seeds, animals, and tools. Then he included a prerogative that spoke of deep alterations in work patterns; he reserved the right to "decide on a transfer of laborers, stock, or land; to...protect my interests in any way of pertaining to the customary routine or exigencies of the plantation."[45] The third contractual obligation of the master awarded one third of the entire crop of cotton, corn, and fodder to the field hands as payment rather than cash. he continued paying the domestic servants money wages, but they were never included in the contracts between himself and field hands.

His fourth obligation was a threat of penalties that would be assessed against scofflaws and lay-abouts; and the fifth was the right to fire anyone guilty

>...Insubordination, gross immorality, Misdemeanor, Disrespect to authority or my family [seeing himself as synonymous with authority] & for Indolence or other habits injurious to the interests of the Partnership.[46]

The sixth obligation was a responsibility so ambiguous that it had little meaning save as a statement of his intentions; if he failed "to comply with the terms of this Agreement," he promised to "make fair & full reparation of all damages done to my Hired Servants."

Although the carefully detailed section on responsibilities of the hired workers exacted more from them than the master, it also demonstrated a change in Stickney's relations with them:

> On our part, for ourselves & those subject to us, we the Hired Servants unite in hearty co-operation with the Master: & pledge ourselves to use all diligence in cultivating the crop & keeping the plantation in a farm like condition; to heed cheerfully & obey faithfully his orders & instructions issued in person or by his agent; to consider this interests in the use of all his property, & to sustain all careless loss or injury to the same; to defray any expense for additional services in making or saving the crop apportioned to us, & to give over any portion of it if unable to cultivate it; to accept One Fifth of the result as our compensation should the crop fail from any fault on our part. [47]

Stickney compressed the 1865 contract in its entirety into the first condition for 1867 and proceeded to enlarge upon his rules and requirements. Two consecutive years of dissatisfied, fussing field hands had taught him that they would not be treated as slaves and that he had to be specific in descriptions of the work to be done.

William Stickney had neither wanted to reorganize the method of work nor had he wished to accommodate the particular family needs of those working for him. But they made him aware that he had to do one in order to affect the other. Both were necessary if he was to continue making good crops of cotton. One of their requirements was to give women with young children a way of being closer to their quarters and children by marking off small plots of land for their domestic use. Some understanding that he had to accommodate them glimmered in a letter to Louisa:

> This began yesterday, I mean, the apportionment of land to the several parties. The entire plantation of open land had to be surveyed by me, & thrown into a dozen shapes before the division could be adjusted with something like equality among them. Poor land to be sliced out

& fitted on to richer equally—a certain quantity needed near home by each party for their women with infants.[48]

Whose demands were these? Had the mothers of babies insisted on these terms? Was the reorganization of labor and redistribution of land important to the older single women who had neither husband nor baby to look after? Had the men decided that it was what was best for their families? Had the men, as Laura Towne had interpreted actions of the freedmen of Port Royal and the sea islands, become jealous of their male prerogatives and sought to subordinate their women?[49] Was the prospect that the best workers (and potentially highest wage-earners) who were women too disheartening to men who had to assert authority in some directions?

The 1867 contract contained obligations of workers to their old master which reinforced an asymmetrical gender system between black women and men in the post-war South. Comparisons between the vaguely defined terms of 1865 and the carefully detailed ones of 1867 indicated that while some changes had taken place in the relations between landlord Stickney and his hired labor, that was not what set the 1867 contract apart as a document revealing a conflict central to the lives of black female field workers. The second obligation shows a step taken by black men in accord with their white labor lord where, as males, they gained greater social authority based on personal and familial relationships with black women.

Enslaved black men were not acknowledged as heads of their families or households or even as fathers because too much social authority devolved from that position. Once slavery was abolished, other social structures affected gender relations between black women and men. However, the exact shape and manner of the gender relations between men and women are historical and some cultural elements vary over time and place. How many African cultural elements had survived and remained vital in their lives? Had Africa's old voice been silenced or heard within the African-American community as it grew in the isolation of Lake Phelps, North Carolina in 1800 or Marengo County, Alabama in 1843? How much had three generations of Christian rhetoric combined with elite white values shaped the expectations of the black women and men of Faunsdale? The exact provenance for the gender system particular to black women and men of the late nineteenth-century South may not be located, but its asymmetrical form can be discerned as Stickney's second contractual obligation of hired servants in 1867 reveals:

> For the distribution of our year's earnings, we submit to be classified according to our respective merits by a committee consisting of the Principal of our company ("Head of the Squad") & two others chosen by us from among ourselves. [50]

Ranking was not imposed from above by the old master, but from within by the men who held the position of squad head. The old master had dictated the terms of the contract straight from his own gender and class ideology. He was part of the white, male-dominated planter class whose interests he served and tried to preserve in relations with the new class of labor. While the contract's second obligation of worker to master reflected the master's construction, he was building on the foundation laid by the demands and actions of the ex-slaves who were now his hired laborers. The contract was written by the old master, but the decisions that had to be made regarding how every worker was to be ranked, i.e., their classification that would determine the share of the crop and wages each hand received, were left up to head men and two others "from among ourselves."

One of the powers wielded by the squad head over members of his squad was his authority to charge fines against them. When Stickney conceded to his laborers and reorganized field labor from gangs into squads, he countered with another mode of control in the form of fines. Pressed to grant more freedom and autonomy to hired hands, he made them pay for what they got. Any deviation from prescribed rules would cost either the individual or the adult responsible for that person. By appointing only men to be squad heads and then giving those to power to reward or penalize squad members with fines that head men chose to levy, Stickney gave them economic control over the other members of the squads.

The list of classified offenses for which workers could be fined numbered twenty-six with each carrying a fine. This was the plan for extending control and discipline over the workers to which he referred in the letter of 13 March, 1867 to his wife:

Another load is yet on me in this same connection: to secure all under full contract in their respective squads, where they will have to remain, with duties towards each other & me to be enforced by skillful [sic] fines written down & agreed to severally. [51]

In his characteristically methodical manner Stickney had the fines grouped into five classes reflective of some hierarchy of his own. However, reading the finable offenses for 1867, 1869, and 1874 reveals in what direction his concerns moved over the nine-year period. In 1867 the offense he considered first was one regarding a proper delegation of authority and the fine if the squad head failed to report all offenses. If he failed to report finable offenses committed by members of his squad, he was liable to pay the fine. Seven of the first nine offenses were for behavior and two for damage to land or crops. [52]

Two more of the twenty-six finable offenses reveal that in 1867 he was particularly concerned about authority and how to effectively delegate this own:

20. Parents & acknowledged Heads of Minors & noncontractors, Responsible for their offenses. [53]

If those to whom he granted authority accepted it, then they in turn had to wield it within their community (and his fields) over wives, relatives, and friends.

The last finable offense listed by Stickney also carried the highest fine other than dismissal. It might also have been the one most personally repugnant to him:

26. "Conjuring" or "tricking" or "dealing in spells" or "charms", or "preaching" $10 or dismissal[54]

If the amount of the fine may be taken as an indicator of how much trouble Stickney was experiencing with specific acts of the hired hands, then conjuring and preaching no longer concerned him in 1874 because it was absent from the list that year.

In 1874 he went straight to the issues of stability of the work force and growing cotton. Where he had once made attendance of religious services and moral behavior topics of joint concern in 166Z, in 1874 he emphasized productivity and profits. The last section on joint responsibilities reveals a contract with much attention paid to percentages and profits:

> I. It is conjointly agreed
> 7. that no portion of the crops shall be claimed or appropriated without the consent of the "Owner" party of this contract, until the same shall have been harvested & duly divided, under penalty of Trespass & Misdemeanor. Nor, after the due division or apportionment to each laborer of his share in the crops, may be claim or dispose of such portion until the Owner shall have been reimbursed in the full sum of all advances made by him to said laborers & his family.[55]

The list of finable offenses showed a shift Stickney's areas of concern and an increase in violence among workers. Of the twenty-five finable offenses listed for 1874, sixteen dealt with either making and protecting the crop or a penalty for disruptive behavior among the workers. Two offenses for which fines were raised related to fighting or quarreling. An increase in aggressive and disruptive behavior among the men and women engaged in field work can be seen throughout the plantation day books which Stickney began to keep in 1867. Concessions won from their labor lord were not sufficient to allay their problems or lessen the tensions created by poverty and oppression. The women and men who worked for William Stickney continued to act with violence against each other in the fields and quarters.[56]

When all four of Stickney's extant contracts for field labor are compared, certain changes are obvious. The contracts after 1865 show that his concerns about the legitimacy of his authority had given way to concerns about productivity; and his prevailing emphasis on religious participation had also lessened. Religious matters were not excluded by Stickney from later contracts, but they no longer held the position of primary importance. The 1874 contract carried the following, less stringent proposal:

## II. Obligation of the Owner:

1. On my part, I claim the set apart certain Festival & Fast week days from all secular right to work, to Almighty God; in which, as well as on stated Sundays I will supply religious Christian services in the Chapel on the place, free of charge.[57]

The second promise included the provision for the employees' temporal and spiritual condition and free coffins. It also differed considerably in tone and expectation from his rule of 1865 and 1867 that there would be "[n]o leaving the place on Sundays but by permission. Prompt attendance in the Church...whenever opened for service" or that all would "set apart...all Sundays & certain week days...to be devoted to His Worship...in His Holy Temple on the place, whenever open for service." Even on this most important issue, the old master had been forced to recognize and concede to their resistance.

The contracts also indicate that at least one pattern had not been altered. As slaves, African-American women were subject to performing any type of productive and reproductive labor for the master or mistress or their own men and families. A Louisiana slaveowner even set some of his male slaves to what he termed womens' work for the stated purpose of humiliating them.[58] Slave women did both field and domestic work for their masters and mistresses, domestic labor and child care for their own families, but were not put in places of authority over slave men. Adult male slaves did not take part in making clothing, in child care, cooking, or domestic chores in the cabins. This omission has been attributed to the demands of masters as long as they retained the power which flowed from the organization of labor permitted by slavery.

But if African-American men and women adhered to the same practices after slavery ended, several conclusions seem logical: African cultures were of a patriarchal or male-dominant nature and many of the surviving cultural elements prevailed; the dominant culture of the white planter class with its emphasis on the subordinate position of women to the power of their men had affected gender relations of an enslaved people who adapted it upon their freedom; slavery permitted white males access to black women and tended to make black men especially protective of them; the new opportunity to direct their labor toward their domestic responsibilities appealed to most freedwomen; and slavery had not produced an egalitarian set of gender relations between black women and men.[59]

What the contracts reveal that did not change between 1865 and 1874 was the superior position of black men relative to black women at Faunsdale Plantation. The contracts were written by a white male of the planter class and expressed his own gender and class ideology, but they were agreed to an supported by the same men who had earlier effected many changes from him; it is a mistake to assume that when African-American women chose to raise their own children or were denied social and economic equality with the men of their family and community that men like Stickney bear total responsibility. What the contracts indicate is that William Stickney and his hired black male workers excluded black women from the highest paying rank of a first class hand and relegated married women to part-time or seasonal status which the re-organization of labor into kinship-based squads facilitated.

# END NOTES

1. For the full text of the contract, see "Labor contracts," Stickney box VII, folder 15, FPP, BPL.

2. Individual authority and personal violence as the social norm of white male behavior in southern society are addressed by W. J. Cash in <u>The Mind of the South</u> (New York, 1969), esp. pp. 44-5, 115-23, 125, 138. For the place of violence in the political economy of southern racial slavery and its importance to the hegemony of the ruling planter class, see Eugene D. Genoveses, <u>Roll, Jordan, Roll: The World the Slaves Made</u> (New York, 1976), esp. pp. 25-49. Bertram Wyat-Brown's <u>Southern Honor</u> gives an excellent study of the male planter-class ideology and the role of both violence and honor. For an application of the ideological concept of honor to action, see Gerald Linderman, <u>Embattled Courage: The Experience of Combat in the American Civil War</u> (New York, 1987). For the constant presence of violence in the lives of enslaved black women and men, see any one of the slave narratives such as the recently published collection edited by James Mellon, <u>Bullwhip Days: The Slaves Remember-An Oral History</u> (New York, 1988). The implications of violence and honor in the lives of white southern women of all classes remain to be presented.

3. See "William Augustus Stickney Biographical Note," prepared by Renee Blalock, Inventories box, Stickney Family folder, FPP, BPL.

4. Op. cit., "Labor contracts," 1865.

5. Copies of contracts between William Stickney and workers exist for the following years and services: field work 1865, 1867, 1869, 1874; social control over persons residing but not contracting with Stickney 1866; one very short agreement between Stickney and a single woman Joanna for 1868; for medical services between workers and Stickney for 1873; and one

agreement between Stickney and the mercantile company of Adler & Bros. in Uniontown to supply credit to hired workers in 1872 may be found in Stickney box VII, folder 15, FPP, BPL.

6. Ibid, 1865 contract

7. Ibid, 1865 contract

8. Ibid, 1865 contract

9. That William Stickney fully expected to continue to command the labor of his hired workers in any direction he chose becomes clear with reading the complete texts of his labor contracts. He included provisions which would have allowed him to direct their work to all tasks necessary to the operation of a large plantation, just as has been customary during slavery.

10. 1865 Diary of William Stickney, Stickney box III, folder 80, FPP, BPL

11. Ibid.

12. Anne Page's death was recorded in Stickney's diary for 1865, but the information about the arrangement of the white and black burials comes from my own observation of the cemetery and interview with a descendent of Louisa's first marriage.

13. Op. cit., 1865 diary

14. Ibid.

15. Op. cit., 1865 contract

16. W. E. Clark to Rev. Wm. A. Stickney, May 28, 1865, Stickney box II, folder 52, FPP, BPL

17. J. A. Young, Judge of Probate for Marengo County, Alabama, 1st day of June, 1865, Stickney box II, folder 52, FPP, BPL

18. Op. cit., 1865 contract

19. For more on jobs held by slaves at Faunsdale in 1864, see the bound register, "St. Winifred's Family & Day School," pp. 21, 22, 23, Stickney box V, folder 55, FPP, BPL.

20. Op. cit., 1865 contract

21. Op. cit., 1865 contract

22. The free labor ideology is probably best analyzed by Eric Foner Free Soil, Free Labor, Free Men: The Ideology of the Republican Party Before the Civil War, (Oxford, 1970).

23. The much touted ideology that labor serves to both set those who work free while making them ore masculine was relevant only among northern white males who were threatened by the degradation of labor from slavery. Labor may have "masculinized" black women of the South by forcing them to act against the created concept of what was "feminine," but it hardly set them free. "Arbeit Macht Frei" was not exactly a lie new to the twentieth century.

24. Howe's quote may be found in Foner, op. cit., p. 27 and Lincoln's p. 23.

25. Op. cit., slave register, pp. 11-17

26. Ibid.

27. T. W. Hall was a neighboring planter. Badenhausen was a man of sufficient social standing to have shared meals with Stickney when the rest of the family was away. He fought as a Confederate soldier and may have been a tutor in the household once. W. B. Shepard was 'Wil Shepard," son of one of Louisa's sisters and the man who married Louisa's daughter Louise. The Freedmens' Bureau agent who certified the contract filed with the bureau was A. C. Washtonstall, a captain in the U.S. Army and Bureau assistant superintendent for Alabama.

28. Op. cit., 1865 contract

29. Op. cit., Stickney 1865 diary

30. "Crop and Labor Accounts, 1865-1869," pages for 1st week of June through 2Dece., 1865, Stickney box V, folder 54

31. Stickney routinely noted the weather in his diary entries.

32. Op. cit., Stickney 1866 diary

33. Ibid.

34. Ibid.

35. "A contract," 1866, Stickney box VII, folder 15, FPP, BPL

36. Ibid.

37. According to his diary entry for 7 April, 1866, William Stickney married Jim Flood and Murriah in his dining room.

38. Op. cit., 1866 Summary of Expenses

39. William Stickney to Louisa Stickney, 13 March, 1867, Stickney Box 1, folder 1, FPP, BPL

40. Two of Louisa's sisters died as young adult women form what appears to have been tuberculosis. Louise's illness was never named in any of the correspondence but she also died before reaching the age of thirty.

41. Louisa's directions to the gardener have not survived because none of her letters to William Stickney are among the Faunsdale Plantation Papers. However, Stickney made frequent references to her instructions in his letters to her.

42. Op. cit., William to Louisa, 13 March, 1867

43. Op. cit., 1867 contract

44. Ibid.

45. Ibid.

46. Ibid.

47. Ibid.

48. Op. cit., William to Louisa, 13 March, 1867

49. See Rupert Sargent Holand, ed., Letters and Diary of Laura Towne Written from the Sea Islands of South Carolina, 1862-1884. (Negro University Press, rep., 1969).

50. Op. cit., 1867 contract

51. Op. cit., William to Louisa, 13 March, 1867

52. Although the list of punishable offenses and fines for each infraction of the rules was attached to the contracts, Stickney also began noting offenses committed and fines levied when he began keeping plantation day books in 1867.

53. Op. cit., 1867 contract

54. Ibid.

55. Op. cit., 1874 contract

56. Plantation Day Books, 1867-1876, Stickney box VIII, folders 8, 9, 10, FPP, BPL.

57. Op. cit., 1874 contract

58. Jacqueline Jones <u>Labor of Love, Labor of Sorrow: Black Women, Work, and the Family from Slavery to the Present,</u> (New York, 1985), p. 38.

59. See Deborah Gray White, <u>Aren't I a Woman? Female Slaves in the Plantation South</u> (New York, 1985), p. 158 and Dorothy Sterling, ed. <u>We Are Your sisters: Black Women in the Nineteenth Century</u>, (New York, 1984), p. 37.

## CHAPTER FIVE

# "12 March, 1867...The 3 squads parted, & began planting..."[1]

When field hands at Faunsdale Plantation began planting corn in the spring of 1867, they worked as squads. Each squad was headed by an adult black male (each of whom had been a slave on that same plantation) selected as head man by his former master William Stickney: Oliver headed squad 1; Cassius was head man for squad 2; and Willis for number 3. Stickney hired each head man, then held him responsible for all members of his squad both in and out of the fields. Stickney's re-organization of field labor from large gangs into smaller discrete units would, he hoped, assure his continued control over the labor force and aid in slowing or reversing the decentralization of management on the plantation. By careful selection of men to head each squad and by encouragement of their domestic authority over their wives and children, Stickney used the squad system to extend his hold over the women who were beginning to leave field labor. Stickney's efforts to manage the plantation were mirrored on cotton plantations across the postwar South.[2]

During the Reconstruction decade under study, most married black women left full-time paid field work. The labor intensive nature of cotton culture played a part in the division of their time between paid field and unpaid home labor, but developing gender demands also played a large part in their absence from field labor. Compelling gender demands on freed women and men acted in several ways; black women wanted to assume the gendered role of providing domestic care for their own families and time to be with their own children; black men were being told to assert themselves as masters of their families and providers for their wants. As slaves, African-Americans could not have been blind to the gender roles of the dominant culture that sanctioned domestic and familial male dominance and what must have seemed to enslaved black women the privilege of domestic responsibility. Coupled with the old master's encouragement that was driven by self-interest and a need to strengthen his weakened control over the freedpeople, freed men were quick to assert themselves as husbands and fathers.[3]

Between 1867 and 1876, in Marengo County, Alabama the number of black female field hands on Faunsdale plantation diminished yearly. Between 1867 and 1877, squad 1 went from an overall total of 25 members to 4, with the number of female hands decreasing from 12 in 1867 to 0 by 1877. For squad 2 during the same time, the overall number of workers went from 21 to 6, with the number of women going from 8 in 1867 to 0 in 1877. The third squad had a 1867 total of 15 workers, 5 of whom were female, and went to 7 in 1877, with 0 women. Squad 4 was formed in 1870 with 7 total, 3 women, to 6 workers in 1877, with 2 women. The fifth squad was formed in 1872 with a total of 6 workers, 2 were females and had the same number of workers in 1877 with 1 woman.[4]

Black women re-directed their labor toward personal, domestic (although unpaid) ends and away from contracted labor that produced cotton for the market. Whether acting on their own desires or directions from their husbands and fathers, most freed black women hired their labor on part-time or seasonal terms. Although this "withdrawal" into the kind of private, familial domesticity that had been denied them while slaves provided an immediate improvement in their lives, it did not give them the same access to cash that contracted field labor did.[5] If black female field workers had any desire to own land, they had to have money to pay for it. However, evidence shows that for field work at Faunsdale between 1867 and 1876, female field workers were systematically relegated to the lower ranks within the squads. The lower ranks, which meant lower wages, were not designated for the women by the old master, but by their husbands, fathers, and male co-workers.

Generally, the re-organization of field labor on persisting large-scale cotton plantations developed at an uneven rate throughout the postwar South. Squads were formed late in the 1860's and averaged from eight to twelve members. These early squads eventually collapsed into smaller single-family groups like that of John Iredell who began as a squad member, progressed to squad head, and then became a sharecropper. Between 1867 and 1869, John Iredell was a contracted squad member working in the squad headed by Cassius and Cassius' brother Wilson. Of the squad of 21 members, John Iredell and his four children were one quarter of the entire number. In 1870, Stickney made Iredell head of a fourth squad which he continued to head until he and his son Henry rented land from Stickney in the 1800s. Between 1870 and 1879, John Iredell's squad numbered about 9 members each year, one half of whom were his own children and the other half young men. By the end of the decade, the only female field hands in Iredell's squad were his own daughters Maria, Eliza, Molly, and Judy. His wife Hester never worked at field labor after emancipation.[6]

"Working shares," the same refinement of the squad system as practiced by John Iredell and family, reached full florescence in the South by the 1880s. For black sharecroppers like Iredell, the male head of the family acted simultaneously as head of a family and labor supervisor for the working family as he mediated between them and the white landowner. Each sharecropper family worked together to produce a cash crop and their own subsistence crops. As was the case with slaveless white yeomen during the antebellum years, black freedmen who worked shares put their own family members to work in the fields because their families were their only available labor force. Men like John Iredell were at an advantage because they had a labor force bound to them by ties of familial commitment and affection and did not have to rely on wages to keep workers.[7]

After slavery ended, William Stickney would have continued his centralized management of the plantation which concentrated all authority in his hands had it been allowed. No longer able to own the bodies and control the labor of black workers through racial slavery, Stickney turned to another tenet of his patriarchal ideology to maintain his position of control over the new social class of workers. He relied on the socially sanctioned practice of male dominance when re-organizing hired black workers into squads. His black male laborers were encouraged to exercise authority over their wives, female relatives, and the other women in their work squads. Planters like Stickney could recognize the benefits of having their male workers act as heads of households as long as that role aided the planter class in maintaining their hierarchical superiority. However, they would not permit black adult males to assume the other male privileges or authority that would challenge their dominance of the entire society. Black men could have only the degree of authority that served the needs of their old masters, and that was to be confined to specific areas. By relying on male dominance in black families, Stickney could retain a systemic method of control over labor. By encouraging them for his own reasons, Stickney would assist the freedmen in obtaining some of the gender authority that had been denied them as slaves and the squad system was an effective means to implement control.

In creating squads, he sought solutions for some of his most pressing problems: he had to motivate the field hands to high productivity without using violence or corporal punishment; he needed a method of payment that would satisfy the workers and keep them from leaving him without using all of his own cash; he had to respond to their demand for some bit of autonomy in their lives without giving up much. His solution was to restructure gang labor into squads and continue to exert indirect control over the workers by choosing the head man for each squad; he then held fathers and husbands responsible for the actions of their wives, children, and various relatives, especially those who had not signed a labor contract. The workers over whom he had least control and eventually rid himself of were single women with children, but without husbands or fathers to keep them in line.

In a letter written to his wife on 13 March, 1867, Stickney outlined his new plan for re-organizing the workers into squads. He pointed out the benefit of introducing competition into the formula:

> Yesterday nearly made the finish; ...all were divided off & delighted with being busy in their new field. The plan is going to work well on me. Each head man will be deeply enough concerned & interested to relieve me of all details by which I should suffer at wages. And the spirit of emulation is so high, that opposition will provoke industry & vigilance to a high degree. Each party sees itself beating all the balance in results already. [8]

The details by which he would suffer if paying wages made him doubly reluctant to do so; he wished neither to give up his much-needed, scarce cash in wages nor would he relinquish the control that debt peonage provided. As long as the field hands remained in squads and unpaid, he had enough leverage to maintain his authority over them. In fact, straight cash wages for clearly defined tasks with no other concerns about social control or religious activities or morality would appear to have meant that Stickney had less work to do, if that had really been his concern.

Stickney reorganized his labor force from indiscriminate gang labor to discrete work units in 1867. He selected the men who would be in charge of each squad, then allowed them to organize their own squad with members of their choosing. Based on the authority and responsibility with which Stickney vested each head man, the squad heads effectively became Stickney's agent in carrying out his wishes and protecting his interests. Throughout 1867, 1868, and 1869, there were three squads; for 1870 and 1871, four; and between 1872 and 1877, he had five squads in operation. Initially, each of the three squads differed in the nature of its composition: Willis' squad contained members of his immediate and extended family; Cassius' squad was a grouping of two or three persons from six different families; and Oliver's was a conglomerate of single persons or young workers lacking a family. In 1867, each of the squads numbered between 15 and 24 members, but as time passed and two more squads were created, each became smaller with about 7 to 10 members by 1877. There was relatively little turnover among the head men, those chosen as head men the first year tended to keep the same squad number. Some turnover took place among squad members, but it was internal with workers shifting from one squad to another, rather than new workers coming into the system from outside the plantation. For the decade under study, 1867 to 1877, almost every member of the squads had been a slave on the plantation. So when Stickney had to negotiate with his hired workers for the next year's contract, he was working with women and men who were well known to him.[9]

Scattered throughout his letters, diaries, and plantation day books were Stickney's observations on the scarcity of workers on neighboring plantations and his dislike of negotiating with black workers. He remarked from time to time that he had "all about me that I wish to retain" or how much trouble one of his neighbors was having in pulling together an adequate labor force past the time for planting. The task of having to negotiate with workers that he had once commanded irritated and angered William Stickney, but he really had no other option.[10]

His reluctance to permit freed men and women to have land and the necessity of reaching a compromise was revealed in a letter to Louisa written in March, 1867:

> They are largely excited at scattering off "into squads." This began yesterday with planting corn—a dreaded job on me, which I got thru' (sic] pretty well. I mean, the apportionment of land to the several parties. The entire plantation of open land had to be surveyed by me & thrown into a dozen shapes before the division could be adjusted with something like equality among them.[11]

In 1866, the year before he implemented the squad system, he paid the field hands money wages, just as he was paying the house servants. His distaste for the negotiations necessary to keep house servants was clear in a diary of 1868:

> Managing with house s'vts for another year—wearisome and sickening work.[12]

Because he had almost exactly the same group of servants for 1868 that had worked for him and Louisa in 1867, his attitude about the negotiations does not reflect a dissatisfaction with the servants so much as the necessity of having to bargain with the same persons whose labor and presence he had once been able to take quite for granted. There is also the possibility that they, Adeline, Scotty, Margaret, Henry, William, Philip, and Ella, had an idea of the value of their domestic skills and were not willing simply to accept whatever he chose to offer. With the exception of Ella who was about thirteen, all the others were mature and experienced domestics who did not require training to become house servants. A look at Stickney's expenses for 1868 shows what he paid them that year:

| | | |
|---|---|---|
| Adeline | Cook | $5.00 @month |
| William | Dining room & garden | $10.00 @month |
| Scotty | Seamstress | $5.00 @month |
| Philip | Hostler & driver | $7.00 @month |
| Margaret | Light incidentals | $2.00 @month |
| Ella | Maid | Clothing[13] |

In addition to these regularly salaried servants, he hired Mary, Jane, and Margarett Ann to do the washing for "house room & fire wood." As was the case with field hands, he disliked the necessity and the process of having to bargain with hired workers whom he regarded as a permanent class of workers whose purpose was to make life easier for his class. But they made him see that it had to be done.[14]

Under Stickney's squad system, the workers were paid at the end of the year after all cotton had been ginned, baled, and sold. Although the Alabama port at Mobile was the usual destination for Faunsdale cotton, Stickney did not always wait until the entire crop was ready to ship before selling what was baled. In September, 1867 he noted:

> 22 days maximum of work (3 lost to rain). Fine weather for cotton pick'g—rapid work all month. Each Squad's Bales sent to market (Mobile) as rapidly as packed.[15]

To each squad accrued a group share of the cotton; within the squad each hand received an individual share calculated from her or his rank, or classification. Classifications were designated in either ordinal or fractional terms from first to sixth or as whole-hands, half-hands, and quarter-hands, etc., with each worker receiving year-end wages based on that rank. While squad shares and individual ranks determined the amount of cash each hand earned, that was seldom the amount received. Stickney deducted amounts owed from the pay of either the person who had made the debt or from the person liable for the worker. Deductions in pay between 1869 and 1876 were usually made for several reasons: cash advances made during the year; dry goods charged by field hands at one of the stores where Stickney kept a charge account; food, whiskey, and tobacco obtained directly from Stickney; payment of fines; various services provided by one worker to another; and the services of a medical doctor.[16]

Stickney's bookkeeping for field hands in 1869 shows that each woman's debts and wages were handled according to her marital status. He recognized male liability for the actions of wives or female relatives. (In some cases, adult women paid the debts made by male or female relatives, but never those of their husbands or fathers.) if debts or fines were paid by one other than the person who incurred it, the person paying was usually the same one who had committed the debtor to the contract. The same kin or marital relationship that granted authority to commit the labor of a dependent also granted the right to receive their wages. This was a commonplace practice among those who worked for Stickney. As a general example, unmarried women who signed for themselves also paid their own debts. Women whose fathers, husbands, or older relatives had signed for them were not held responsible for those debts. Adeline (house) signed contracts which committed her nieces Gabriella and Amy and nephew Jackson, the children of her sister Penelope, to work although their mother was still living.[17]

The adult who had authority to commit the labor of dependents also had the responsibility to pay their fines and be paid their wages. Charity, an unmarried mother of three children, signed contracts in 1869 for her children Lydia (aged 19), Margiana (aged 16), and Alexander (aged 14). Kinship ties also prevailed in determining Charity's fiscal responsibility for her dependent workers. Charity's "final settlement" with Stickney for 1869 indicates that she was expected to pay the $8.65 fine owed to Stickney by Lydia, the $10.00 fines assessed against Margiana, and two fines of $7.10 and $2.50 for her son Alexander. On the credit side of her account, Stickney owed Charity a total of $441.67 as the head of the family. Of that amount, she had earned $93.95, Lydia earned $187.88, Margiana made $63.70, and Alexander earned $96.14. From that amount Stickney deducted $28.25 that Charity owed to him and thus he owed Charity Paine $413.2 in December, 1869.[18]

Another 1869 example shows that the married women were treated differently. Henrietta was considered the dependent of her husband Tom who committed her labor to the contract, was liable for her debts, and could be paid her wages. Tom was fined $2.35 for allowing some animals to run free. Tom also obtained a cash advance of $58.57 against his part of the cotton, another $11.00 cash advance, and money to pay a $2.00 debt he owed to Oliver, probably for Oliver's treatment of a minor ailment. Tom's share of the cotton was $158.79 and Henrietta's, which was accounted for in Tom's account, was $80.00[19] As Henrietta's husband, Tom could now act in a manner which black men had not been permitted when slaves: Tom had the right to both protect and take charge of his wife. The authority which legal marriage gave a man over his wife was acknowledged by William Stickney when he accepted Tom's actions of signing the labor contract which committed his wife's labor for a year. And Stickney settled with Tom for 1869 by paying him the amount he and Henrietta had earned from the cotton crop minus the cash advances and fine, in a total of $164.97. Had Tom not received Henrietta's share, his settlement would have been $84.97.

Stickney's field hands were neither docile nor as easy to manage as he would have liked, but he found ways other than debt peonage to aid in controlling them. He noted their "fusses" and "flare ups." He complained in his diary about the onerous task of keeping account books for the workers. His satisfaction in winning a contracting battle with them is apparent in a gloating remark from his diary of January 2 and 3, 1866:

> Ordered all the Quarters cleared by the morrow morning. Point gained & contracting began at night.
>
> Out at the Quarters—all busy, some moving & others contracting. Occupied till after tea with them. [20]

Stickney won only a partial victory. Seven women and one old married pair, Delphy and Joan, defied him by staying on and not contracting with him for 1866. Their resistance was met in June with another contract aimed specifically at them in which someone had to agree to be held responsible for each non-contracted resident. [21]

The refusal of seven women to perform either domestic or field labor for the old master was a patent assertion of their own will and determination to seek their own freedom. Of the nine who would not contract in January, 1866 and refused to leave the plantation, some were old enough that age was a likely reason why that they would not work. Delphy, Joan, Hannah Paine, and Becky Parsons were all between the ages of 58 and 70, all past the time they could have expected to "retire" according to past practice. However, the remaining five women, Murriah, Hester Iredell, Nancy Paine, Penelope, and Mary Newbern ranged in age respectively from Murriah's 18 to Mary Newbern's age of J0. These women did not work because they did not want to and each one had a family member who would claim responsibility for her. And each one of those workers who took the responsibility was a valuable enough worker to Stickney that he had to tolerate the defiance among the women. Murriah's man Jim Flood signed for her, Mary Newbern's husband Allen took responsibility for her, John Iredell signed for his wife Hester, and Jack Jones signed for Nancy Paine. Adeline took the responsibility for her sister Penelope. Stickney disliked the situation, calling the women "drones," but he made the concession to keep the others.[22]

Another major concession from Stickney was doing what he had called the "dread job" of creating squads and parceling out the plantation cotton land accordingly:

> Poor land [is] to be sliced out & fitted on to richer equally. A certain quantity [is] needed near home by each party for their women with infants. [Each squad needs a] body of land to be complete in itself, & not to lap on another squad with rows half one's & half another & still to preserve the proportion to their unequal numbers. These are a specimen of the perplexities in the job, which I have long dreaded.[23]

Each squad would maintain its group integrity by signing contracts as a unified group, working the same divisions of land for the entire year, and then dividing their collective share of profit from the cotton sold:

> Another load is on me in this same connection; to secure all under full contract in their respective squads; where they will have to remain, with duties toward each other & me to be enforced by skillful fines written down & agreed to severally. I'll be lightened no little when this

is done, [which] I hope to see in the course of the present week or next...[24]

Stickney retained the prerogative to choose the head men, granting them the specific authority to act as a sub-contractor of labor by selecting their own squad members. Before sharecropping prevailed as the common mode of farming in the cotton south, the right to select squad members reinforced a black male's authority over women of his own family who worked in his squad. In spite of giving up this specific authority, Stickney did not relinquish all to the head men as the "Obligations of the Master" of the 1867 contract reveal where he asserted his right to

> ...direct the proportionate quantity of land to be planted in corn & cotton, & how they shall be worked; [I] will decide when they are in need of additional labour, & procure it; will decide on a transfer of labourers, stock, or land....[25]

In giving over a relative degree of authority to certain males, Stickney not only place them over all women and the other men in making decisions on who would work, he also expected a reciprocal relationship between the head men and himself in which they became his agents for maintaining social control over their squad members.

Stickney delegated to the head men the authority to classify the other workers. Each squad member's rank was to be decided by a committee made of the head man and two other squad members. Although Stickney retained the right to move workers from one squad to another, he did not rank them, as another section from the 1867 contract ("Obligations of the Hired Servants") shows:

> For the Distribution of our year's earnings, we submit to be classified according to our respective merits, by a Committee consisting of the Principal of our Company ("Head of the Squad") & two others chosen by us from among ourselves.[26]

This portion of the contract clearly states that the right within each squad to classify members and to choose those who would make up the classification committee was to be vested in the squads. However, since each committee was composed of the squad's head man (chosen by the old master) and two members from the squad, there was a decided tilt toward the selection of men and men of whom the old master would approve. If the committee members were selected by simply majority, then the men would have an advantage since they always outnumbered the women by a large percentage. This must have been quite a large concession for the old master to make, but once he gave over the right to make those choices, it was up to the mostly-male squads to classify themselves.

Following through on his plan for classification of hands, Stickney noted their selections for the coming year in a diary:

Mon. 1 [January] Raw, cloudy & muddy. Rec'd their classifications from the various squad's committees. [27]

Although classification criteria were not included in the contracts, one patent criterion for holding a first-class or full hand rank was sex. Black female field hands at Faunsdale between 1867 and 1875 did not hold the highest rank in spite of being very productive workers. [28] A list of each squad member's rank in 1871 was attached to Stickney's bookkeeping accounts for distribution of the com due each person based on their labor toward making the crop. The list of ranks reveals that only males held first-class or full hand ranks regardless of the amount of cotton each person had picked that year. The numerals following the names are the rank of that person (with an asterisk by names of females):

1871
Classification[29]

| Squad 1 | | Squad 2 | | Squad 3 | | Squad 4 | |
|---|---|---|---|---|---|---|---|
| Solomon | 1 | Willis | 1 | Cassius | 1 | John Iredell | 2 |
| Sam | 2 | Milford | 3 | Edward | 1 | Henry | 3 |
| Tom C. | 2 | Richard | 4 | Jackson | 2 | Judy* | 4 |
| Manuel | 2 | Noah | 2 | Amy* | 3 | Anderson | 1 |

| | | | | | | | |
|---|---|---|---|---|---|---|---|
| London | 2 | Alick | 2 | Osceola | 1 1/2 | Tom W. | 1 |
| Keziah* | S | Mose | 3 | Jeff | 2 | Allen | 2 1/2 |
| Tom W. | 2 | Shepherd | 2 | Milly* | S | Wellington 2 | 2 |
| Albert | 2 | Joe C. | S | Josiah | 3 1/4 | Elizabeth€ | 3 3/4 |
| Joe Hunter | 6 | Augustus | 2 | Boston | 4 | Maria• | 4 |
| Stephen | 3 | Isaac | 2 | | | | |
| Quomine | 3 | Andrew | 2 | | | | |
| Will | 4 | Joanna• | 6 | | | | |
| Sime | 5 | Grace* | 6 | | | | |
| Lucy* | 5 | | | | | | |

*female

In 1871, the four squad held a total of 45 workers, with only six men from a possible 36 were ranked as first-class. Of the total number of 9 women on the combined squads, none were rated as whole or first-class hands. The highest rank any women held that year was third-class held by 2 women; 2 were ranked fourth-class hands; and 5 were either fifth- or sixth-class. During the Reconstruction decade, neither Stickney nor the black men employed by him selected women to positions of authority or the highest paying rank.

When the war's end made slavery's end obvious, the freed African-American women and men still had to learn what freedom would mean for them. At the most immediate and personal level, they had to reconstruct fractured families and establish gender relations outside the dictates of slavery. Locating lost relatives, husbands, wives or children was not so formidable a task for the black families of Faunsdale because white members of the Collins family had taken pride in what they saw as their benign treatment of slaves and they seldom sold anyone. Even after her first husband's death in 1858 altered her plans to leave Alabama for the new and unpaid-for plantation in Louisiana, Louisa Collins Harrison refused to sell slaves. Harrison purchased the Louisiana land in 1857, then moved some slaves from Alabama to Louisiana in anticipation of moving all his family, white and black, to the new plantation. His death in 1858 ended the transferal, but left slaves in Louisiana and a wife in debt in Alabama who offered only the Louisiana land for sale, refusing all offers for the labor force there.[30]

Some freedwomen and men left Faunsdale immediately in June, 1865. Other waited until their contract ended in December. Most remained and eventually worked as members of a squad. An examination of squad membership lists shows the names of those workers with whom each head man filled his squad. This lists also reveal what part familial and marital ties played in filling the squad with workers. A comparison of the three squads as each was composed in 1867 also shows the differences among them. By charting the membership of the original squads over nine years, one can see the diminishing number, or what has been called the withdrawal, of black women from field work as represented by their membership in squads.

William Stickney (either as a deliberate plan or ideological reflex) was actively involved in ridding the field labor force of unmarried black women. At the same time that he was getting rid those certain troublesome women that he wanted to have off the plantation and out of his life, he was encouraging men to assume dominance within their families in order to extend his own reach of social control into their cabins. A recalcitrant, strong-minded black woman with no man to help Stickney keep her at work and in line was not the kind of worker he wanted.[31]

In 1867 Willis Collins, another ex-slave of Faunsdale, assumed the responsibility and authority of being head man of a labor squad that was also his extended family:

| Willis | [136-head man) |
| Adeline | [31-Willis' wife] |
| Augustus | [17-Fanny's son, Willis claimed as his son) |
| Milford | [13-Adeline's son, Willis claimed as his son] |
| Joe | [21-brother of Willisl |
| Shepherd | [27-brother of Willis] |
| Lucy | [24-sister of Willis, married to Sam] |
| Teresa | [32-sister of Willis, married to Noah] |
| Noah | [40-married to Teresa, Joanna's bro., Sol.'s uncle] |
| Alick | [14-Willis' nephew, son of Teresa & Noah] |
| Mose | [12-Willis' nephew, son of Teresa & Noah] |

| | |
|---|---|
| Sam | [23-married Lucy, Willis' brother-in-law, brother of Solomon, Noah & Joanna's nephew] |
| Solomon | [29-brother of Sam, Noah & Joanna's nephew] |
| Hannah | [26-wife of Solomon) |
| Joanna | [28-Solomon's aunt, Noah's sister][32] |

When Willis directed his squad to plant corn, he was directing his wife Adeline (black) and the two young men, Augustus and Milford, who were referred to on the contract as his sons. However, according to the slave records from Faunsdale which spanned the years from 1843 to 1865, during that time Adeline (black) had been wife to neither Willis nor any other man. Hers was the only name listed as parent for the children born to her between 1848 and 1865: Milford (1854); Joyce (1856); Richard (1859), and Amanda (born 1861 - died 1865). If Willis was the biological father of Adeline's children, he was not so recognized by the master or mistress. Perhaps Willis and Adeline (black) waited until they were no longer under the control or scrutiny of a master to openly assert their parental rights.[33]

When Willis signed the contract for the boys in January, he acted on an authority previously assumed only by white males, as a married man, head of family and household. Willis committed the name of Adeline's son Milford and Fanny's son Augustus to a contract based on his claim as their father. Willis had been the husband of Ruth while a slave and Adeline had no husband listed, but it is uncertain if Willis derived his parental rights from a biological or social concept of parenthood 30 Both boys were in the squad with Willis and Milford's mother Adeline, but Augustus' mother Fanny was in another squad. Mose and Alick, Willis' nephews, were also in his squad. Despite the presence of their parents, Teresa and Noah (Willis' sister and her husband), in the same squad, Willis was the one held accountable for the boys when they were at work.

Four of Willis' siblings (Teresa, Lucy, Shepherd, and Joe) were members of his squad. The only member of his squad whose connection to Willis was indirect rather than familial or marital was Solomon Littlejohn whose place in the squad came from Sol's brother Sam who was married to Willis' sister Lucy. Still, Sol, his wife Hannah Paine, his brother Sam and sister-in-law Lucy were members of the extended family that was Willis' work unit. For Willis and every member of his squad, no separation existed between family and work.

Stickney delegated authority to squad heads to be exercised within parameters he established and with the expectation that each head man would wield it at his direction. The lines along which that authority flowed are clear from the contracts that recognized the right of one person to commit another person to labor: husbands and fathers held authority over wives and children; single mothers over their own children and unmarried or feeble female relatives. The 1867 labor contract between Stickney and Willis' squad offers an example of those emergent patterns:

Signatures
W. A. Stickney, Master

Hired Servants
I.  Willis his mark (Head of Squad)
1. for himself
2. Adeline his wife
3. Augustus his son
4. Milford his son
5. Joe his brother

II. Solomon Littlejohn his mark
6. for himself
7. Hannah his wife

Signatures
III. Noah his mark

8. for himself
9. Teresa his wife
10. Alick his son
11. Moses his son

IV. Sam his mark

12. for himself
13. Lucy his wife

V. Shepherd his mark

14. for himself

IV. Joanna her mark

15. for herself

I...attest that the foregoing contract was read & fully explained to the Hired Servants in my presence; that they severally assented to the same, & then signed it.[35]

The emerging pattern was one in which married men could commit the labor of all members of their family while married women could not. Willis signed for his wife Adeline (black)—who two years earlier was not permitted a husband's protection or the choice of limiting her labor within private domesticity—and her children as well. Willis also signed for two adolescent males whose mothers lived at Faunsdale (one of whom must have needed what a seventeen-year son earned) and his two married sisters had their names signed by their husbands. Joanna, an unmarried sister, signed for herself.

Willis' squad membership changed between 1867 and 1868, but the number remained fairly steady with fifteen for 1867 and fourteen in 1868. The year 1867 was the last that Adeline (black) contracted her labor for field work at Faunsdale. She signed no more contracts and was noted in the 1870 federal census as living in the same dwelling with Willis and "keeping house." Teresa also gave her occupation in 1870 as keeping house, while her husband Noah worked intermittently on the plantation for Stickney. Willis' brother Joe did not work with any squad in 1868, but returned to Willis' in 1870 when his mother signed a contract for him. Solomon shifted from being a member of a squad in 1867 to becoming the head man of another in 1868, and when he moved he took Willis' sister Lucy with him. Apparently Sam left Faunsdale during 1868 and did not live with Lucy again after his return in 1869. New members added to Willis' squad for 1868 were Adeline's eleven-year old son Richard, Orpah's seventeen- year old son Isaac, a woman identified only as Henrietta, and the married pair Albert and Maria. Although the number of workers in Willis' squad remained nearly the same, fewer of his extended family were in it the second year.

Willis was head man at least until 1877. The chart below lists members of Willis' squad between 1867 and 1877. It shows how the composition of his squad continued to change over the eleven-year span from 1867 to 1877.

| name: | 1867 | '68 | '69 | '70 | '71 | '72 | '73 | '74 | '75 | '76 | '77 |
|---|---|---|---|---|---|---|---|---|---|---|---|
| Willis | y | y | y | y | y | y | y | y | y | y | y |
| Adeline | y | - | - | - | - | - | - | - | - | - | - |
| Augustus* | y | y | y | y | y | y | - | - | - | - | - |
| Milford | y | y | y | y | y | y | y | - | - | - | - |
| Joe | y | - | - | y | y | y | y | y | y | y | y |
| Sol L.^ | y | - | - | - | - | - | - | - | - | - | - |
| Hannah | y | y | y | y | - | - | - | y | - | - | - |
| Noah | y | y | - | y | y | y | y | y | y | - | - |
| Teresa | y | - | - | - | - | - | - | - | - | - | - |
| Alick | y | y | y | y | y | - | - | - | - | - | - |
| Mose | y | y | - | y | y | y | y | y | y | y | y |
| Sam | y | - | y | - | - | - | - | - | - | - | - |
| Lucy | y | - | y | - | - | - | - | y | y | y | - |
| Shepherd | y | y | - | y | y | y | y | y | y | y | y |
| Joanna | y | y | - | y | y | y | - | - | - | - | - |
| Richard | - | y | y | y | y | y | y | y | y | y | y |
| Tom | - | - | y | y | - | - | - | - | - | - | - |
| Henrietta | - | y | y | - | - | - | - | - | - | - | - |
| Luke | - | - | y | - | - | - | - | - | - | - | - |
| Grace | - | - | - | y | y | - | - | - | - | - | - |
| Andrew | - | - | - | - | y | - | - | - | - | - | - |
| Isaac | - | y | y | - | y | - | - | - | - | - | - |
| Will Jones | - | - | - | - | - | y | y | - | - | - | - |
| Wellington | - | - | - | - | - | y | - | - | - | - | - |
| John Wills | - | - | - | - | - | y | - | - | - | - | - |
| Susan | - | - | - | - | - | - | y | - | - | - | - |
| Sime | - | - | - | - | - | - | - | - | - | y | y |
| Solomon M.# | - | - | - | - | - | - | - | - | y | y | y |
| Albert` | - | y | - | - | - | - | - | - | - | - | - |
| Maria | - | y | - | - | - | - | - | - | - | - | - |
| total | 15 | 14 | 12 | 13 | 13 | 12 | 9 | 8 | 8 | 8 | 7 |
| men | 10 | 10 | 9 | 10 | 11 | 11 | 8 | 6 | 7 | 7 | 7 |
| women | 5 | 4 | 3 | 3 | 2 | 1 | 1 | 2 | 1 | 1 | 0 |

*died 1873
^headed own squad after 1868
#not Solomon Littlejohn, another, younger man
`on another squad after 1868 until headed his own in 1872

By 1875, Willis' squad had diminished in number from the original fifteen male and female members of his and Adeline's extended families to a unit of eight workers. The seven adult males were Willis, his brothers Joe and Shepherd, his son Richard, his nephew Mose, his sister Teresa's husband Noah, and

Solomon. The number of women in the squad was down to one, his sister Lucy; after that year, none. By 1877 his squad was a small group of related males that no longer reflected the age and sex-inclusive corporate family.[36]

The squad which Cassius headed differed from Willis' because it was a coalition of several small families rather than one large corporate family group. Cassius' 1867 squad, composed from six separate families, was less dependent on his own extended family than Willis' was. Cassius' squad numbered twenty-one and contained, in Stickney's words,"9 men, 7 women, 4 boys, 1 next to woman:"

| | | |
|---|---|---|
| (1)a | Cassius | [29 head man, 1st wife Hester died 1865]* |
| (2) | John Iredell | [45 - unrelated to Cassius] |
| | Maria | [19 - John and Hester Iredell's daughter] |
| | Elizabeth | [18 - John and Hester Iredell's daughter] |
| | Henry | [11 - John and Hester Iredell's son] |
| | Anderson | [21 - John and Hester Iredell's son] |
| (3) | Allen | [58 - not related to Cassius] |
| | London | [20 - son of Allen and Mary Newbern] |
| | Sarah | [16 - daughter of Allen and Mary Newbern] |
| (1)b | Wilson | [26 - Cassius' brother] |
| | Lavinia | [28 - Wilson's wife] |
| | Josiah | [11 - Lavinia's son] |
| (1)c | Edward | [23 - Cassius' brother] |
| | Mary Ann | [ - Edward's wife] |
| (4) | Orpah | [37 - wife of Cassius' cousin Providence] |
| | Issac | [16 - Orpah's son] |
| (5) | Cyrus | [43 - cousin, brother of Providence] |
| | Fanny | [45 - married to Cyrus] |
| | Grace | [20 - daughter of Cyrus' 1st wife Ruth] |
| | Will | [13 - son of Fanny] |
| (6) | Osceola | [ - new to Faunsdale since freedom][37] |

\* not Hester Iredell

Since his squad consisted of workers from families other than just his, Cassius may have had less control of it than he would have had if his position as squad head been reinforced by the same strong family ties that bound the members of Willis' squad together. The nature of Cassius' squad membership may have had an effect on the amount of friction and violence that erupted in it in 1869. Cassius had been head man in 1868, but Stickney demoted him from head man to worker in 1869, placing Cassius' brother Wilson over him as the new head man. Wilson remained head of the squad throughout 1869 and for the first month of 1870 when Stickney replaced him in February with Cassius. Judging by the fines leveled against squad workers in Solomon's and Cassius' squads, they seemed to have lacked something that Willis had. He also had far fewer fines against his squad members for 1869 than either Cassius or Solomon.[38]

The year 1869 was one of antagonism, abusive behavior, and rebelliousness among the field hands. Those most often fined for violence, disrespect, disruption, or damage, were the women. It was the responsibility of the head man to note infractions of rules and list the offenses by the offender's name. A sampling of some of the offenses committed by squad members in 1869 shows what kind of behavior was thought belligerent or abusive by the head men who represented the old master's authority in the fields and kept the records for him: Lydia was "impudent to Head"; Maria was "impudent to Head" and fined for "quitting work before time"; John Iredell "quit ploughing to report on Head"; Samson was "impudent to Head"; Maria and Sarah were "quarreling in the fields"; Amy was "abusive to Albert"; Albert was fined for a lack of respect to the head man; Maria and Elizabeth were "impudent to Head"; and Lavinia for "taking Lydia's socks."[39]

Not all of the resistance and disruptive behavior was directed against the head men nor was it all overtly expressed. Many workers were fined for not coming out to work on time or leaving the field early or without permission. Many stayed in long periods of time because they were ill, an explanation that may have covered illnesses real or feigned. The head men did not easily assume the respect and willing cooperation from all of their squad members, although Willis had far less trouble than any other head man. And when a fourth squad was formed in 1870 with John Iredell as head over his family members, he too had less trouble than the other head men.

Another form of expressing their anger and dissatisfaction with either the squad head or Stickney could have been the lack of care with which the field workers treated the cotton they were cultivating. Stickney's list of finable offenses included one of $.10 per stalk of cotton broken. Many of the field hands were fined for damaging or breaking down stalks of cotton. While the formations of squads might have been received by the freed women and men as an improvement over slavery-style gang labor in 1867, many seem to have had trouble accepting the authority of the men that Stickney had selected as their squad heads. Of the four squads formed between 1867 and 1870, the two headed by men whose closest family members made up the majority or entirety of his squad had the least trouble. Willis and John Iredell had the least number of fines against their squads and at least amount of disruptive behavior within them. The most troubled squad was the one headed first by Cassius in 1868, his brother Wilson in 1869, then back to Cassius again in 1870.

The most serious recorded non-fatal injury to a Faunsdale field hand happened in the Cassius/Wilson squad only four days after Stickney pulled Wilson out and replaced him with Cassius on 25 February, 1870. All involved in the fracas were members of Cassius' squad, no other squad ever had a similar brawl. Entries from the plantation day book for 1870 unfold the events:

January

Sat. 29   Josiah ran away.

February

Tue. 1   Manuel off for Josiah (Lavinia's boy)
Thr. 24   Changed the Head from Wilson to Cassius

March

Tues. 1   Josiah hurt by Amy - lost 1/2 day Jackson off for doctor - 1/2 day Amy for injuring Josiah - fined 5.00 Amy quarreling with Lavinia - 5.00 Lavinia quarreling with Amy - 5.00
Tues. 8   Josiah in for a season (Amy's loss)

April

Mon. 11   Josiah still in from leg-break
Thr. 14   Lavinia abusive & quarrelsome to Head in consequence Gned3.00
Wed. 20   Lavinia abused Head of Squad - fined 5.00 Lavinia abused Amy - fined 2.00[40]

Lavinia's angry and often violent behavior may have been what prompted Stickney to get rid of her, although there may have been another reason since Albert, a man on the same squad, had far more fines against him than did Lavinia. Albert was a violent and abusive man toward his wife, his head man, and even showed disrespect toward Stickney. In 1870 alone Albert received more fines than any other field hand. Lavinia came in second.

In 1870 Albert was fined for the following offenses: in April, "profane and abusive to Head," losing four days' work; in May, for "fighting with his wife in field" and "oppressing wife," "cursing at Head and upsetting work" and "going off without permission" and "oppressed several, cursing them at meeting," and "in without permission." This kind of behavior continued through the year. Lavinia was fined for days lost from illness, for her part in the brawl that resulted in her son's broken leg, for being "abusive and quarrelsome to Head," and for quarreling with Amy. When contracting time came in 1871, Albert was on the new contract, but Lavinia was not. However, since her sons were, she must have remained in the local area, or even lived with them in the quarters because Stickney finally took drastic action to rid himself of her, as he noted in the day book for April, 1872:

[This] [a]fternoon discharged Josiah & Boston—Lavinia's boys, mainly to get rid of her.[41]

Cassius seems to have lacked the personality, leadership, or ability to instill respect in his squad members. Stickney had to make some hard choices in choosing his head men. If he selected a man too independent who identified too much with the workers, then Stickney's interests would suffer. If he picked a man too lacking in the necessary leadership ability, then he was likely to have a head man like Cassius. Nothing in Cassius' background or family structure suggests why he was not an effective head man. He came from the large family of Chloe Pain and Fed Blacksmith. His mother was Chloe's daughter Becky Parsons, who had traveled to Alabama in 1843 when Louisa Collins Harrison's husband moved them from North Carolina. Cassius had no sisters and two brothers, Edward and Wilson.

Cassius seems to have a rather unsteady marital life. Although he had no wife working in his 1867 squad, he had been married until his first wife died in the 1865 measles epidemic at Faunsdale. Cassius was married to Amy by 1874, and may have been married to a woman named Sally in between, since Stickney referred to her as Cassius' wife. Had she not been legally wed to him, Stickney would have been quick to label her in the same derogatory way that he did the woman who lived with Solomon without the sanction of marriage. The Rev. Stickney strove (in vain) to make his now free workers adhere to his own morality, maintaining a watch over the legality of their marriages.[42]

If Sally was married to Cassius in 1867, she was not living with him in 1870 when the federal census showed that Cassius lived not with a wife, but with his brother Wilson. Cassius eventually married again and his new wife was someone he had known her entire life. Sometime between 1876 and 1879, he married Amy Dickinson, one of Penelope's daughters and Adeline's (house) niece. Amy and Cassius had at least two children, Penelope (born 1879) and Gabriella (born 1886), who were named for Amy's mother and her sister Gabriella. Her aunt Adeline exercised the kind of responsibility for Amy usually assumed by a parent. Since Penelope lived close enough to her children to act for them, yet her sister had assumed the parental role for her children Amy, Gabriella, and Jackson, it may be that Penelope's health had deteriorated and left her unable to take responsibility for her dependents. In other words, perhaps Adeline took care of her niece because Amy's own mother could no longer do it. Placing Amy in Cassius' squad in 1868 after she had been in Oliver's the year before may have been Adeline's decision to provide for her niece. Amy did not honor her childless aunt by naming one of her daughters after her. Cassius assured himself the restoration of his family life and probably thought that he had a dependable worker/wife when he married Amy. However, Amy seems to have been a source of irritation to his squad members, if not to Cassius.[43]

Unlike most of Faunsdale's female field hands, Amy continued at field work as late as 1876. Perhaps she stayed because of her relationship with Cassius, a dependable farmer whom the old master came to trust after the one year that Cassius was replaced as head man in 1869.[44] Amy was not favored by Stickney, since she was one of the troublesome women who was both disruptive and, in Stickney's eyes, immoral. In his baptismal records, Stickney noted in 1869 that

Amy had given birth to child for whom no father was listed and in 1874 "Amy and Sin" had a child. Since he often rid himself of women like Amy, perhaps her relationship to Adeline, and then Cassius, protected her. Amy was not living with a husband in 1870, but with her mother and Penelope's new husband, Gregory, the old man Stickney described to Louisa in a letter:

> I took leave of cousin Thos. who had been with us since the day before at dinner & went over to [the] Chapel to marry old Penelope (!!) to old Gregory, a sv't of Mr. Adams, brother of Sally the wife of Cassius. Adeline came up with them & acted the part of giving away the bride. She fixed up something of a supper for them also. I think in the main she was interestedly glad of the step taken by the old stagers;... [45]

Amy's continuation as a field worker for at least ten years went against what most of the female field hands had done. Most of the women worked as contracted field hands for a year, or two, or even three, after emancipation. Then they worked at home or were seasonal workers that Stickney would hire by the day during the peak of harvest. However, Amy differed from women like Hester Iredell or most of the others because she was unmarried until she was about thirty years sold. She had two children that she had to rear and provide for, and until she married Cassius in the late 1870s, there was not husband to provide for her or share in living expenses. If Amy left field work, it was only following her marriage to Cassius, not the birth of her children.

John Iredell and most members of his family, wife Hester (big) excluded, were in the 1867 squad with Cassius. Even in her youthful days under the demanding oversight of Louisa Collins Stickney's first husband Thomas Harrison, Hester was not much of a field hand. From the extant plantation records which Harrison kept for 1844 to 1849, his first years as owner of an Alabama cotton plantation, it is apparent that Hester was often absent from field work and was not a strong worker when present.[46] Twenty years later when Louisa's new husband and Faunsdale's new master, the Rev. William Stickney, prepared the Confederate tax list enumerating the plantation slave population for 1864; he listed Hester as a "nurse to the sick". Whatever her job had been as a slave, once free she worked no longer for the old master. Hester was one of the recalcitrant ones who remained at Faunsdale after Stickney ordered all non-contracting "drones" off the plantation unless one of his contracted workers would agree to vouch for the person.[47] Because his wife would not cooperate, John Iredell had to sign the special contract of 1866 if she was to live with him. Still, she performed no contracted labor for Stickney.

In 1870 Hester told the federal census taker that her occupation was keeping house. Although she no longer hired her labor with Stickney, her daughters Maria, Elizabeth, Molly, and Judy worked for several years at Faunsdale as field hands, but always under the eye of and in the squad with their own father. From 1867 and 1869 they were in the squad headed by Cassius and Wilson; from 1870 to 1877 they were in one headed by John Iredell. The membership of John Iredell's squad from 1870 to 1877 and the kinship, if any, with the head man were:

| name: | | | 1870 | 1871 | 1872 | 1873 | 1874 | 1875 | 1876 | 1877 |
|---|---|---|---|---|---|---|---|---|---|---|
| Hester | - | wife | - | - | - | - | - | - | - | - |
| Anderson | - | son | yes | yes | yes | yes | yes | yes | yes | yes |
| Maria | - | dau. | yes | yes | - | - | - | - | - | yes |
| Eliza. | - | dau. | yes | yes | yes | yes | yes | yes | - | - |
| Henry | - | son | yes | yes | yes | yes | yes | yes | yes | yes |
| Judy | - | dau. | yes | yes | yes | yes | yes | yes | yes | yes |
| Molly | - | dau. | - | - | - | yes | yes | yes | yes | yes |
| Allen | - | not | yes | yes | yes | yes | yes | - | - | - |
| Wel'ton | - | not | - | yes | - | yes | yes | - | - | - |
| Alick | - | not | - | - | yes | - | - | - | - | - |
| Parker | - | not | - | - | yes | yes | - | - | - | - |
| Stephen | - | not | - | - | - | - | - | yes | - | yes |
| Betsy | - | not | - | - | - | - | - | yes | - | - |
| Tom W. | - | not | - | - | - | - | - | - | yes | yes |
| Harrison | - | not | - | - | - | - | - | - | - | yes |
| Jackson | - | not | - | - | - | - | - | - | - | yes |
| Tom C. | - | not | - | - | - | - | - | - | - | yes |
| Quomini | - | not | - | - | - | - | - | - | - | yes |

No evidence links John Iredell as kin to any of the workers in his squad other than his own children. No name of a parent, wife, or child of John Iredell was ever listed in the slave records of Somerset. His own name suggests that his birth family had not been owned by the Collins, but by their Edenton neighbor, James Iredell.[48] As a young slave John Iredell was taken from North Carolina to Alabama where he chose to remain when he became a free man with a family of his own and a squad to manage. He did not move straight from being a member of a squad under Cassius to full-blown sharecropper status with land rental; he first headed a squad for ten years before renting land from the old master. In 1881 his son Henry Iredell rented land and a mule from William Stickney for which he payed $2.75 per acre for 42 acres and $16.20 20 for Julia the mule. John Iredell was seldom in trouble, seldom missed time from the fields when a squad worker, and generally was a man upon whom Stickney could rely as a farmer and head of a family that produced good cotton.[49]

When William Stickney encouraged the men to assume the place as the head of the household, it was an authority that he did not intend for them to assume in any public arena. If any black man was to be so bold and self-confident that he tried to exercise his private, familial male authority publicly, it would have been a great affront to Stickney's patriarchal position. When Oliver Harrison extended his interests outside his domestic sphere, he was not tolerated. Oliver had been a man praised and relied upon as long as he gave the appearance of being at the command of his old master, but was later vilified by Stickney as dishonest, devious, ambitious, and too influential in the black community of the quarters, and too much a sycophant with members of Stickney's white household.[50] Had Oliver confined himself to managing his own family rather than audaciously usurping white male authority, Stickney could have been satisfied with him. However, part of a letter by Stickney to Louisa in January, 1870 reveals his scorn:

> Yester morning he [Oliver] left for Va., I learn, in quest of hands for Mr. Alexander [neighbor planter who has moved into the Weaver house with his large family. After all his quiet boasting of having more hands than he wanted for working this place, ñ therefore could not let have any of the land, he has only the old dog & his puppies [Oliver and family) carried from here at the "Shelterplace."[51]

As long as Stickney's gender, class, or race standing was not challenged by his re-shuffling authority among the hired black workers, he supported the domestic authority of black males. Oliver had a large (and apparently scattered) number of children whose labor Stickney expected to direct. Oliver and his wife Scotty had at least eight children, but after 1865 Oliver claimed parental rights over some laborers who were not Scotty's children:

> There your old Scotty is at rest, with nothing to do at last but sit down, & gravitate into deeper sloth & uselessness. When forced to maintain herself, which must inevitably be the case soon, she will be too far impaired for a position of mediocrity requirements. Poor old Nancy, too, was taken along in order to prove that he [Oliver] would support her & draw John's earnings from me. ...She is hereabouts...all the time, worse crazy than ever,...[52]

Nancy Wills, usually referred to as crazy, and her son John Wills were taken from Stickney's influence and protection by Oliver, who was competing directly with Stickney for the control of young workers over whom Stickney thought he held authority. After getting rid of Oliver, Stickney became the legal guardian of Young wills.[53]

On another occasion Oliver had tried to lure away Jane, a young woman from Faunsdale, but her husband William exerted his domestic authority to stop her leaving with Oliver. Stickney valued the labor of William and it was in Stickney's interest to keep the married couple together, thus Stickney supported William against Oliver. Oliver was a man who put his own welfare ahead of his squad members' and if they were alone or very young, they lacked familial support against his machinations. But William made it clear to Oliver that Jane would follow her husband's instructions and that Oliver had nothing to say about where Jane would go:

> He [Oliver] has fallen out with William. ...he [William] put down his foot against Jane's following on after him this year. W. tells me that he is determined to beat him with severity if he touches his wife (Jane), which has been threatened ever since she refused to follow him... The

old dog tells Adeline that he is coming over to take Ella [his daughter] away as soon as she arrives here.[54]

William threatened Oliver with a beating if he continued to bother Jane. Oliver must have thought that since Jane had no family or relatives at Faunsdale other than her husband, he may be successful in taking her away with him.[55]

Oliver also tried to recruit workers for other planters from among the Faunsdale labor force. He wanted the younger workers over whom he thought he held some power or authority, such as his "ward" John Wills, a young man named Isaac whom Oliver had brought to Faunsdale from another plantation, and his daughter Ella to be in his own squad. However, he may have been working on a commission to recruit workers for other planters. Stickney mentioned that Oliver made "every base overture to seduce them away" by lying about Stickney and his head men:

> Poor old Samson actually came to let me know, that he was compelled to leave the place, from the manner in which his head man (Sol) treated him all the year; when less than <u>three</u> days before he was in rapture over the same man, & assured me that he could & would work with him always, as a "man all over," & the "best farmer of all." Cassius had the promise "of $100 if he would just go right up <u>that night</u> & and sign with my [Oliver's] chaps." And the simpleton was entirely unbalanced, not willing to trust so base a liar, & yet upset.[56]

When Stickney finally realized that Oliver was undermining his authority on the plantation, he fired him. Stickney was disturbed enough about the series of events that led to the rupture that he wrote a fourteen page letter to Louisa, most of which were details of the conflict.

Before Stickney fired him, Oliver Harrison had been one of the men that Stickney selected to be squad heads in 1867. Of the three squads, Oliver's was the largest, with twenty-four members. Size was not the only way that his squad initially differed from the other two. Where both Willis and Cassius relied on kinship ties of either their own families or of small groups of families to fill the ranks of their squads, Oliver went outside family ties and beyond relatives to fill his. l'sfeither Oliver's wife Scotty nor any of her children were on his squad although they remained at Faunsdale (Scotty was Louisa's seamstress on whom she relied for her more ordinary clothing, even when she was away):

| | | | |
|---|---|---|---|
| Oliver Harrison | | head | |
| Billy | - | Oliver's ward, new to Faunsdale | |
| Betsy | - | 48 | - husband Tom Mutton just died |
| Dave (Davy) | - | 19 | - Betsy's son |
| Alethea | - | 11 | - Betsy's daughter |
| Charity Paine | - | 39 | - signed for self, unmarried |
| Lydia | - | 17 | - Charity's dau., mother signed for |
| Margiana | - | 14 | - Charity's dau., mother signed for |
| Alexander | - | 12 | - Charity's son, mother signed for |
| Jack Jones | - | | new to Faunsdale, Nancy Paine's husband |
| Lafayette | - | 16 | - Jack Jones' step-son, signed for by him |
| Tom Mitchell | - | new to Faunsdale | |
| Emma | - | new, signed for by husband Tom Mitchell | |
| Gabriella | - | 22 | - signed for by aunt, Adeline |
| Amy | - | 20 | - signed for by aunt, Adeline |
| Jackson | - | 18 | - signed for by aunt, Adeline |
| Samson Collins | | 42 | - was a slave at Faunsdale from Somerset |
| Emily | - | 39 | - Samson's wife, signed for by Samson |
| Louisa | - | 11 | - Samson & Emily's daughter, Samson signed |
| Albert | - | 27 | - no family left except brother & wife |
| Anne Maria | - | signed for by husband Albert | |
| Matilda | - | new to Faunsdale, signed for herself | |
| Stephen Brine | - | new, signed for himself | |
| Luke | - | probably Nancy's older son, signed fro self | |
| Lawson | - | new, signed for himself[57] | |

Many of the younger workers who signed the contract to work under Oliver's supervision in 1867 had no family in the squad to protect them against mistreatment or dishonesty by the head man. Unlike Willis' squad where his workers knew that their interests were protected by a relative, Oliver's squad reflected his opportunist bent and assertive seeking of his own interests.[58] One of Oliver's tricks was to charge twice for the same services:

> From negro after negro he would collect, or attempt to collect, his medical bills twice-first from or rather through me, & then from them;

telling in some instances he would not require pay, but leave the matter to their honor & time, when I had regularly settled with him two or three days before for them, by his own request & for his own convenience, after having duly entered the same charge for him during the year in his book.[59]

Although Stickney contracted with a medical doctor to provide care for the workers, he also relied on Oliver to attend their needs and paid him for his services to various workers.[60]

Most of the members of Oliver's 1867 squad remained as field workers on the plantation for several years after his departure, moving about from one squad to another. Amy moved to Cassius' and continued to work in the fields. Charity Paine signed the contracts but "kept herself" rather than receiving housing and food from Stickney as her daughters Lydia and Margiana continued to work as field hands and live with Charity.[61] Several of the young women who had been in Oliver's squad later married and no longer signed labor contracts with Stickney. Some may have gone (or been sent) along the same path away from Faunsdale as did old Betsy's daughter in 1873 when, at age fourteen, Alethea moved to another plantation in the county. From Stickney's perspective, she had not left Faunsdale by choice, but was "enticed" away. It added an insult to his injury that he lost her to the same man who had also employed Oliver and family:

> 10 Jan.   After dinner rode over to see Mr. Alexander about Alick & Lethea.

> 18 Feb.   A cold [black] Constable (John) out in field after me, as witness vs. J. C. Alexander for en6cing Alethea (old Betsy's child) from the mother's disposition of her on my contract, to go tomorrow to Magistrate's Court.[62]

Apparently Stickney and Alexander were not on close terms. Alexander was a newcomer to the area who was not abiding by any agreement of solidarity with other planters regarding the hiring away of black workers. Mr. Alexander seems to have been eager to take any Faunsdale hands who wanted to leave and was not above using Oliver to recruit them away from Stickney, as Stickney's letter to Louisa illustrated.

Stickney was suspicious of Oliver before he and his family left Faunsdale for Mr. Alexander's "Shelterplace" in late 1869 or early 1870. He reminded Louisa in the same letter of the problem of the barn and smokehouse keys that had involved Oliver:

> You may remember when I took the barn keys from him, that I was confounded with the fact of my corn's disappearance-18 loads of inferior corn, under a system of checking I had adopted, was not standing against 56 of the very best close-slipped corn, the year before. I now hardly doubt how my corn went. His gang of boys were fat always. And if he could occasionally make me suspicious of some negro around me, why that made capital in his [plan?] for keeping me blind.[63]

And in spite of his professed early suspicions of Oliver, Stickney still sided with him against Adeline in a patent power struggle between the two former slaves. Adeline's housekeeping responsibilities had included keeping the keys to the smokehouse and other locked stores of food and goods for the white household. Oliver cast suspicion on Adeline with the old master. However, as she did when she had something to say to either the master or mistress, Adeline "unburdened herself" to Stickney by telling him how Oliver had managed to get the keys away from her possession. Since this information was included in the letter of 13 January, 1870 to Louisa, the events had taken place previously over a period of time:

> When he [Oliver] began...to see his fall drawing on, he came up and urged Adeline to give up the keys, to send them straight in the house & have no more to do with them; that he had informed her what I thought of her; that I would drive her off immediately only I wanted her to cook, & that I thought nothing of her otherwise, as I had told him so. Upon this her unburdening, I informed her that he worried me with so many hints against her keeping the smokehouse keys years

ago, I could only get rest by taking them from her; & that very soon them, he advised me to let him keep the same for convenience to himself & me. She said that she always believed that from the time it occurred.[64]

Although there was a conflation of time and events within the letter, at some point in the past, Oliver had convinced Stickney that the keys should be taken from Adeline and given over to Oliver's keeping.

Oliver's authority at Faunsdale challenged the old master's. Stickney's postwar selection of Oliver as the supervisor over the other hired workers was meant to aid him in controlling his workers. Oliver was clever enough to see his position as an opportunity to improve his own lot and seized the chance. However, if a black (or as with Oliver, light-brown) man were to overstep the white patriarch's prescribed bounds for acceptable behavior by a black male, he was in trouble. Having a black man usurp what white planters jealously guarded as their authority would not be tolerated.[65]

Oliver Harrison must have been an attractive and persuasive man. He persuaded many of the black men and women who had known him for years when slaves at Faunsdale that they could trust him. Or perhaps they depended on Oliver before becoming accustomed to freedom and though they were still at the old master's mercy. A smart man like Oliver was a good ally. Perhaps he was a natural leader they turned to for advice or help. Stickney had even trusted Oliver to accompany his wife and step-daughter to North Carolina on various trips. But the version of Oliver Harrison that was written by Stickney presented a different picture:

> In other words, where he cannot be the big man, his envious, ambitious heart wishes nothing to succeed…that he may be able to say, "I knew when I left, the place would never get along—I was the only person that kept it up all this time," …Your regrets & contempt for his heartless malicious ingratitude might be expressed, if the old dog comes fawning about you. I find that our negroes are light- hearted at his departure…. These four years they have heard him boast that it was in his power any time to break up this plantation— he could carry off

every hand with him. The older ones laugh now in derision at his huge, long swell which he was much wont to strut under when he felt he had put one of them down by my sanction, or when some fear would be entertained of being superseded by successful squad heads.[66]

Stickney had ignored what he later thought of as Oliver's depredations against the other workers until he recognized that Oliver's actions were possibly undermining his own authority with the workers. When he realized how much influence Oliver had in the black community, Stickney suddenly heard the complaints from the quarters and acted against Oliver. He listed Oliver's many character flaws and probable crimes in the same long letter in January, 1870 to Louisa:

> All knew him to be so false & mean that he could do no more than temporarily upset them—make them to defer to me for solution of the difficulties which he would put in their simple heads. Of course I would have them there in my own hands, & allay the mischief he had sown in them... I always heard, from both white & black, that old Oliver was a vile liar, & he even manifested the greatest fear that I would suspect him of...his true character. I did a few times discover the trait in his dealings. But he was satisfied if only he could keep up appearance with me....[67]

In spite of Stickney's protestations that he had long suspected Oliver of dishonesty, another passage from the letter shows that when previously faced with a choice of either granting authority to Adeline or supporting her in her dispute with Oliver, Stickney failed to legitimate Adeline's authority and gave his support to the male servant. The passage from the letter, quoted earlier, reveals that the conflict between the two servants was not one which had just developed. Oliver had used the possession of the keys as a way in which he could discredit Adeline's influence and standing within the white household and obtain a strong position with Stickney. In his letter, Stickney pointed out that he had been taken in by Oliver, yet even when Oliver's deception was clear, once Stickney realized that Adeline had been maligned by Oliver to serve his own ends, Stickney could not bring himself to hand over the authority to Adeline. Stickney focused on Oliver's accusation that Adeline was unimportant to Stickney in any capacity other than as a cook and thought that she was more concerned over his opinion of her than of her dismay over her probable loss of authority in the household. In reminding Louisa of past events which had led to the current conflict between Adeline and Oliver, Stickney seemed oblivious to the possibility that Adeline had more at stake than just the regard of the old master.

William Stickney continued to relate to Adeline in a highly paternalistic manner, as the old master who would always look after his good servants. He did not regard her as an independent woman who had a great amount of responsibility which she handled with success. Undoubtedly, Oliver's accusation disturbed her. Adeline was accustomed to holding a position of authority in the white household and wanted to maintain it, but she may have also seen that it was the old master and not the old mistress that she had to please. Still, Stickney could not grant to her the same degree of authority that he had been willing to give to Oliver, the struggle for the keys indicates. When he had to decide which of the two slaves and then servants would keep the keys, he gave them to Oliver until he could no longer close his eyes to Oliver's actions. Once aware of them, Stickney still did not return the keys, the symbols of domestic authority, to Adeline.

Louisa probably had no objections to Adeline's authority. She had always depended on black women to carry out her domestic responsibilities and to do the domestic labor of her household. She relied on Adeline to oversee its management. Adeline had a position of significant influence within the household; Oliver's jockeying for a stronger position in that domestic arena was a real threat to her place in it.[68] During Reconstruction, not all political battles fought were of the formal type, nor were all the struggles for authority between white and black men.

When the old master and mistress, William Stickney and Louisa Collins Stickney, faced changes in their society brought on by the end of racial slavery, they had to make new decisions. Louisa continued in the same gender-bound role of deferential acquiescence to most decisions of the male head of the family (with the noticeable exception of long visits to North Carolina), thus leaving

Stickney a free hand in managing the plantation. One decision that he made, heavily weighted as it was by demands from the workers, was to organize them into squads and delegate some of his authority to the men he selected to head the squads. Since they were free to fill their squads as they wished, their choices reveal much about each head man's organizing motive. Willis turned to his and his wife's blood kin; Cassius enlisted several men and each one's wife or older children; and Oliver acted in what was already the norm in northern cities by relying less on kinship and more on personal persuasion and even the relations of the marketplace.[69]

What the outcome of the new squad system might have been had Stickney chosen some women as squad heads or encouraged those to act independent of male relatives cannot be known. Such an action would have gone so much against all social forces which shored up male dominance that they would have soon perished as experimental efforts. William Stickney generated most of the documents and records which have preserved the data concerning the lives of the freed black women and men of Faunsdale, so there is an inherent bias in what he left behind. However, some conclusions can be drawn from his records: Stickney perceived himself and all white men of his class to be patriarchs for whom Biblical sources sanctioned authority; he depended on the squad system to implement his social control over an ostensibly free labor force; the hired black women and men wanted the change to squads and increased control it brought over their domestic and work lives; the squad system as structured at Faunsdale relied heavily on marital and kin ties; Stickney encouraged adult black males on the plantation to exert their authority over their wives and children while black female field hands held only lower ranks within the squads. For black female field hands at Faunsdale plantation who remained unmarried and provided the old master with no male head of their households to respond to his reliance on male dominance in domestic matters, other arrangements were required.

# END NOTES

1. Plantation Day Books, 1867-1876, Stickney box VIII, folders g, 9, 10, FPP, BPL

2. For more on postwar decentralization of plantation labor, see Gerald D. Jaynes <u>Branches Without Roots: Genesis of the Black Working Class in the American South 1862-1882</u> (New York, 1986) and Gavin Wright <u>Old South, New South</u> (New York, 1986).

3. For an analysis of organization of labor into the task system task system on rice plantations of the coastal South, see the work in progress by Leslie Schwam, University of Michigan.

4. Op. cit., squad books 1867-1877

5. The term "withdrawal of female labor" from postwar cotton production refers specifically to the diminishing number of black female field hands who worked for hire. It is a term that has been used without distinguishing whether the black women had ceased all field labor or just contracted work for white planters' market-bound cotton. See Roger L. Ransom and Richard Sutch <u>One Kind of Freedom: The Economic Consequence of Emancipation</u> (Cambridge, 1977).

6. Jaynes, pp. 158-190; Wright pp. 85-90

7. Single-family sharecropping was not invented in the postwar American South, but by the end of the 1880s it was the prevailing mode of raising cotton. An example of the problems of family farming of another's land in eighteenth- century England may be found in Ivy Pinchbeck <u>Women Workers and the Industrial Revolution 1750-1850</u> (Virago Press, London, 1981), esp. pp. 1-110.

8. William A. Stickney to Louisa Collins Stickney, 13 March, 1867, Stickney box I, folder 1, FPP, BPL

9. Op. cit., squad books 1867-1877

10. Stickney hired all of the domestic house servants from the ranks of his ex-slaves and paid them in cash wages.

11. Op. cit., Stickney letter to Louisa

12. 1868 Diary, William A. Stickney, Stickney Box III, folder 80, FPP, BPL

13. For lists of Domestic servants from the years 1867 - 1876, see Stickney Box VII, folders 8, 9, 10 FPP, BPL

14. Ibid.

15. Ibid. Op. cit., 1867 Plantation Day Book

16. Stickney keep account books for worker from 1869 through 1893. For more data from them, see Stickney box VII, folders 5, 6, and 7, FPP, BPL.

17. Such parenthetical descriptive terms as black, house, big, tiger, old were routinely attached to the names of slaves and then servants at Faunsdale to distinguish between different women and men who bore the same first name. Using a last name was not done because it granted too much respect to a person for whom white masters and mistresses were determined to withhold it. As for specific women referred to in the text, Adeline (house) was the unmarried domestic servant who functioned as the housekeeper and Adeline (black) was a field hand who was married to Willis.

18. Op. cit., 1869 account book

19. Ibid.

20. Op. cit., 1866 diary

21. The second contract referred to in the test was one drawn by Stickney in a effort to hold the contracted workers responsible for their relatives living with them, but not under contract to him. It may be found in Stickney box VII, folder 15, FPP, BPL.

22. Ibid.

23. Op. cit., letter of 13 March, 1867

24. Ibid.

25. Labor Contracts, Stickney box VII, folder 15, FPP, BPL

26. Ibid

27. Op. cit., 1872 diary

28. Sufficient documentation exists for the years 1845-1848 and 1865-1871 to determine how much cotton each field handpicked for the two times periods.

29. Stickney box 9A, folder 1871, "1871 Corn Crop - adjusted for division" and "1871 Classification," FPP, BPL

30. The Louisiana land continued to be a problem for Louisa and Stickney because they were unable to sell it for several years. It almost cost them Faunsdale as well. There is much, but very scattered, data within the Faunsdale collection on the Louisiana property problem.

31. Passim. Stickney's critical remarks about such women as Lavinia are numerous, but widely scattered throughout his records.

32. Squad lists for the years 1867 through 1877 may be found in Stickney box VII, folders 1, 2, 3, FPP, BPL.

33. See the bound slave chapel register, "Baptisms," Stickney box V, folder 51, FPP, BPL.

34. For a fuller discussion of social parenthood among postwar black families in the South, see Jo Ann Mantra and Robert R. Dykstra, "Serial Marriage and the Origins of the Black Step family," <u>Journal of American History</u>, V.72, n.1 (June, 1985), pp. 18-44.

35. Op. cit., 1867 labor contract

36. Op. cit., squad books 1867-1877

37. Ibid.

38. For more on inherent intra-squad dissension, see Jaynes pp. 160-164.

39. Op. cit., 1869 plantation day book

40. Op. cit., 1870 plantation day book

41. Op. cit., 1872 plantation day book

42. Stickney received a response from R. Christian, otherwise unidentified, from Uniontown, 1 January, 1870 regarding Solomon which referenced a state legislature's approval of an ordinance regarding marriage and divorce of freed men and the writer stated that Solomon's right to remarry depended on the mutuality of his parting with his wife. Another came in October, 1879 from the Office of the Clerk Circuit Court, Linden, Alabama, signed C. B. Cleveland and was in apparent response to two cases brought to his attention by Stickney. One was "the woman who left the man for North Carolina seven years ago gives the husband a divorce for her desertion" and "No. 2 was divorced by law this is [torn] U.S. Government & state legislature divorced all who were not living together in 1869 or who parted before that years." Stickney made a reference to "Sol and his concubine" in his 1872 diary for 9 March, Stickney box III, folder 80, FPP, BPL.

43. The names and birth dates of Amy's two daughters comes from the "Baptisms," 1869-1886, Faunsdale Chapel, Stickney box V, folder 51, FPP, BPL.

44. See the fragmented letter from William Stickney to Louisa, 9 September, 1874, Correspondence, Stickney Box 1, f. 4, FPP, BPL in which Stickney mentioned his concern about the theft of baled cotton and wanted her to "[t]ell Cassius to have a close eye to Edmund's corn & cotton in the field (privately to Cassius); that I trust him to see all is..." [the rest is lost].

45. Op. cit., letter 18 February, 1867

46. For the daily amount of cotton picked by Hester during the picking season of 1845-1848, see Thomas A. Harrison's account book, Harrison papers, box 1, folder H27a, FPP, BPL.

47. Op. cit., 1866 contract

48. For more on James Iredell, see Don Higginbotham, ed. <u>The Papers of James Iredell, Volume I, 1773-1778</u>, (Raleigh, 1976).

49. For more of Iredell's expenses from Stickney for 1881, see "Final Settlements" and Labourer's Accounts, 1870-1881, Stickney box VII, folder 6, FPP, BPL.

50. From 1865 to 1870, Stickney's letters and diaries make constant reference to Oliver and the many ways in which the old master continued to rely on him.

51. Op. cit., letter 13 January, 1870

52. Ibid.

53. See Stickney's diary, February 1872 and for more on the Freedmen's Bureau and apprenticeship of black children, see Rebecca Scott, "The Battle over the Child", <u>Prologue,</u> Vol. 10, summer 1978.

54. Op. cit., letter 13 January, 1870 Stickney to Louisa

55. Jane was the daughter of Ester and grandchild of Celia, both of whom were Collins' slaves in Edenton before being moved to Alabama in 1843. Ester was last noted on the 1848 list of slaves at Faunsdale and Jane remained with her grandmother. Little is known of them or their relatives.

56. Op. cit., letter 13 January, 1870

57. Op. cit., Oliver's 1867 squad list

58. The 1870 census taker listed "Oliver Harrison" as a "Mulatto" whose place of birth was Virginia, which was Harrison's state of origin. There is no mention in any Somerset documents of a slave who meets his age and name. He was probably Thomas Harrison's personal slave when Harrison married.

59. Op. cit., letter 13 January, 1870

60. Op. cit., Plantation Day Books, 1867-1870 and Account Books 1969-1870

61. Stickney had different arrangements with several workers for providing their housing and food. Charity "found" herself, meaning that she provided her own food.

62. Op. cit., 1873 diary

63. Op. cit., letter 13 January, 1870

64. Ibid.

65. Oliver's skill as a carpenter was noted in the 1864 inventory of taxable slaves for the Confederate government found in "St. Winifred's Family & Day School Register," p. 31, Stickney Box V, folder 55, FPP, BPL.

66. Op. cit., letter 13 January, 1870

67. Ibid.

68. No letters from Louisa after 1844 are extant and no diary from any period has survived.

69. For a different interpretation of the relationship between the head men and their squad members, see Jaynes, pp. 173-187, who describes them as essentially capitalistic in nature rather than based on kin networks.

# CHAPTER SIX

# "Jan. 6 Charity began work for 1/2 the crops, on self-maintenance, 1/2 the mules, & 1/2 their risk"[1]

Only in the absence of a male head of household did black women contract directly with Stickney for domestic or field labor. However, by negotiating directly with unmarried women and recognizing their right to commit their labor to a contract, he had not relinquished his authority over them. In the case of house servants or those working on the grounds of the house, he could oversee their labor, while the head men of the squads oversaw those at work in the fields. Stickney expected head men to maintain authority over every person in the squad without regard to their marital status. Freed black women—like Lucy, Amy, Lavinia, Elizabeth, Joanna, Hannah, Matilda, Adeline, and Charity—unmarried, self-supporting women who signed contracts for themselves—did not fit into the customary arrangements where the male head of the household took responsibility and authority to act for them. Stickney's usual contract recognized and reinforced the still-new right of black men to represent their women and children. It was the arrangement that the men of Faunsdale adhered to, and only when there was no male head of the household did black female workers exercise that right.[2]

William Stickney did not admit to a greater dislike for having female field workers than males, but he did not make the same sort of critical or disparaging remarks about the men as he made about the women. He resented having to negotiate with any of the laborers who had so recently been under his command as slaves, calling the process of contracting and negotiating with them "wearisome & sickening work" and "trying and wearying" or "tiresome as usual."[3] His distaste for contracting and negotiation with all of the freed black workers only served to harden his attitude that black women were a source of trouble and dissension within the household and field labor force. And even while he encouraged black men to assume some aspects of patriarchal authority over their own families or other workers, Stickney did not put them in authority over anyone white. He routinely put them in charge of female field hands, encouraging the men to become the heads of their households even if they were all still living in the old slave quarters. Under slavery, to have command of the labor of black women and children was a white male prerogative which was jealously protected and one from which black males were excluded. To act with authority over others was part of what made a male a man. Above all else, male slaves were not to think of themselves in that way or they might become rebellious and refuse to be enslaved. By acknowledging black men's authority in their own families, Stickney inadvertently legitimated and upheld a prerogative which accrued to a man based on his sex over one of race and class.[4]

Stickney strongly favored hiring men whom he could trust to comply with his instructions, follow his orders, manage the women and children of their families, and farm well. In order to pick such men, he hired those who were already well known to him, men he considered to be stable and settled who would not cause trouble or defy him. He did not favor hiring women who had ambitions reaching past being a field and or troublesome ones who were hard to control:

> [from a 1867 letter] Our old Nancy fi Martha were in the yard a week ago, They came around to see me & inquire after "Misses Lou & Miss Lou." Then they came again to tell me goodby. I can't say how relieved I felt on seeing them,...not about us. Old Nancy not quarreling in the yard & Jno. not in everybody's way,...[5]

Nancy was thought to be insane and lost the right to custody of her son, John Wills. Oliver claimed the right to commit John to work and signed his name as a member of his own squad, but it was Stickney who eventually became the legal guardian of the boy. Nancy seems never to have had a husband and continued to live on or near the plantation, a source of irrita8on and dependency for Stickney. Nancy Wills may have actually suffered from insanity or she may have been smart enough to use it as a kind of shield against the harshness of enslavement and later as a method of getting what she wanted from the old master who hired her for the simplest menial work at small wages. Stickney continued to hire her, often paying her only in food and quarters as he noted her sporadic bouts of insanity. A mentally unstable woman who was apparently not fit for heavy labor was also not one that Stickney's religious beliefs or nearby federal troops would allow him to turn out to starve.[6]

Troublesome, independent, demanding, or ambitious women, no matter what their race, did not work well for a man like Stickney who was so accustomed to deference from women. He had little to do in the way of admonishing the white women within this household to cease being too self-assured or ambitious since their gender role successfully kept them confined within the limited parameters of Southern Ladyhood.[7] The same gender expectations of behavior did not apply to black women because no white man or woman expected them to assume class and race prerogatives of being a lady. A black woman did not have to assume the role of "playing the lady" to offend or threaten the old master. All it took was having too much ambition or being too assertive. Stickney let men go that he would otherwise have kept had it not been for their women. Troublesome women were not worth keeping even if it cost him compliant men:

> [from a 1871 letters I hardly think Jane will suit any longer. [Y]ou can never stand your premises to be appropriated to raising young negroes. As the little things are growing older & larger, they make the place unendurable with their noise, fighting, playing, & etc. Then their mothers put in & just such you never heard & cannot stand. The fathers are useful to us. But I am afraid they will have to be given up.[8]

Jane had been a domestic slave at Faunsdale before emancipation. She was the daughter of Easter, one of the original group of slaves who walked from Edenton, North Carolina to Alabama with Dr. Harrison in 1843. Although Jane was born and reared on Faunsdale and was probably well known to Stickney from his earlier years when he had been the priest there before he wed the widowed mistress, he did not hire Jane after emancipation and would not tolerate her ambitions. Jane was too much trouble, but Stickney was more tolerant of her husband's unruly behavior. He kept William as the gardener in spite of frequent drinking sprees in Uniontown from which William would return drunk to Faunsdale. Even the dissipation of drunkenness in a black male was less offensive to William Stickney, Episcopal priest and plantation manager, than the kind of independence that he saw in Jane and "lady Mary." He noted with smug satisfaction in a letter that their "high money plans" had not worked and predicted that their idleness would only make them into poor domestic servants for any future employment. Perhaps Jane lost enough of her ambitions and plans to suit the old master by 1871 since he finally hired her that year as a cook.

William wanted his wife to work. According to Stickney's assessment of their situation, William was eager for Jane to resume her place as a cook within the white household. From his comments in a letter to Louisa in February, 1867, Stickney knew that Jane and William were concerned because she had no job:

> They (Jane & Mary) are tired out with idleness. Lady Mary concludes that she "feels perfectly foolish doing nothing." The Watts & Weavers may get them—some negotiation finding....William is at your garden,...He is troubled about his wife-not having a place for her since you were carried off so suddenly, & no cook beside Adeline is needed in your & Lou's absence.[9]

Several black women besides Jane and Mary worked as house servants in William and Louisa Stickney's household and were paid wages. Between 1869 and 1873, as an example, several women (and men) worked for William and Louisa. They were paid in cash on a monthly basis to perform the domestic labor necessary to keep house for three or four white adults of the planter class. Adeline, Mary, Mary Newbern, Jane, Scotty, Grace, Nancy, and Caroline were all hired as domestic workers at different times during the four years to be a washerwoman, cook, diary maid, cow and sheep tender, chambermaid, and seamstress. The men, Henry, Philip, Abram, and Joe Hunter, were hired during that period as the hostler and carriage driver, gardener, butler, and a house servant. The following list shows who performed which jobs.

1869
Adeline - cook
Scotty - chamber maid, washer, seamstress
Henry - Dining room, etc.
Philip - Carriage & stable
Mary - washes for Mr. Baden, 1870
Adeline - cook
Mary - diary maid Mary
N. - washer & ironer
Philip - Hostler, carriage driving, gardening

1873
Jane - cook
Adeline - Nurse to "little Lou"
Nancy - Diary maid
Caroline - Laundry & chamber
Philip - Ostler, carriage driver, gardener
Joe H. - Cow & sheep ñ poultry minder
Abram - Dining room & general house sv't.[10]

For each of these domestic servants, contracts and agreements had to be devised that differed from the standard one that Stickney relied on when contracting for field workers. One difference was that he was hiring more women than men and paying them monthly wages in cash rather than the share of the squad's production of cotton, which female field hands received.[11]

Not hiring Jane and getting "Crazy Nancy" out of the yard about his front door was not enough to solve all the problems of dealing with obstreperous and recalcitrant black women. An example of the rowdy behavior that the old master associated with black females and found intolerable can be seen in the conflict that broke out between Amy and Lavinia in March, 1870. A dispute erupted on 1 March which involved Lavinia, Amy, and Josiah that resulted in a serious injury to Josiah, Lavinia's fifteen-year old son. Amy broke his leg. Her brother Jackson then left the plantation to find a doctor for Josiah while Lavinia and Amy went on with their dispute, and for which each was fined five dollars for quarreling. The quarrel and injury probably happened in the quarters since Lavinia had stopped working earlier in the year because she was pregnant and no longer went to the field.[12]

It was the kind of altercation that fueled Stickney's dislike for having as employees freed black women and their children underfoot; loud and disruptive arguments where women squabbled with each other, with their white employer, and even with their own men. Stickney disliked it that the women working for him behaved in such a markedly different manner than the white ladies of his class upon whom he could count to be tractable, genteel, and willing to comply with what their husbands required (or demanded). Lavinia had no husband and was not lady-like or compliant or tractable. The loud, demanding, unruly Lavinias and Amys that elite male planters had to deal with once they were free and hired labor were, for their old masters, unpleasant challenges to their war-damaged pride and authority. If southern men needed the soft and tender domestic mercies of their women to ease the pain of defeat, women like Lavinia stood out as an anathema to what they prized in women. Men like Stickney did not have to tolerate any behavior from female subordinates that disturbed their shaky sense of hierarchical order.[13]

Several options for controlling hired black workers, female or male, were available to planters once they had been forced to see that the old ways of corporal punishment and violent coercion would not be permitted. Stickney relied on several methods, but two that were especially successful were his opening charge accounts at local dry goods stores and the account books that he personally kept for each worker. Stickney's ledgers were very detailed individual accounts on each worker, with each divided in either separate pages or columns to reflect a credit and debit side. The credit side reported what he owed the worker while the debit side showed what was owed to Stickney by either a contracted laborer or one of their dependents. Some debts were made directly to the merchant with whom

Stickney had opened the charge account, but some had been made with him for what he had provided. Still, Stickney was ultimately responsible for all money his laborers owed the merchants. A comparison of credits and debits of accounts suggests why Stickney had to work so hard so many late nights on his accounts. Hours spent over the books were necessary to ensure that no hired black worker would get far enough ahead that he or she could collect a large cash payment in December and walk away from the plantation. Working late into the nights by bright lamplight was required if he was to keep the workers in debt peonage.[14]

All Stickney's financial arrangements with local merchants may have followed the same pattern as the one he made with Adler and Brothers of Uniontown in 1872. He may have made a similar agreement with one merchant each year who would keep open charge accounts for workers and from whom Stickney also could draw cash advances for his own use. This agreement for 1872 shows that he had cash from the merchant Adler before his cotton had been sold. It also underlines the role merchants played in providing credit to planters. The terms of Stickney's agreement with Mr. Adler of Uniontown were enumerated in a letter to him:

> 1st Such Dry Goods, as I or my labourers may need the current year, or credit, without interest;
>
> 2nd to furnish us with Groceries (meat included) on credit, at 8 per cent interest;
>
> 3rd to advance me money along when called for, to the extent perhaps of a thousand ($1000.) or Twelve hundred ($1200.) dollars, at 8 per cent interest.[15]

The agreement included the disposition of the cotton through the "House of Webster & Wilson, Cotton Factors, Mobile, Alabama" with proceeds going directly from the factors to the merchants to satisfy Stickney's debts with them. Anything left after those were paid would be remitted by the factors to Stickney. He also reminded Adler not to restrain the hands from going in debt, but to (l)et there be no seeming constraint on them, to excite their suspicions. They mainly prefer dealing in your house, expecting none other than fair treatment. But there's no accounting for African whims & suspicions...[16]

In spite of his hard work to keep the books reflecting more debits than credits for each worker, some of the women managed to stay out of debt, often for a short time only, but some came out ahead in their dealings with the old master. Amy and Charity had different degrees of success financially, but both seemed to have fought against the trap of debt peonage to Stickney. Amy stayed single and self-supporting for several years before she married Cassius in the latter part of the 1870s. But until then she had earned her own way. Not that she ever made much, but she stayed out of debt for a few years, clearing $14.21 for an entire year's labor for 1870 after paying (among other items charged to her), $1.00 for the crutches for Josiah after she broke his leg, $9.36 for his time that was lost from the fields, and an additional charge of $.41 for time lost by her younger brother Jackson when he left the field to bring back a doctor for Josiah. The credit side of Amy's account received the $2.00 levied against Lavinia as a fine for her "tongue abuse" against Amy. In all, perhaps $14.21 was not too bad for a young woman who paid all her debts, owed no one, and could live with her mother and step-father.[17]

For the next few years, Amy remained single, paying her debts, earning a bit more in 1871, then less and less each year that followed. After she married Cassius, the head of her squad, she did not earn a larger share or wage, but did have his to share. Amy cleared $28.26 in 1872 and $13.39 the next year, but when she began with Stickney in January, 1874, Amy had a debt of $3.69 that had been brought over from 1873 and again ended the year in debt $3.03.[18]

With the birth of her child Victoria in 1874, Amy had two children for whom she had to provide who were too young to help by working in the fields also. Amy tried to be frugal in January by having her old shoes repaired for $.90 before she spent $2.50 on a new pair in August. She charged coarse materials such as plaid and osnaburg and thread to her account so that she could make clothes for herself and her children. From the small amounts of food charged against her account, Amy must have been growing much of her own food or even getting help from some other quarter because what she charged was not enough to feed them for a year. Seven years later in 1881 when her options of places to purchase food and dry goods had widened, Adler and Brothers was no longer the only merchant to whom Amy and other Faunsdale workers could go for their needs. Amy ended 1881 owning $1.20 to Ernst Brothers for shoes, $2.06 to Brown and Company for shoes and calico for herself and her seventeen-year old sister Sophy, and $1.75 to Price and Watkins for more shoes. Their large extended family of children, step-children, and relatives needed more than the pork and corn meal that Amy and Cassius received as rations from Stickney. Pooling her resources with those of a man who had the old master's trust as Cassius did looked like a good move for Amy since she managed to clear $20.00 in 1881. However, Cassius was not able to stay out of debt and her twenty dollars probably went to pay the $17.77 that he owed Stickney.[19]

Although most of the women who signed contracts for themselves had children, motherhood alone did not confer upon them the adult status which made legitimate their right to sign contracts and be paid their own wages. Most of the married women whose men signed for them were also mothers with children ranging in ages from infancy to adulthood, yet their husbands or fathers still represented them. While motherhood may have retained its original African meaning as the most significant rite of passage for a girl into womanhood within the black community, that condition alone conferred upon the freed African-American women of Faunsdale neither the rights possessed by free men to own their labor nor to receive the wages earned by it.

Many women with children did not marry, remaining single during the Reconstruction decade even though it was a survival strategy for a woman with small children to combine her resources with those of a man. Several factors besides motherhood must be considered in determining what contributed to the single status for so many black women: factors such as an unbalanced sex ratio that left black women at a statistical disadvantage in finding a marital partner; living without a man by choice; and the lack of gender restrictions against black women working for hire.[20]

Every county in Alabama suffered a loss in the population of black males in their twenties by 1866. In his work on freedwomen and freedmen, <u>First Freedom: The Responses of Alabama's Blacks to Emancipation and</u>

Reconstructions Peter Kolchin points out that for Alabama, the 1860 federal census showed a population with a higher number of black males than females in the twenty- to twenty-nine-year old age cohort, but the 1866 state census found a substantial state-wide loss of black men had occurred from the same age group. This resulted in an imbalanced sex ratio between freedmen and women in 1866 that Kolchin attributed to war-related deaths. He also thinks that the imbalance put the men in that age group at an advantage in selecting mates, making young black men the premium and created what he termed a "buyer's market" for black women.[21]

Some freedwomen did not want one of the premium males and chose to be without a marriage partner or separated from the ones they had as Lucy Skipwith did late in 1865. She was married, but left her husband. Her decision to live without Armistead, whom she had married when both were slaves, may be taken as an example of what other Alabama freedwomen did as soon as they were able. In "Dear master": Letters of a Slave Family, editor Randall M. Miller writes that Lucy Skipwith had been characterized by her master John Hartwell Cocke as the "vilest sinner" on his Alabama plantation of Hopewell. Her "sins" were probably sexual in nature since she gained his trust after she married and became a settled, religious slave. She earned his trust in part by doing such things as telling him what she discovered about her husband Armistead's plan to destroy Hopewell's cotton so that the white overseer would look bad. From this bit of information, it appears that her relationship with the master mattered much more to her than did her marriage. While a slave, Skipwith lived at Cocke's Alabama plantation located in Hale County, just north of Marengo. As the absentee master of Alabama plantation, John Hartwell Cocke lived in Virginia on his home plantation of Bremo after he had established Hopewell in 1840. He left several members of the Skipwith slave family there in positions of responsibility with the intention of training them for freedom in Liberia.[22]

Placed by the master to be a surrogate housekeeper/mistress, Lucy learned to align herself with him and made efforts to carry out his desire that all of the other slaves be instructed in his Protestant religious beliefs. Her position was precarious and depended on pleasing the master. In spite of her deep religious belief, demonstrated piety, and energy spent trying to win other slaves to the masters' religion, Lucy's letters to "dear master" reveal that her goal was frustrated. And her husband's piety was rather less than Lucy's as he caused her ex-communication from their church when she ended the marriage in 1865. In spite of his lesser degree of piety, he seems to have gained one of greater authority within the church.[23]

Lucy Skipwith's letter to her "dear Master" written in December, 1865 informed him that she had parted from Armistead and made it clear that she was setting out on a path of her own making. She wanted Cocke's approval, but if he withheld it, Lucy meant to refocus her aim and life's meaning by serving another less earthly master rather than the one she had depended upon for so long. She also clearly intended to live without a man to direct or interfere with that work:

> my dear Master
>
> I received your letter a few days ago dated oct 14th it being nearly two months on the way. ...I was sorry that I had to part from Armistead but I have lived a life of trouble with him, & a white man has ever had to Judge between us, & now to be turned loose from under a master I know that I could never live with him in no peace, therefore I left him for I wish. to live a life of peace & die a death of both Joy and peace & if you have any hard feelings against me on the subject, I hope that you will forgive me for Jesus sake.[24]

Most freedwomen lacked the knowledge or opportunity to preserve their reasons and intentions in letters. Lucy Horton, another ex-slave who also seized her own freedom as Skipwith had done, lived fifteen miles south of Hopewell at Faunsdale. Horton expressed her desire for freedom from her husband Sam in action rather than written form. Stickney had listed them as one of the six "new families" formed at Faunsdale during 1865. Lucy Horton, as she soon named herself, and Sam remained together for a while after 1865, but by the 1870 census they lived apart. Sam still took some responsibility for Lucy when he committed her name in 1867 to Stickney's contract, but she made her own mark on the one for 1869 and received her own wages. Lucy Horton and Sam stayed as workers in the same squad, but did not live together; he lived with another male field hand named Albert and Albert's wife Maria while Lucy headed her own household that she shared with her two children. No man was included. She signed her own contracts, worked as a field hand for whom Stickney provided food and quarters un8l 1875 when she and a freedwoman named Joanna agreed to work "outside the contract" for Stickney.[25]

Lucy Horton left no letters that might explain why she decided to live apart from her husband as Lucy Skipwith had done, but Stickney's correspondence reveals that several freedmen and freedwomen at Faunsdale had ended their marriages. Some of the once-married couples had separated and formed new unions which Stickney considered illicit, such as Sol's. Stickney called the woman who lived with Sol his concubine. Acting in both his capacities as employer and priest, William Stickney pursued the matter of the legality of some marriages that had taken place between some of his hired workers. He received written responses to his inquiries from men in two county offices.

Mr. R. Christian wrote to Stickney on 1 January, 1870 and gave him information about the legal basis for Solomon's divorce and for his possible freedom to remarry. Solomon and Hannah were considered a married pair when slaves, but parted after emancipation. Seeking a legal opinion, the Rev. Stickney wrote to an officer of the county court system to learn if they were still married. Mr. Christian's reply was based on an ordinance passed by Alabama's Reconstruction government in which he expressed his low regard for that body and what had been done

> by the so-called State Convention on 30th Nov'b, 1867 which covers Solomon's case, provided the separation is by mutual consent. His right to remarry...depends upon whether the parting was by mutual consent.[26]

Legal or not, the separation had taken place by the time of the federal census of 1870 because Solomon Littlejohn was living with a woman identified as his wife Margaret while Hannah lived with her grandmother Hannah, her brother Jackson, and a five-year old child named Sa1lie.[27]

At least two other marriages of freedmen and women were investigated by Stickney after the one of Solomon and Hannah. A second letter from Mr. C. B. Cleveland came from the office of the Clerk of Circuit Court in Linden, Alabama bearing the date of October, 1879. Cleveland had also written in apparent response to another request from Stickney about two other marriages that had been made under slavery and dissolved in freedoms:

> Rev & Dear Sir,
> ...The woman who left the man for N. Carolina seven years ago gives the husband a divorce for her desertion. No 2 was divorced by law that is the U.S. government & state legislature divorced all who were not living together in 1869 or who parted before that year. [28]

As I have stated before in this work, the pairings of men and women or "new families" of African-Americans that took place when the men and women were slaves should not be taken as prima facie proof that the marriage reflected the desires of the slaves involved. They may have been regarded as married and a family by only a master who based their marriage on the woman's pregnancy. Stickney disapproved of what he regarded as illicit unions and tried to influence both slaves and freedpeople to live in what he considered a properly sanctioned, legitimate marriage. His six "new families" in the ledger of slave family were these: Albert and Eliza (m. January, 1865) and infant (b. July, 1865); Dunkey and George Washington (29 January, 1865) and infant (b. March, 1865); Philip and Mary (no date) and infant (b. December, lfiii5); Sam and Lucy (no date, no child listed); William and Jane (no date, no child listed); Willis and Adeline and infant (b. July, 1865). Of these six families, only two remained together after emancipation.[29]

One young freedwoman created her own family without marrying and as a black woman, no generic restraint prevented her from working or compelled her to marry. The combination of motherhood, wages earned through a place in a squad, and support from members of her family allowed Elizabeth Iredell to live independent of a husband and still support herself and two young children. Prior to 1870, the year her first child was born, Elizabeth Iredell's father John Iredell had regularly committed his daughter's labor to the contracts as a field hand at Faunsdale, making his mark by her name to show that she would work for Stickney. Elizabeth always worked in her father's squad and under his supervision, but did not live with him. The 1870 census located her living in a dwelling that was close by but separate from her parents' quarters and identified her occupation as "keeping house" rather than "farm laborer." Since she was living with her small children and sister Maria, also a field hand, she may have taken some time off after the birth of her child while her sister worked in the squad. Maria Iredell did not remain in the house and a single woman for long; Stickney conducted her marriage ceremony when she wed David Washington in 1872. Elizabeth's mother Hester may have taken care of the babies while Elizabeth went back to the field work, living alone and with the limited rights allowed a "free" black woman in postwar Alabama.[30]

By 1873 John Iredell was no longer signing contracts for his daughter Elizabeth or collecting her wages as he had earlier. She continued as a member of his squad, but signed the contracts for herself. The size of her own family increased with the birth of her second child in 1872, a boy she named John Wilken. As it had been two years earlier with the baptism of baby Moses, no man's name was carried on the baptismal record as the infant's father. The Rev. Stickney regarded such births with intense disapproval and saw them as evidence of the "depravity" of freed black women who lacked understanding of religion and morality. In spite of his deep distaste for such births, he still baptized both of Elizabeth's children into the Episcopal Church, but took care to record them as illicit. His blame was directed against the women and reveals his perspective that they were the real culprits. It was against freedwomen and their unsanctioned unions that he railed when he attributed the fatherhood of Lucy's children:

| Children | | Parents |
|---|---|---|
| John | - born Jan., 1870 | Lucy & bastardy |
| Moses | - born May, 1870 | Elizabeth & base born |
| Corra | - born May, 1871 | Maria John &k adultery |
| Merinda | - bap. Nov., 1871 | Lavinia & sin |
| Lizzie | - born Oct., 1870 | Lydia & bastardy |
| W. Henry | - born Aug., 1871 | Lucy & sin[31] |

Like classes, genders function in opposition to each other. We may neither apply the analytical concept of gender to just one sex nor think of gender roles as applicable to only one. Male and female members of every society are both subject to material rewards, restrictions, and ideological assumptions inherent in their specific society's social construction of gender. Every culture has gender roles and each person knows what it means for a male to "be a man" and for a female to "be a woman." Each sex also learns what characteristics and behaviors are appropriate and permitted the different class of the society and those must not challenge the elite class's control of society. With the end of slavery, gender relations would be affected and the roles for each sex might alter, but to what extent depended on race and class. Military and political events swirling about the periphery of the community of Faunsdale imposed great changes in the lives of the slaves, but it would remain for them to work out a gender system that accommodated their new social class and did not deny their African heritage. [32]

Race and class, but especially race, had a profound effect on shaping variations in female gender roles. If race had not been the variable, then African women would not have been shorn of all the protective proscriptions that guarded white women. If class had been the only criterion to elevate a farm wife into the upper rank of a planter-class mistress, then any black wife who wed a white man of land and wealth would not have had to "play the lady" because she would have simply followed into the class standing of the man she married. The physical conditions of race and sex provide easily identifiable characteristics, in a way that economic class does not, for those who would be made into permanent workers based on either sex or race. If being a member of the elite class of a society is predicated upon either sex or race, or a combination of the two, that class condition cannot easily be overcome or changed. For black men the road to Manhood began with the right to assume the role of the head of their family, to assume the authority over their women and children which had been reserved for white men only. At least that one aspect of Manhood would not be withheld from the freedmen because it would benefit the planter class. But for black women, the meaning and definition of Womanhood was too enmeshed with the role of the white Lady to permit it to be usurped by women whose practice of being a lady would not benefit the elites.

The freedpeople themselves generated almost no written testaments or contemporary accounts of their daily lives in that first decade of freedom as an illiterate people struggling with overwhelming barriers and restrictions. What was written about them by their white contemporaries was usually too polemical to serve the cause of an accurate appraisal of the times. Most of those who wrote had their own ideological as to grind and used the lives of freedwomen and men as exemplars for what was either right or wrong with slavery. White abolitionists who wanted to test their ideas in a living laboratory went south while white defenders of slavery predicted that the black race would perish once freed from the guardianship and care of masters. Some of our present imagery and data from the ten to fifteen years of the transition from slavery to freedom and through Reconstruction in the South derive from the first-hand accounts of white northern women like Sarah Foster and Laura Towne who went from northern homes to the South to educate those black men, women, and children who were in the process of becoming free people.[33] Laura Towne made the following entry in her diary for 1 June, 1867 in regard to the unfolding of a new, yet still asymmetrical gender system between the freedpeople of Port Royal, South Carolina:

> The people are just now in a state of great excitement over their right to vote, and are busy forming a Republican Party on the island. At their first meeting they had an informal time; at the second there was some business done. Our school was invited to sing at this one, and it seemed the main attraction. But two or three white men, one of them Mr. Wells, got up and said women and children ought to stay at home on such occasions. He afterwards sent us an apology, saying he had no idea of including us or our school, but only outsiders who were making some noise. Nevertheless, the idea took. To-day in church Mr. Hunn announced another meeting next Sunday. "The females must stay at home?" asked Demas [black elder of church] from the pulpit. "The females can come or not as they choose," said Mr. Hunn, "but the meeting is for men voters." Demas immediately announced that "the womens will stay at home and cut grass," that is hoc the corn and cotton fields—clear them of grass! It is too funny to see how much

more jealous the men are of one kind of liberty they have achieved than of the other! Political freedom they are rather shy of; but domestic freedom—the right, just found, to have their own way in their families and rule their wives— that is an inestimable privilege! In slavery the woman was far more important and was in every way held higher than the man. It was the woman's house; the children were entirely hers, etc., etc. Several speakers have been here who have advised the people to get the women into their proper place, never to tell them anything of their concerns, etc., etc.; and the notion of being bigger than women generally is just now inflating the conceit of the males to an amazing degree. When women get the vote too, no people will be more indignant than these, I suppose.[34]

Obviously, Towne lacked the experience with slavery to have made a fully informed judgment concerning the importance of black female slaves relative to males. From Towns' perspective, the added burden of familial domestic labor that slave women had to perform when they came in from field work looked like a kind of familial authority that was denied to males slaves. For Laura Towne the ideology of domesticity was well known and had probably influenced her thinking about the domestic lives of freed women and men. However, she applied it inappropriately to the meaning of family and domestic labor of enslaved black women and her evaluation of their importance and power was miscalculated.[35]

Towne had been in Port Royale for five years when she made the diary entry and had grown sufficiently acquainted with the contemporary culture to make an informed opinion. Observations and daily experiences give that part of her evaluation legitimate explanatory power and authenticity, but Towns still made the same error that so many of her peers made. She imposed her values onto their lives, making judgments drawn from her own culture. Her judgments reflect a white, middle-class, northern Protestant perspective with little regard for the African-American cultural norms or tire black community of Port Royale. Like many members of "Gideon's Band" who went south from Boston, Philadelphia, New York, and other northern cities, Laura Towne brought as great a commitment to inculcate her black charges with her brand of Victorian morality as to teaching them to read or write.[36]

The ideology of domesticity and its desirability as a model for freedwomen and men to emulate in the postwar South was often invoked by a variety of speakers and writers, but how much freed black men and women internalized it remains to be proven. They were subject to scrutiny and advice which seemed to emanate from many different quarters. White teachers from the North who lived among them, the few officers who had commanded black troops, bureaucrats who found niches for themselves in the Freedmen's Bureau field offices, and many others who passed through the moribund Confederacy wrote of their experiences from an immediate and personal association. Other distant advocates of middle-class morality such as abolitionist Lydia Maria Child had no direct experience of life among freedpeople. Lack of first-hand knowledge did not deter Child, a northern white supporter of emancipation who wrote an advice book ostensibly for freedpeople and paid the publication costs. However, since about ninety per cent of ex-slaves were still illiterate when her book, The Freedmen's Book, was published in 1865, it had no value in their lives and raises the question of who she had in mind for an audience of readers.[37]

Writer and abolitionist Frances Harper also had advice for freedwomen and men on "the need for education, temperance, and a higher standard of domestic morality among Negroes." Harper differed in kind from Lydia Child but her advice ran along the same lines of self-improvement for freedpeople through a higher morality. She was a free black woman who had been educated in Maryland and supported abolition before the war by trying to raise the moral indignation of the white audiences she addressed. After emancipation her interests shifted toward the morality of freed blacks, taking form in the organization of Sunday Schools for black children in Philadelphia for which she wrote didactic materials. Turning to fiction, she wrote a rather florid book, Iola Leroy, or Shadows Uplifted, a novel about the problems of a beautiful light-skinned black woman sold into slavery and saved through marriage. Harper intended it as more instructional reading for Sunday Schools.[38]

General Clinton B. Fiske was another promoter of white middle-class culture for African-Americans. Fiske lived in the postwar South and should have been aware of how the freed women and men were actually living, but his advice indicates that he was insensitive to what their greatest needs were. However, his physical proximity and position as head of the Tennessee Freedmen's Bureau did not give him a better understanding of their lives than those who advised form a distance. He lectured publicly, giving "Plain Counsels to Freedmen," where he advised freemen on how to "be a man'.

> Husbands must provide for their families. Your wives will not love you if you do not provide bread and clothes for them. They cannot be happy and greet you with a kiss, when you come home, if they are hungry, ragged, and cold. By industry and economy you can soon provide a good home and plenty of food and clothing for your family; and you should not rest until this is done.[39]

This advice must have warmed the hearts of white plantation owners who feared the loss of their labor force at the same time that it warmed hearts and pocketbooks of northern men of capital and manufacturers looking south toward potential new customers. Wage-earning free laborers needed wives and families to support and upon whom they could spend those dollars.

Fiske offered this advise to freed women on how to get and keep a husband:

> Do not think of getting married until you know how to knit and sew, to mend clothes and bake good bread, to keep a nice clean house and cultivate a garden, and to read and write. A wife should take good care of her person, be clean, neat, tidy, and look as pretty as possible. I do not see how a man can love a slovenly woman.[40]

Such advice given by Childs, Harper, and Fiske could not ameliorate the harshness and daily grinding down of black women and men who remained on isolated plantations like Faunsdale or the small rural communities that stretched across the South. Their advice was not what the freedpeople needed and was probably never heard by anyone working for William Stickney in Marengo County, Alabama. Such advice offered no solutions for their problems, had they ever heard any of it. White planters also had their own advice for freedmen and women and thought they knew best what "their Negroes" needed as may be read in one of the sermons preached by William Stickney in 1866. Having written the sermon, "How to rule the masses & keep the negro true to us," the good priest then put his words into practice. His sermon laid out his plan for educating the new class of laborers so that they would remain useful to white planters without permitting radical and dangerous northern ideas of social equality to be introduced to the ex-slaves. He called on fellow patriarchs (his term) to remember their class responsibility and supervise the education of their freed slaves while furthering their own interests by a judicious handling of the workers. His account books prove that what his hired freedpeople needed was not advice from anyone local or distant, but adequate wages.[41]

Advice from any quarter which directed black women in their manner of dress or conduct around men or the importance of being a good home-maker while remaining dainty and fresh not only lacked any relevance but was patently ludicrous in such material barreness as lived by black women like Charity Paine or Lucy Horton or Lavinia Bennet. These women could barely keep themselves and their children fed as they labored six days a week, twelve hours a day trying to stay out of debt working for the old master who kept very strict accounts.

Stickney kept carefully detailed accounts, to the penny of each dollar and the 1/12 portion of a workday, of what each of his workers owed in money and time, what had been advanced, charged, broken, or time missed from field work. His entries reflected what each hand charged at stores in the surrounding area s where he had established charge accounts. Dry goods and food purchased by the freedmen and women of Faunsdale, everything that added to their impoverished world was itemized in ledgers kept by the old master. And contrary to what Lydia Maria Child or Clinton B. Fiske might have advised to help the new class of free labor become part of the capitalistic economy and practice Victorian morality, female field workers at Faunsdale had as hard and poor a life as Stickney's ledgers reflect. The bareness of material comforts and their oppressive surroundings are apparent in those books.

Although fewer and fewer women remained as contracted field hands to face the likelihood of debt peonage to the old master themselves, those who did were not getting ahead, as the account books show. Married women still had problems of indebtedness and living with scarcity when their husbands owed the old master so much that they could never get ahead, as was the case with two married pairs, Eliza and Manuel and Albert and Maria. In 1870 Manuel was $218.60 in debt to William Stickney and $102.50 in 1874 in spite of Eliza's share of the profit from the crop being added to Manuel's. Albert was in better financial condition than Manuel in 1870 because he came out $10.83 to the good at the end of the year. By 1874, he too had slid inexorably into debt, owing Stickney $180.33 even after Maria's share of $37.84 had been added to her husband's account. In 1874, both men were married and their wives were on the contract, but what each woman earned or charged went on her husband's account. By 1875 Manuel and Eliza were off the contract and so was Albert's wife, Maria. The women whose full-time field labor was lost to the planter class and whose absence was lamented by ex-masters were not living a life of leisure and ease or even eating well. Stickney's books attest to a poor diet of pork, corn meal, and molasses that was supplemented by whatever men could hunt or women could grow. The material deprivation of their lives was slightly improved by the cheap clothing, shoes, toys, and other dry good items while their spiritual nourishment was occasionally relieved with a pint of whiskey, or a plug of tobacco, or a visit to Uniontown to see a circus. Stickney forbade them their own expression of religion and insisted as a prime term of employment that they keep the Episcopal calendar, observing that religion's tenets of belief. For a while, the drudgery of farming might be broken up such attractions as Republican-sponsored barbecues and other vote-getting entertainments, but even those were stopped as soon as Alabama's "Redeemers" were elected in 1876.[42]

Having been freed from slavery did not free the black women of Faunsdale plantation from the difficulties of a hard life. Medical care from a physician was available only if they paid for it through a contract agreement with a doctor provided by the old master, and summoned only at his decision. More often, treatment of injury or illness was what the women could muster themselves or get Oliver to perform: they delivered babies, treated the common injuries of a farming life, treated the persistent and debilitating intestinal parasites with "worm candy," tried to find ways to combat the chronic respiratory ailments that plagued so many black farm workers, and put home-made ungents on the damaged hands of the workers who had to apply poison to cotton plants. Poorly heated quarters and lack of sanitary facilities did not improve with freedom and were much more likely to have eroded as a spiteful response from planters who abrogated any responsible oversight of their "free" laborers.[43]

Another responsibility that fell on women, whether working in contracted field labor, domestic service, or in their own family, was to keep their own family, was to keep their children fed enough to get them into their adulthood. What was available for the female field hands at Faunsdale had to come from their own labor. One of the provisions that Stickney had to make in 1867 to keep this labor force working for him was to agree to organize them into squads, while at the same time he had to provide land of "[a] certain quantity needed near home by each party for their women with infants." Since he also raised a variety of fowl on the plantation, black women were probably also raising turkeys and chickens for their own families while they printed and tended gardens, All of the food available to the freedwomen had to be either grown, raised, or charged at Adler and Brothers.[44]

Stickney's commitment to set aside garden land for women with infants came from their pressing for it. By achieving that, some of the same gender rights that had previously accrued only to white women were being permitted to freed black women. Or, a more accurate statement might be that they had taken some of those rights for themselves. White women often expressed resentment over what they saw as a usurpation of their privileges that were derived from legal marriage. Once black women and men were free to marry and establish their own domestic lives, the ex-mistresses had more trouble appropriating the labor of black women to carry out the domestic labor within the white household. However, the reverse side of the freedom that marriage granted was that it also sanctioned male dominance within families by the male head of a household, imposing the same restraints upon the sexuality of black women that Stickney so often expressed in his criticisms of black women who had children outside of marriage, an act that had hardly been discouraged under slavery.

Charity Paine, one of the freedwomen who were first a slave, then a hired field hand at Faunsdale, may be considered a modal representation of the options available for freedwomen of her time in a society undergoing structural alterations. What makes Charity Paine my focal point is the intriguing ambivalence of her life as she tried to take up the freedom that she had earned, only to be frustrated in that by a personal relationship with a black man and an economic one with a white one. I have often hoped that she managed to make a good life for herself later.

Charity's first contract with Stickney in 1865 was the same blanket agreement on which all the freedpeople made their marks of assent in June, 1865. Very few of the ex-slaves failed to enter the first contract. Charity's name appeared just below that of Manuel, her husband, and was followed by the names of her two older children, Lydia and Margianne, which indicated that all the members of her family old enough for field labor were under contract and expected to work. Her contract terms for 1867 and 1868, after leaving Manuel, show how fluid the possibilities were for women if they were not married. The 1867 contract had Charity signing for her own labor and that of Lydia 17, Margianna 14, and Alexander 12, and receiving as payment one-third of the cotton and corn crops and one half of their rations in meal, but only while working for Stickney. Charity appears to have concluded the contract as the head of her own family with no man usurping her adult prerogatives, until one reads the last page of her account in Stickney's ledger book dated 27 December, 1867 and reads "Cash Settlement [of] $108.00 in Oliver's hands."[45]

Since there is not evidence that suggests Oliver and Charity were related either by family or marriage, his right to be paid her wages in 1867 was based on some relationship other than a marital or familial one. He was the head of a squad made up of single persons and those without family ties and was also the general overseer for the plantation until Stickney fired him in 1870. He and his wife Scotty had a long-standing marriage and a very large family of children. Charity and her husband Manuel parted that year and she may have turned to Oliver for some type of help in establishing herself since she had no husband at a time when the old master was implementing his new labor system of squads. Oliver was a very persuasive man who may have insinuated himself into her life or been able to convince Stickney that he was acting for Charity when it was not so. For whatever reason, he was paid her wages for 1867, but it was never repeated and in the following years Charity signed for herself and took her own wages directly.

The second year of the squad system at Faunsdale brought a different manner of payment to Charity. She signed a contract for herself and children for field labor and again had a fairly large amount owed her by the old master in

December. Regardless of the amount that field hands received that year, they had made 160 bales of cotton at Faunsdale which weighed an average of 500 pounds per bale in 1867. The cotton sold for $13,292.57, from which Stickney deducted his expenses, including the "[e]ntire Nett for division (after deducting labourers' share of Bagging & Rope)" with his share $10,154.32, from which he (presumably) paid the hands. However, his final accounts ledger for 1867—debts that he paid in late December or early January, l86Mshows that Stickney did not have sufficient cash to pay Charity all that she was due as her share of the crop for the past year. Instead of paying everything he owed her, he gave her a partial cash payment of $89.55 and a note for $300.00 that came due in January 1870.[46]

In spite of giving her the note and taking care to record it, no evidence in his books indicates that it was paid. Charity was in Oliver's squad in 1867 and Solomon's in 1868 and 1869, but did not enter another squad or work at Faunsdale after 1869. She may have been another one of the ambitious and troublesome women that he got rid of rather than tolerate. Perhaps Charity's challenge to Stickney and Oliver was that she was smart enough to manage for herself.

In 1867, the first year she worked in a squad, Charity earned $159.94 from the cotton, owed $51.94, and cleared $ 108.00. The charges which totaled $51.94 were for a large iron wash pot, the account book in which Stickney itemized her debts, a book for Margianna and Alex, five pairs of shoes, fifty pounds of bacon, two and one half gallons of molasses, thirty-three dozen herring, and several yards of cloth. Since she was not charging food items to the general account, Charity must have had some cash for buying her own food. She again contracted herself and children to work for Stickney the following year to earn her share of half of the crops, but maintained herself and was responsible for paying one half the cost of care for the mules she used in field work.[47]

Entrusting the use and care of mules to a hired field hand was not an uncommon practice for Stickney during the decade which followed emancipation. But Stickney only extended the privilege to the men who had a position of authority and responsibility and never to an unmarried woman—except Charity. She had a separate agreement with the old master that gave her more autonomy and more latitude that most of the men under contract.

However, she did not remain as a field hand at Faunsdale for more than five years after she became free. Since her name disappears from the records at the same time that Oliver was fired and moved away and she had some kind of relationship with him, it is tempting to speculate that his leaving affected hers. Whether she left with him or not, while she worked for Stickney she managed to convince him that she could farm as well as any man, better than most, and proved it.

Charity Paine, or rather her symbolic value for the present, challenges a too-ready willingness to accept a male model of what freedom meant to emancipated slaves. If black men sought their legal and political manhood through the same means available to mid-nineteenth-century white males, to own their own labor, to not experience the same "civil death" in marriage as women did, to own the labor of their wives and children, to possess real or personal property, to bear arms in the protection of a state or the nation, to have legitimate open access to participation in formal politics, and be recognized as the head of their family in domestic matters, then what path were black women to take to prove their womanhood and become free women?

While slaves, male and female African-Americans could not assume most of the same gender roles that their mistresses and masters held. Part of the proscription against their usurpation of the privileged roles was class-related and also worked against whites of the small-farmer class, but the greatest barrier was race. Race had been the determining factor in slavery and only black men and women were enslaved with their children born into a condition they could not escape. Racial slavery was a method of creating a permanent laboring underclass whose members could be recognized immediately because of the biological and genetic fact of race. Sex is the other permanent class into which one is born that is also based on biology and genetics. Both are immutable physical conditions from which one may neither rise nor fall. Gender is not immutable, but is malleable and responsive to the needs and pressures of the material world into which all are born and where men and women become both the actors and acted upon. Their responses, concrete and abstract, create the culture which sustains them.[48]

But what of the freedwoman? How was she to become a woman instead of a female slave? What had she to do in order to gain her womanhood, her freedom, in the postwar South? Should she be the head of her household and agitate for enfranchisement? Was she to buy land and plant cotton for the market? Could she be regarded as a woman rather than a female worker by pursuing any of the same avenues that her husband, father, or brother would have to take? The logic that prescribed those actions as the defining acts of a free man denied it to females because those were the pursuits that affirmed manhood. The customs and laws of the land reinforced each other, upholding proscriptions against females acting in the same ways that defined maleness.

Should she take as her example of how to be a free woman from what had been demonstrated for her by women of the planter class and emulate her mistress? If we read the northern givers of advice, then she should have made herself into a carbon copy of the white original and assume the dominant class' dictates by moving the Cult of True Womanhood from its northern provenance to the South. But True Womanhood rested on having the middle-class options that working-class black women of the South lacked, although some did manage to find their own source of respectability outside the South or in all-black communities where they set the standards. That kind of community developed too late in the nineteenth-century to help Charity Paine in 1865.

Since no real precedent had been set for freedwomen in gaining the kind of legal and cultural freedom available for men, they had to find ways for themselves. They could not gain it by following the avenues open to men because they were females and barred from those paths; and while they might have envied the privileges they knew women of the planter class to have, they were privileges that could be withdrawn and were not available to black women. White women were bound to the dictates, legal and cultural, of their gender roles. They did not have the means to free themselves or to demonstrate a useful example to ex-slave women. What being a free black woman meant would have to be invented and it had to be done in the shadow of both racial and genderic denial of rights. And as black men were adapting the old masters' system of patriarchal control into one of male dominance that could include them, then black women had very few allies in their search for their own freedom.

For the freedwomen of Faunsdale, and by extension all other black female field hands in the postwar South, emancipation gave them the rewards and the penalties of legal marriage. That they did not necessarily see it as restrictive or limiting but a dearly treasured privilege does not alter what it was in fact. As slaves, African-Americans were not allowed to fulfill gender roles of either the planter class or white yeoman farmers. Since they were female and human beings, yet denied the right to act out the gender role for women because of their race, enslaved women were living examples that gender roles for women (and men) were as mutable as the patriarchal political economy of slavery needed. Once freed from slavery, African-American women were not freed from the restraints that marriage imposed on all women. As slaves, they had not been allowed to marry so they could neither gain the benefits nor pay the penalties that marriage imposed on women of the nineteenth-century south. With freedom, some of the racially determined gender expectations for black women changed, but they did not experience even the limited political freedom afforded to black men who had gained it based upon their sex.[49]

What William Stickney imposed on his labor force in terms of who could earn the highest wages, garner most shares, and hold the greater degrees of authority derived from his own gender, race, and class biases and is distinctly expressed in his own words and action; how much of it was accepted and internalized by the black men and women who worked for him is less easily discerned. However, that Faunsdale's freedmen held positions of authority in both the fields and quarters, denying women of their families and work units the same places cannot be disputed. If slavery had created a rough equality between African-American men and women because both were equally degraded, that equality did not carry over into freedom. Freedwomen still performed their own domestic labor, child care, and wage labor while their husbands and fathers were being denied admittance into the public arena, turning them back into their personal lives and private relations for everything they needed to see themselves as men. Slavery taught black women they were capable of doing the hardest kind of labor and not to depend on the gender privileges afforded white women. Freedom would teach them the restrictions of being female without the benefits of being white.

# END NOTES

1. Charity's 1868 arrangement with Stickney is in "Charity Acc'ts, 1867-1868" Stickney Box VII, folder 5, FPP, BPL.

2. "Contracts," Stickney Box VB, f. 15 and Stickney Box 9A, f. 1868, FPP, BPL

3. Passim, Stickney diaries 1865-1870, Stickney Box III, f. 80, FFP, BPL

4. Frederick Douglass made the point in his autobiography, <u>My Bondage and My Freedom</u>, New York, 1855, that he did not feel like a man as long as he was under the control and ownership of another man.

5. Letter from William Stickney to Louisa Collins Stickney, 26 March, 1867, "Correspondence to Louisa C. Stickney," Stickney Box I, f. I, FPP, BPL

6. Nancy and Margaret Wills were twins and while Stickney referred to Nancy as suffering from insanity in the 1865-1881 period, as early as 1843, Louisa's first husband had identified Margaret as having bouts of insanity.

7. For an interesting discussion on how "Southern womanhood" differed from other regional gender ideologies of upper-class women, see Ann Godwyn Jones <u>Tomorrow Is Another Day: The Woman Writer in the South 1859-1936</u> Baton Rouge, LSU Press, 1981, pp. 3-12. For an in-depth examination of the patriarchal origins of "Southern womanhood," see John Carl Ruoff "Southern Womanhood, 1865-1920: An Intellectual and Cultural Study," Ph.D. dissertation, University of Illinois, 1976.

8. Letter from William Stickney to Louisa Collins Stickney, 2 September, 1871, Stickney Box I, f.3, "Correspondence to Louisa Collins Stickney 1871-1873," FPP, BPL

9. Op. cit., letter from W.A.S. to L.C.S., 12 February, 1867

10. The list comes from Stickney's separate account books kept for domestic workers, Stickney Box V, f.15, "Domestics 1869-1873" FPP, BPL.

11. Ibid. Stickney paid house servants monthly wages in cash.

12. Plantation Day Book 1870, Stickney Box VII, f. 9, FPP, BPL

13. For more on the difficulty for ex-masters to accept their altered condition and loss of authority as a master, see James L. Roark Masters Without Slaves: Southern Planters in the Civil War and Reconstruction, New York, 1977.

14. For more details of his accounting system, see "Laborers Accounts, 1869-1893," Stickney Box VII, f. 5, 6, 7, FPP, BPL.

15. Stickney Inventory Box, f. "Correspondence"

16. Ibid.

17. The account books, or "final settlement ledgers," that Stickney kept for thirty years are a hidden source of information about the material world of freedpeople on at least one plantation in postwar Alabama; Stickney Box VII, folders 5-7, FPP, BPL.

18. Ibid.

19. Ibid., for "Amy" and "Cassius."

20. For more on the right of husbands to own their wives' labor and to receive their wages, see Stanley, op. cit.

21. Peter Kolchin, First Freedom: the Responses of Alabama's Blacks to Emancipation and Reconstruction, Westport, Conn., 1972.

22. Randall M. Miller, editor, "Dear Master": Letters of A Slave Family, Cornell University Press, 1978.

23. Ibid. In the few surviving collections of postwar black church records that I have seen, it was commonplace to punish the woman caught in illicit sexual activity more severely than her male partner, even when both were members of the congregation.

24. Ibid, Miller, p. 262.

25. The term "outside the contract" appears to refer to a working arrangement that Stickney made with some field hands to work for him, but with no contract between them—in fact, they may have been his first real sharecroppers since that was the way the organization of labor and land was moving across the entire South, that small acreage farms would be worked by a family without the kind of labor contract that had prevailed since 1865.

26. See the letter to "Rev. W. Stickney" from "R. Christian," Stickney Inventory Box, f. "Correspondence, FPP, BPL.

27. It has been a bit hard to keep straight which women Sol actually married after Hannah because he was noted as living as a married man with at least two others.

28. See the letter to "Rev. W. A, Stickney" from "C. B. Cleveland," op. cit.

29. The list drawn up by Stickney in 1865 of six new families formed at Faunsdale during the year is in Stickney Box V, f. 55, FPP, BPL.

30. Hester Iredell, John's wife and Elizabeth's mother, continued to live at Faunsdale with her husband, but never worked in the fields again. She would have been available to help with her grandchild for Elizabeth.

31. See the old slave chapel baptism records which Stickney kept up to date well into the 1880's, Stickney Box V, f. 51, FPP, BPL.

32. For a more anthropological approach to the relationship between formation of gender roles, the economy, and systemic devaluation of "female" labor, see Esther Boserup, <u>Women's Role in Economic Development, London,</u>

,1970; Peggy Reeves Sanday <u>Female Power and Male Dominance: On the Origins of Sexual Inequality,</u> Cambridge University Press, 1981; <u>Genders</u> Ivan Illich, Pantheon, New York, 1982.

33. Sarah Jane Foster was one of the women who took part in the efforts to educate newly-freed slaves during and after the war. Her extant letters and diaries have been edited by Wayne E. Reilly in <u>Sarah Jane Foster: Teacher of the Freedmen,</u> University of Virginia Press, 1990.

34. Rupert Sargent Holland, editor, <u>letters and Dairy of Laura M. Towne,</u> New York, 1969, pp. 183-4.

35. Probably the best single source for more on the "ideology of domesticity" is Katheryn Kish Slar's <u>Catherine Beecher: A Study in American Domesticity,</u> New York, 1973.

36. The standard starting point for more on "Gideon's Band" has to be Willie Lee Rose's <u>Rehearsal for Reconstruction: The Port Royal Experiment,</u> Oxford University Press, 1964.

37. Lydia Maria Child, <u>Notable American Women: A Biographical Dictionary,</u> Vol. I, A-F, editors Edward T. James, Janet Wilson James, Paul S. Boyer, Harvard University Press, 1971, pp. 330-333.

38. Frances Ellen Watkins Harper, Op. cit., Vol. II, G-O, pp. 137-139.

39. For more documentary examples of the intense effort to inculcate the prevailing Victorian Cult of True Womanhood and middle-class morality in freedwomen, see Dorothy Sterling, ed., <u>We Are Your Sisters: Black Women in the Nineteenth Century,</u> New York, 1984. The quoted Fisk material is found on p. 319.

40. Ibid., p. 320

41. Op. cit., Stickney's account ledgers

42. For the complete run of accounts kept by Stickney on individual workers, see "Labourer's Acc'ts, 1870-1881" and "Labourer's Acc'ts, 1882-1893," two bound account books found in Stickney Box VII, folders 6 and 7, FPP, BPL. For three different perspectives on the end of Reconstruction in Alabama and waning of the Republican party in the state, see Walter L. Fleming, Civil War and Reconstruction in Alabama, Columbia University Press, 1905; W. E. B. DuBois, Black Reconstruction in America, 1860-1880 (nineth printing), New York, 1983; and Eric Forner, Reconstruction, 1863-1877, New York, 1988.

43. Op. cit., Stickney's account ledgers

44. Passim, Stickney's diaries, letters, plantation day books, and workers account ledgers.

45. Op. cit., last page of Charity's "Final Acc'ts, 1867"

46. Plantation Day Book 1867, Stickney Box VII, f. 8, FPP, BPL

47. The terms of the contract between Charity Paine and William Stickney were simply those first quoted at the beginning of the chapter and were noted in her separate account book.

48. Op. cit., Gender, Illich.

49. Every dissertation seems to either end or begin with the author calling for more study of some special interest or thorny question which she had to leave unanswered. If ever there was an issue that deserved further serious work, it is a gender analysis applied to the entire ideological assumption inherent in "free labor = free men."

# Epilogue

Freedwomen faced "freedom" with a formidable array of forces acting on them. Racism, the psychological and physical effects of slavery, remnants of their African heritage, the restrictive and misogynistic tenets of most religions to which slaves had been exposed or allowed to practice, the persistent power of patriarchal institutions, confining gender roles, and the needs of the developing capitalistic economy combined to create an environment that was hostile to real freedom for freedwomen. Slavery had distorted the functioning gender systems that had existed between men and women from various African tribes and cultures into one that was intended to benefit slave masters and mistresses. The gender system that developed between freedwomen and men after emancipation differed from the one in place between white women and men of the planter class in many ways, but the subordination of women, black or white, was one key element of both sets of relationships.

Questions remain: why did freed black women leave field work in the postwar South? Was it their own desire to spend more time with their children and establish a domestic life for themselves free of white interference? Was it the desire of their husbands and fathers, as Laura Towne assumed, that the freedwomen learn to subordinate themselves to the male head of the family and to the black men of the community? To continue searching for the one reason that black women left contracted or wage-earning field work is not the most productive avenue to take if we could know more about the nature of gender relations in general or the specific history of African-American women in the postwar South.

Women labor either for wages or for keep. They are and always have been part of the productive and reproductive forces of society. Women reproduce the rising generation, reproduce the ephemeral daily cultural lessons for that generation, and produce the wealth and material goods necessary for consumption and trade. The questions that we need to ask are not about whether or not women work, but what are the relationships between their race, their gender role, and the labor that they perform.

Social classes exist in opposition to each other. A single class does not function in a social vacuum. Gender also functions in oppositional relationships. It is without meaning to refer to only one group of persons or an entire people as being a race unless it is made clear what other races are thought to exist, or have existed, in the same time and place. If we would know what gender means, we must apply it as an analytical tool to both men and women just as we must recognize that the men and women of the planter class had a race as well. "Black" has no meaning unless we know about "White." Which one of the powerful troika of gender, race, and class should take primacy in the study and writing of social history is a wrong-headed approach. That all three have been and remain powerful forces acting upon each of us is the more important lesson.

The black women who had been slaves as children or adults at Somerset and then Faunsdale plantations were acted upon and were actors in their own lives. They left fewer records behind than their literate mistresses or masters, but they lived and acted and influenced their own surroundings. If we have not arrived at all of the answers to our questions about their time and their actions, perhaps we have been asking the wrong questions. If I have not provided enough answers here, I hope to have raised some provocative questions.

# Bibliography

## PRIMARY MATERIALS

### Manuscripts

Collins Family Papers, Private Collections, North Carolina State Archives, Raleigh, North Carolina

Darden, John, "The Story of Washington County," North Carolina State Archives, Raleigh, North Carolina

DuBose, John Witherspoon Papers, Alabama Department or Archives and History, Montgomery, Alabama

Faunsdale Plantation Papers, Lim-Henley Research Library, Birmingham Public Library, Birmingham, Alabama

Lay, Henry Champlin Papers, Southern Historical Collection, The University of North Carolina, Chapel Hill, North Carolina

Records of the Bureau of Refugees, Freedmen, and Abandoned Lands (Record Group 105), National Archives, Washington, DC

### Government Documents

U.S. Bureau of the Census, Nineth Census of the United States; 1870, Population

U.S. Bureau of the Census, Tenth Census of the United States; 1880, Population

## SECONDARY MATERIALS

### Books and Articles

Andrews, Sidney. The South Since The War. Boston: Houghton Mifflin, 1971. Aptheker, Herbert. Nepro Slave Revolts. New York: International Publishers, 19&4.

Armstrong, Margaret. Kemble: A Passionate Victorian. New York: The MacMillan Company, 1938.

Basch, Norma. The Eyes Of The Law: Women, Marriage, And Property In The Nineteenth-Century. New York: Cornell University Press, 1982.

Bell, Malcolm, Jr. Major Butler's Legacy: Five Generations Of A Slaveholding Fam{_yl. Athens: University of Georgia Press, 1987.

Berlin, Ira; Barbara J. Fields; Thavolia Glymph; Steven F. Miller; Joseph P. Reidy; Leslie S. Rowland; and Julie Saville, editors. Freedom: A Documentary History of Emancipation: Series I, Volume I, The Destruction Of Slavery: (1985); and Volume III, The Wartime Genesis of Free Labor: The Lower South. (1990) Cambridge: Cambridge University Press.

Bethel, Elizabeth, "The Freedmen's Bureau In Alabama," Journal of Southern History XIV (1948): pp. 49-92.

Blair, William A. and W. A. Clark. A Historical Sketch of Banking in North Carolina And The Banking Institutions Organized In South Carolina Prior To 1860. New York: Arno Press, 1980.

Blassingame, John W. The Slave Community: Plantation Life In T e Antebellum South. New York: Oxford University Press, 1979.

Boles, John B. Black Southerners, 1619-1869. Lexington: University of Kentucky Press, 1984.

Boserup, Esther. Women's Role In Economic Development. London: George Allen and Unwin, 1970.

8oyd, Minnie Clare. Alabama In The Fifties: A Social Study. New York: AMS Press, 1966.

Cash, J. W. The Mind Of The South. New York: Vintage Books, 1969.

Clinton, Catherine. The Plantation Mistress: Women's World In The Old South. New York: Pantheon, 1982.

Cott, Nancy F. The Bonds of Womanhood, Woman's Sphere In New England, 1780-1835. New Haven: Yale University Press, 1978.

"Passionless: An Interpretation Of Victorian Sexual Ideology, 1790-1850," A Heritage Of Her Own,. Nancy F. Cott and Elizabeth H. Pleck, pp. 162-181, New York: 1979.

Cutrufelli, Maria Rosa. Women of Africa: Roots Of Oppression. London: zed Press, 1983.

Demos, John. A Little Commonwealth: Family Life In Plymouth Colony.

Oxford: Oxford University Press, 1970.

Dennett, John Richard. The South As It Is, 1865-1866. Edited by Henry M. Christian. Athens: University of Georgia Press, 1986.

Douglass, Frederich. My Bondage And My Freedom. Dover Publications, 1969. Dublin, Thomas. Women At Work: The Transformation Of Work And Community In Lowell, Massachusetts, 1826-1860. New York: Columbia University Press, 1979.

DuBois, Ellen, Mari Jo Buhle, Temma Kaplan, Gerda Lerner, and Carroll Smith- Rosenberg, "Politics and Culture In Women's History: A Symposium," Feminist Studies V. 6, n. 1 (Spring 19g0): pp. 26-64.

Du Bois, W. E. B. Black Reconstruction In America 1860-1880. New York: Atheneum, 1983.

DuBose, John Witherspoon, "Chronicles Of The Canebrake 1817-1860" Alabama Historical Quarterly (Winter 1947).

Elkins, Stanley. Slavery: A Problem In American Institutional And Intellectual Life. Chicago: University of Chicago Press, 1968.

Escott, Paul. Hill: University of North Carolina Press, 1979.

Faragher, John Mack, "The Midwestern Farming Family, 1860," Women's American ed. Linda Kerber and Jane DeHart Mathews, New York: 1982, pp. 114-129.

Fleming, Walter. Civil War And Reconstruction In Alabama. Gloucester, Massachusetts: Peter Smith, 1949.

Friedman, Jean E. The Enclosed Garden: Women And Community In The Evangelical South, 1830-1900. Chapel Hill: University of North Carolina Press, 1985

Forner, Eric. Free Soil, Free Labor, Free Men: The Ideology Of The Republican Party Before The Civil War. Oxford: Oxford University Press, 1970.

Nothing But Freedom: Emancipation And Its Legacy. Baton Rouge:

Louisiana State University Press, 1983.

Reconstruction: America's Unfinished Revolution, 1863-1877. New York: Harper and Row, 1988.

Fox-Genovese, Elizabeth. Within The Plantation Household: Black And White Women Of The Old South. Chapel Hill: The University of North Carolina Press, 1988.

Genovese, Eugene. Roll, Jordan, Roll: The World The Slaves Made. New York: Pantheon, 1874.

Gidden, Paula. When And Where I Enter: The Impact Of Black Women On Race And Sex In America. New York: Bantam Books, 1985.

Green, Michael D. The Politics Of Indian Removal: Creek Government And Society In Crisis. Lincoln: University of Nebraska Press, 1982.

Gutman, Herbert. The Black Family In Slavery And Freedom 1750-1925. New York: Vintage Books, 1977.

Gavin, Minrose. Black And White Women Of The Old South: The Peculiar Sisterhood In American Literature. Knoxville: University of Tennessee Press, 1985.

Herskovits, Melville J. The Myth Of The Negro Past. Boston: Beacon Press, 1958.

Higginbotham, Donald, ed. Papers Of James Iredell, Volume II. Raleigh: Division of Archives and History, State of North Carolina, 1976.

Holland, Rupert, ed. Letters And Diary Of Laura M. Towne Written From The Sea Islands Of South Carolina 1862-1884. New York: Negro University Press, 1969.

Hull, Gloria; Scott, Patricia Bell; and Barbara Smith, editors. But Some Of Us Are Brave: Black Women's Studies. Old Westbury, New York: The Feminist Press, 1982.

Illich, Ivan. Gender. New York: Pantheon Books, 1982.

Jacobs, Harriet. Incidents In The Life Of A Slave Girl Written By Herself. Edited by Jean Fagan Yellin. Cambridge: Harvard University Press, 1987.

James, Edward T.; Jane Wilson James; and Paul S. Boyer, eds. Notable American Women, 1607-1950: A Biographical Dictionary, Volume I. Cambridge: Belknap Press of Harvard University, 1971.

Jaynes, Jerald. Branches Without Roots: Genesis Of The Black Working Class In The American South, 1862-1882. Oxford: Oxford University Press, 1986.

Johnson, Michael P., "Smothered Slave Infants: Were Slave Mothers At Fault?"

Journal Of Southern History 47 (November 1981): pp. 493-520.

Jones, Anne Goodwin. Tomorrow Is Another Day: The Women Writer In The South, 1859-1936. Baton Rouge: Louisiana State University Press, 1981.

Jones, Jacqueline. Labor Of Love, Labor Of Sorrow: Black Women, Work, And The Family From Slavery To The Present. New York: Basic Books, 1985.

Jordan, Winthrop D. White Over Black: American Attitudes Toward The Negro, 1550-1821. New York: W. W. Norton & Company, 1977.

Joyner, Charles. Down By The Riverside: A South Carolina Slave Community. Urbana: University of Illinois Press, 1984.

Kelly, Joan. Women, History and Theory. Chicago: University Of Chicago Press, 1984.

Kemble, Fanny. Journal Of A Residence On A Georgia Plantation In 1838-1839. Chicago: Afro-Am Press, 1969.

Kerber, Linda. "Separate Spheres, Female Worlds, Woman's Piace: The Rhetoric Of Women's History," <u>Journal Of American History</u> V. 75, n. 1 (June 1988): pp. 9-39.

Kessler-Harris, Alice, "Where Are All The Organized Women Workers?" <u>Women's American</u> eds. Linda Kerber and Jane DeHart Mathews, New York: 1982, pp. 225-242.

Kolchin, Peter. Firs Freedom: The Response Of Alabama's Blacks To <u>Emancipation and Reconstruction</u>. Westport: 1972.

Kulikoff, Alan. <u>Tobacco And Slaves: The Development Of Southern Cultures In The Chesapeak, 1680 1300.</u> Chapel Hill: University of North Carolina Press, 1986.

Lane, Ann J., ed. <u>The Debate Over Slavery: Stanley Elkins And His Critics</u>. Urbana: University of Illinois Press, 1971.

Leavitt, Judith Walzer, "Under The Shadow Of Maternity: American Women's Responses To Death And Debility Fears In Nineteenth-Century Childbirth," <u>Feminist Studies</u> V. 12, n. 1 (Spring 1986): pp. 129-154.

Lebsock, Susan, "Radical Reconstruction And The Property Rights of Southern Women," Journal Of <u>Southern History</u> XLIII. (May 1977): pp. 195-216.

<u>The Free Women Of Petersburg: Status And Culture In A Southern Town, 1784-1860.</u> New York: N. W. Norton & Company, 1984.

Lemmon, Sarah McCulloh, ed. <u>The Pettigrew Papers, 1685-1818</u> Volume I. Raleigh: Division of Archives and History, State of North Carolina, 1971.

ed. <u>The Pettigrew Papers, 1819-1832</u> Volume II, Raleigh: Division of Archives and History, State of North Carolina, 1988.

Lerner, Gerda. <u>The Creation Of Patriarchy.</u> Oxford: Oxford University Press, 1986.

Levine, Lawrence. Black Culture And Black Consciousness: Afro-American Folk Thought From Slavery To Freedom. Oxford: Oxford University Press, 1978.

Linderman, Gerald. Embattled Of Combat In The American Civil War. New York: Free Press, 1987.

Littwack, Leon F. Been In The Storm So Long : The Aftermath Of Slavery. New York: Vintage books, 1980.

Mantra, Jo Ann and Robert R. Dykstra, "Serial Marriage And The Origins Of The Black Stepfamily," Journal Of American History V. 72, n.1 (June 1985): pp. 18-44.

Marx, Karl. A Contribution To The Critique Of Political Economy, Chicago: Kerr, 1911.

Masterson, William H., ed The John Gray Blount Papers, Volume III. Raleigh: Division of Archives and History, State of North Carolina, 1965.

Mellon, James. Bullwhip Days: The Slaves Remember. New York: Weidenfeld & Nicolson, 1988.

Miller, Randall M., ed. "Dear Master": Letters Of A Slave Family. Ithaca: Cornel University Press, 1978.

Norton, Mary Beth, "The Paradox Of 'Women's Spheres,"' Women Of American pp. 139-149. Carol Ruth Berkin and Mary Beth Norton, eds. Boston: Houghton Mifflin Company, 1979.

Patterson, Orlando. Slavery And Social Death: A Comparative Study. Cambridge: Harvard University Press, 1982.

Pinchbeck, Ivy. Women Workers In The Industrial Revolution 1750-1850. London: Virago Press, 1981.

Powell, William S., ed. Dictionary of North Carolina, Volume I. Chapel Hill: University of North Carolina, 1950.

Pratt, Fletcher. Preble's Boys: Commador Preble And The British Of American Sea Power. New York: 1950.

Rabinowitz, Howard. Race Relations In The Urban South, 1865-1890. Urbana: University of Illinois Press, 1980.

Raboteau, Albert J. Slave Religion: The "Invisible Institution" In The Antebellum South. Oxford: Oxford University Press, 1978.

Ransom, Roger L. and Richard Sutch. One Kind Of Freedom: The Economic Consequences Of Emancipation. Cambridge: Cambridge University Press, 1977.

Redford, Dorothy S. Somerset Slave community: An Antebellum Genealogical Stud (published and distributed by the author): 1986.

Reilly, Wayre E., ed. Sarah Jane Foster, Teacher Of The Freedmen: A Diary And Letters. Charlottesville: University of Virginia Press, 1990.

Roark, James L. Masters Without Slaves: Southern Planters In The Civil War And Reconstruction. New York: 1977.

Rose, Willie Lee. Rehearsal For Reconstruction: The Port Royal Experiment. Oxford: Oxford University Press, 1964.

Rosenthal, Ida D., "Legal Status Of Women In Alabama," (pamphlet held by Birmingham Public Library) Birmingham: 1940.

Ruben, Gayle, "The Traffic In Women: Notes On The Political Economy Of Sex," Towards An Anthropology Of Women ed. Rayna R. Rapp. New York: 1975. pp. 157-210.

Ryan, Mary P. Cradle Of The Middle Class: The Family In Oneida Country, New York. Cambridge: Cambridge University Press, 1981.

Womanhood In America From Colonial Times To The Present. New York: Franklin Watts, 1983.

Sanday, Peggy Reeves. Female Power And Male Dominance: On The Origins Sexual Inequality. Cambridge: Cambridge University Press, 1981.

Scott, Anne Firor. The Southern Lady: From Pedestal To Politics, 1830-1930. Chicago: University of Chicago Press, 1970.

Scott, Joan Wallace. Gender And The Politics Of History. New York: Columbia University Press, 1988.

Scott, Rebecca, "The Battle Over The Child: Child Apprenticeship And The Freedmen's Bureau In North Carolina," Polo e 10 (Summer 1978): pp. 101-113.

Sklar, Kathryn Kish. Catherine Beecher: A Study In American Domesticity. New York: W. W. Norton & Company, 1976.

Smith-Rosenberg, Carroll, "The Female World Of Love And Ritual: Relations Between Women In Nineteenth-Century America," A Heritage Of Her Owns eds. Nancy F. Cott and Elizabeth H. Pleck. New York: 1979. pp. 311-S42.

Spellman, Elizabeth V. Inessential Woman: Problems Of Exclusion In Feminist Thought. Boston: Beacon Press, 1988.

Spruill, Julia Cherry. Women's Life And Work In The Southern Colonies. New York: W. W. Norton & Company, 1972.

Stanley, Amy Dru, "Conjugal Bonds And Wage Labor: Rights Of Contract In The Age Of Emancipation," Journal Of American History V. 75, n.2 (September 1988): pp. 471-500.

Sterling, Dorothy, ed. We Are Your Sisters: Black Women In The Nineteenth Century. New York: W. W. Norton & Company, 1984.

Stuckey, Sterling. Slave Culture: Nationalist Theory And The Foundations Of Black America. Oxford: Oxford University Press, 1987.

Tarlton, William S., "Somerset Place And Its Restoration," Division Of State Parks, North Carolina Department Of Conservation And Development: 1954.

Trowbridge, John T. The Desolate South, 1865-1866. New York: Duell, Sloan and Pearce, 1956.

Vlach, John Michael. The Afro-American Tradition In Decorative Arts. Cleveland: Cleveland Museum of Art, 1978.

Warren, Edward. A Doctor's Experiences On Three Continents. Baltimore: Cushings and Bailey, 1885,

Watson, Alan D. Money And Monetary Problems In Early North Carolina. Raleigh: Division of Archives and History, State of North Carolina, 1980.

Wertz, Dorothy C. and Richard L.

White, Deborah Gray. Aren't I A Woman? Female Slaves In The Plantation South. New York: W. W. Norton & Company, 1987.

White, Kenneth, "Wager Swayne: Racist Or Realist?" Alabama Review XXXI (April 1978): pp. 92-109.

Whites, LeeAnn. Gender And The Origins Of The New South, Augusta, Georgia 1860-1890. Chapel Hill: University of North Carolina, (forthcoming).

Wiener, Jonathan M. Social Origins Of The New South, Alabama 1860-1885. Baton Rouge: Louisiana State University Press, 1978.

Williams, Sherley Anne. Dessa Rose. New York: 1987.

Williamson, Joel. The Crucible Of Race: Black-White elations In the American South since Emancipation. Oxford: Oxford University Press, 1984.

Wood, Peter, "Digging Black History," Southern Exposure (March/April 1983): pp. 62-65.

Woodward, C. Vann, ed. Mary Chesnut's Civil War. New Haven: Yale University Press, 1981.

Woodward, C. Vann and Elizabeth Muhlenfeld, editors. The Private Mary Chesnut: The Unpublished Civil War Diaries. New York: 1984.

Wright, Gavin. Old South, New South: Revolutions In The Southern Economy Since The Civil War. New York: Basic Books, 1986.

Wyatt-Brown, Bertram. Southern Honor: Ethics And Behavior In The Old South, Oxford: Oxford University Press, 1983.

# DISSERTATIONS

Ash, Stephen V., "Civil War, Black Freedom, And Social Change In The Upper South: Middle Tennessee, 1860-1870." (Ph.D. Dissertation, University of Tennessee, Knoxville, 1983)

Cooke, Michael Anthony, "The Health Of Blacks During Reconstruction, 1862- 1870." (Ph.D. Dissertation, University of Maryland, 1983)

De Boer, Clara Merritt, "The Role Of Afro-Americans In The Origin And Work Of The American Missionary Association: 1839-1877." (Ph.D. Dissertation, Rutgers University, 1973)

Jones, Maxine Deloris, "A Glorious Work": The American Missionary Association And Black North Carolinians, 1863-1880." (Ph.D. Dissertation, Florida State University, 1982)

Myers, John Benjamin, "Black Human Capital: The Freedmen And The Reconstruction Of Labor In Alabama, 1860-1880." (Ph.D. Dissertation, Florida State University, 1974)

Ruoff, John Carl, "Southern Womanhood, 1865-1920: An Intellectual And Cultural Study." (Ph.D. Dissertation, University of Illinois at Urbana-Champaign, 1976)

Wheeler, Edward Lorenzo, "Uplifting The Race: Black Ministers In The New South, 1865-1902." (Ph.D. Dissertation, Emory University, 1982)

# Carol Lemley Montgomery

*April 25, 1943 – September 15, 2022*

Preceded by parents and son Mark Hamilton Gary, sister Rhoda Jane Hall.

Survived by her loving husband Mac Montgomery, son John Paul Gary (Colleen), daughters Rhoda J Gary, Mary Montgomery, Grandchildren Katie Nannini (Michael), Hannah Reed (Brittany), Emily Gary. Brother Ed Lemley (Camille). Nieces and nephews, Mary Alvice Davidson, Ruth Lemley-Goodman (Jeff), Mark Lemley (Roxanne) and three great grandchildren.

Carol was born in Birmingham, AL to Edwin and Mary Frances Lemley. Carol and Mac were married in 1970 in Columbus GA while he was assigned to Ft Benning after his first tour to Viet Nam. Their adventure together went on from there for 52 years and it was time filled with accomplishments, travel and growth.

Shortly after they were married Carol started taking flying lessons while Mac was in flight school. It was a bold move for an Army wife at that time but she loved going to the flight line and pulling her Cessna 150 out of the hanger for lessons. She continued her flying lessons for the next two years while raising four children with a husband back in Viet Nam again. The stories of. her solo flights were great.

Carol and Mac went off to Florida Atlantic University where she began her studies and worked in the College theater. The they were all off to Germany for over three years. Living in a small German village, Carol mastered shopping in

German and being the liaison for local town guests to the base. She pushed and shoved past Secret Service and Army Colonels to get her assigned Mayor to meet President Ford during his visit, never one to take no for an answer.

Carol enrolled at Armstrong State in savannah on their return and graduated in three years, Magna Cum Laude (she got a B in College Algebra). The they were off the southern California where Carol had been accepted into the doctoral program in history at University of California Irvine. She studied there four years and then they were off to New York City. Carol worked on her dissertation and taught at St John's University (where Mac was assigned). It was days of long trips for research to New York libraries, the National Archives in DC and on-site visits to former plantation sites in Alabama.

Carol completed an absolutely great dissertation and was awarded her PhD in 1991 with all the family there in California to include her mother. They moved to North Carolina in 1988 after Mac was stationed at Ft. Bragg. After he retired, they moved to Hamlet, NC. In 1989, the bought a little place in Kure Beach. In 2000, they retired to the beach and used that house as home base while traveling in their Airstream.

Retirement was good but needed a little extra. Carol joined the Board of the Foundation at Cape Fear Community College and Mac was elected Mayor of Kure Beach. Carol immersed herself in support of the environment working as a volunteer for sea turtle nesting and supporting efforts to stop industrial pollution of our air and water. Then they discovered volunteering for National Parks, Wildlife Refuges and Federal recreation areas in New Mexico. After six tours of welcoming the public to these wonderful spaces, Carol decided to stay home and enjoy being retired.

Carol was a strong and very intelligent woman who carried with her a deep sense of equity, fairness and goodness. She was at home arguing politics, women's rights and as well as the taste of food at a particular restaurant. And for over half a century Carol and Mac visited many places, met and loved many people, watched family grow and bond and never stopped loving each other.

www.ingramcontent.com/pod-product-compliance
Lightning Source LLC
Chambersburg PA
CBHW070051080526
44586CB00013B/1008